WHO ARE
THE
ILLUMINATI?

Conspiracy Books is a topical range of titles dedicated to publishing the truth about all conspiracies – whether ancient or modern, theoretical or real. The series is informative, entertaining, subjective and incisive, and will endeavour to bring the reader closer than ever before to the reality of the conspiracies that surround us.

WHO ARE THE ILLUMINATI?

LINDSAY PORTER

COLLINS & BROWN

First published in 2005 by Collins & Brown
The Chrysalis Building
Bramley Road
London W10 6SP

An imprint of **Chrysalis** Books Group plc

Produced by Conspiracy Books
PO Box 51726, London NW1 9ZH

British Library Cataloguing-in-Publication Data:
A catalogue record for this book is available from the
British Library.

ISBN 1-84340-289-0

The author and publishers have made every
reasonable effort to contact copyright holders. Any
errors that may have occurred are inadvertent and
anyone who has not been contacted is invited to
write to the publishers so that full acknowledgement
may be made in subsequent editions of this work.

1 3 5 7 9 8 6 4 2

Printed and bound in Great Britain by
Creative Print & Design (Wales), Ebbw Vale

Contents

Introduction

In the Communist Manifesto of Marx, we find again all the
points of Weishaupt – abolition of property, inheritance,
marriage, and all morality, of patriotism and all religion. Is it
not obvious that the plan has been handed down to the
succeeding groups of Socialists and Anarchists by the secret
societies which had carried on the traditions of the
Illuminati?

Nesta Webster, 1922

It is historical fact that the Illuminati vowed vengeance
against the Vatican in the 1600s. The early Illuminati – those
of Galileo's day – were expelled from Rome by the Vatican
and hunted mercilessly. The Illuminati fled and went into
hiding in Bavaria where they began mixing with other
refugee groups fleeing the Catholic purges – mystics,
alchemists, scientists, occultists, Muslims, Jews.

Dan Brown, Interview, 2001

The Illuminati, the clique which control the direction of the
world, are genetic hybrids, the result of interbreeding
between a reptilian extraterrestrial race and humanity many
thousands of years ago.

David Icke, 2003

Who are the Illuminati? Seventeenth-century mystics and alchemists? Demonic masters behind the Russian Revolution? Extraterrestrial lizards pursuing a cosmic plot against humankind? Is there any truth at all behind the accusations, or is it all legend and hearsay? This much we know for certain: the Illuminati were a short-lived secret society, founded in 18th-century Bavaria by one Adam Weishaupt and modelled on the Freemasons. The group's name, the Illuminati – the "enlightened ones" – was chosen by Weishaupt to reflect the society's quest for knowledge, particularly the egalitarian, rational philosophies that were gaining ground in the rest of Europe during this period of the 18th century that became known as the Enlightenment. How does this historically documented Illuminati relate, if at all, to such disparate – and in some cases, frankly crazy – beliefs as extraterrestrial genetic hybrids, the New World Order, the Communist Manifesto or a centuries-old vendetta against the Catholic Church? Why and how would a word that conjures notions of light, illumination and clarity come to symbolize darkness, fear and obfuscation?

To begin to answer that, you need to look at where each theory originated, and how each developed. In doing so a common thread begins to emerge, joining each apparently unconnected theory, and providing a genealogy that can be traced from today's beliefs all the way back to the time the Illuminati first fell into disfavour. And once this genealogy has been established, it becomes clear that the Illuminati legend originates with just a handful of people, who, through the ages, interpreted the myth in light of their own anxieties, embellished it, and bequeathed it to the next generation.

Historian Richard Hofstadter identified in the mid-1960s a recurrent but growing preoccupation – obsession even – with a conspiratorial view of history, one which dwelled upon the idea that world events were brought about through subversion and secret plots. He called this the "paranoid style". This tendency is characterized by the belief that historical events, rather than resulting from a complex series of factors, have been consciously manipulated behind the scenes, usually by a minority with malign intent. Hofstadter initially identified this tendency with the extreme right, who historically have targeted minorities as scapegoats to carry the burden for the world's ills – among them immigrant communities, ethnic minorities, Jews, Catholics, communists or, in the more distant past, Freemasons. More than 40 years after Hofstadter introduced his theory, the paranoid style is thriving, but it is no longer the preserve of the extreme right, and it is no longer limited to political theory. Maybe we've all become too cynical in the age of 24-hour news coverage; maybe the post-war era has revealed too many admissions of cover-ups and official lies, but conspiracy theories are now part of life's daily fabric. Within days of the attacks on the World Trade Center a veritable swarm of conspiracy theories challenged the official version of events coming from the White House; the death of Princess Diana in Paris had a similar effect in the UK, as though the authority of the police and the coroner's report are merely distracting details to be discarded in the quest for the hidden truth. Even in the mundane business of living, conspiracy and doubt are part of common discourse. It's as if we expect politicians to lie to us, or that somehow, as in the slogan of *The X-Files*, "The Truth is Out There".

What characterizes today's "paranoid style" is that the idea of a vast, overarching conspiracy has moved firmly centre stage. For example, in the immediate aftermath of the Kennedy assassination, countless theories were put forth in opposition to the official version contained in the Warren Commission report, which represented any number of political ideologies and concomitant scapegoats, among them, the mafia, international communists, Freemasons, Texas oil barons or the CIA. Whereas today, it is common among conspiracy theorists to see a connection between all these disparate elements: everything is connected in a vast conspiratorial web. The most prevalent of these mega-conspiracy theories is the idea that the world is ruled by an elite group of secret powerbrokers. Once this basic premise has been accepted then a whole parcel of assumptions seem to go with it, and even seemingly innocuous actions can be seen in a sinister light; for example, the government's issuing of social security numbers is seen as evidence of its working toward a one world government, a New World Order.

Former goalie-turned-New Age guru David Icke is clearly one of the most extreme examples of this tendency, devising a theory that transcends time, space, and even species, wrapped up in a New Age interpretation of the world that considers the ultimate weapon against the human race to be a band of negative energy encircling the planet. But he is far from alone in subscribing to a vast, umbrella conspiracy theory. Christian fundamentalist and former US presidential candidate Pat Robertson sums up a surprisingly common belief when he described in his 1991 book, *The New World Order*, a single thread connecting the White House, State Department, Council on Foreign Relations and Trilateral Commission to secret societies and what he called "extreme New Agers". In charge of this is a "world government, world police force, world courts, world banking and currency, and a world elite", which necessitates either a "complete redistribution of wealth" or the complete destruction of the Christian faith.

Wrapped up in these all-encompassing theories, glimpsed here and there, are references to the Illuminati. Many of today's conspiracy theorists see the Illuminati as the shadowy elite that connects all bodies working toward a world government, Robertson's "single thread" that links high-ranking government organizations. Robertson repeats a popular allegation that this elite seeks to destroy the twin pillars supporting the edifice of

Western civilization – capitalism and Christianity. For many of today's Christian right wing, this allegation is taken further still: the Illuminati are often referred to as being synonymous with the Antichrist, illustrating once again just how slippery the conspiracy theory slope can be. For example, the US Patriot movement, an umbrella term for a number of extreme right, Christian fundamentalist groups, adheres to the idea that white Christian men have a rightful superiority – a God-given right – over any other creed or race. Among this milieu, it is but a short hop to the conclusion that non-Christian faiths represent a threat, bent on destroying this alleged supremacy. And who is the archnemesis of the Christian faith but Satan himself? But how, exactly, have the Illuminati become entangled in this premise? Is there any truth in the idea that the Illuminati were sworn enemies of the Vatican in the 17th century, as Dan Brown asserts in his best-selling novel *Angels and Demons*?

It might appear that the Christian right and New Age conspiracy theorists had conjured the idea of the Illuminati from thin air, as a convenient metaphor for faithlessness in the modern age. But they weren't the first to blame the Illuminati for the world's ills. In the 1960s the Illuminati were compared to an even more pressing threat: the spread of communism. One of the most vocal advocates of the "shadowy elite" theory of government was sweets manufacturer Robert Welch, founder of the ultra-conservative John Birch Society in the late 1950s in the US. Robert Welch single-handedly revived the fear of the Illuminati in the post-war era, writing in his 1966 essay "The Truth in Time":

Whether or not this increasingly all-powerful hidden command was due to an unbroken continuation of Weishaupt's Illuminati, or was a distillation from the leadership of this and other groups, we do not know. Some of them may never have been Communists, while others were. To avoid as much dispute as possible, therefore, let's call this ruling clique simply the Insiders.

When Welch formed the John Birch Society to combat the spread of communism in the US, he was part of a wave of anti-communist activity sweeping the country. Communism, according to FBI director J. Edgar Hoover, aimed at nothing less than to "destroy Western civilization and roll history back to the ages of barbaric cruelty and despotism", and Welch was doing his part to eradicate this influence. He had been an active supporter of Senator John McCarthy – of the infamous McCarthy witch hunts – in the 1950s and was to increase his crusade by forming his society. He had obviously identified a need: in the early 1960s the JBS counted members in the tens of thousands. However, Welch's anti-communist rhetoric was unique in his choosing to believe in, and identify, a hidden group behind the scenes, the puppet masters pulling the communists' strings. In this he was continuing, whether he knew it or not, a much more sinister tradition of scapegoating, a hangover from the beginning of the century, whose roots were much older still.

Even though Robert Welch took the Illuminati myth to new heights and reworked it for his highly idiosyncratic political agenda, he cannot be credited with originating the story. Nor was he the first to weave the idea of secret plots and shadowy forces into his anti-communist crusade. In the 1930s the radio priest Father Coughlin led a popular groundswell of anti-communism through a series of radio programmes that, at the height of his popularity, entered the homes of millions. Coughlin's anti-communist diatribes were based on the idea that a secret elite were quietly plotting behind the scenes – even at the heart of the US government. And a decade earlier, in the 1920s, US automobile mogul Henry Ford had used the same template – the idea of a secret force conniving behind the scenes –

to spread his own political agenda. But anti-communism was not Ford's aim. He perpetuated a more unpleasant legacy – now largely forgotten – in a series of articles printed in the *Dearborne Independent* in the 1920s, in which he gave voice to a vehement and sustained campaign of anti-Semitism, suspecting a Jewish plot to infiltrate and undermine all aspects of American life (through the most extraordinary of avenues: from baseball to Jazz, to Prohibition-era bootleg liquor). Within his bigoted stream of vindictiveness he alluded to a secret society and the alleged Jewish influence upon it; the Illuminati in all but name: "a pseudo-Masonry, of French origin, given to atheistic and revolutionary purposes, strongly patronized by Jews", who were hiding "behind the name of Masonry" to further their nefarious agenda. With Ford, the triumvirate of popular scapegoats, the Jewish-communist– Masonic conspiracy, comes together under the guise of the Illuminati.

Ford, in turn, was influenced by a notorious forgery, the *Protocols of the Elders of Zion*, which surfaced in the early years of the 20th century and purported to be the transcript of a meeting between members of a Jewish cabal plotting to take over the world. From the details of its tangled origins, it is now believed to have been the work of the Soviet secret police, intended to incite anti-Semitic feeling and garner support for the vicious pogroms sweeping the country at the turn of the century. In incorporating the secret society myth into his anti-Semitic agenda, Ford was inverting a theory put forward by the revisionist historian and fascist Nesta Webster, who provides the next clue in the development of the Illuminati legend. Webster, writing in the 1920s, decided that the idea of a secret Jewish cabal was merely a smokescreen, devilishly contrived by none other than the Illuminati to perpetuate their agenda of world domination through the spread of world communism. The *Protocols* were merely a diversionary tactic, as she explained in *World Revolution* in 1922:

> Here was the whole explanation – a conspiracy of the Jewish race that began perhaps in Golgotha, that hid itself behind the ritual of Freemasonry, that provided the driving force behind the succeeding revolutionary upheavals, that inspired the sombre hatred of Marx, the malignant theory of Trotsky, and all this with the fixed and unalterable purpose of destroying that Christianity which is hateful to it. Is this theory true? Possibly. But in the opinion of the present author it has not been proved – it does not provide the whole key to the mystery.

The key to the mystery could be found in Weishaupt's writings, in which Webster, reflecting the fads of her day for theosophy and other forms of spiritualism, claimed to see evidence of occult practices:

> Let us not forget that the cult of Satan which flourished in Bavaria at the same time as Illuminism, and was in all probability connected with it, is practised today in our own country. The powers exercised by the modern Illuminati are occult powers and range from hypnotism to black magic, which, since the days of the [18th-century] magician Cagliostro, have always formed part of the stock-in-trade of the sect.

In doing so, Webster can be credited with personally introducing the Illuminati story to the 20th century and laying the groundwork for much of the theories that persist to this day: the occult allegations resurface in the fears of the Christian right and reinforce the Illuminati's reputation for Satanism; the order's republican philosophy is contorted to embody the threat of communism, and underlying it all is the nasty and inescapable taint of anti-Semitism. What a legacy. And yet, even today, her work is often quoted as a valid historical reference, as proof of the Illuminati's existence – even among mainstream, reputable publishers – and her titles are continually reprinted.

But where did Webster's ideas about the Illuminati stem from? Why, in the 1920s, when there was no shortage of ideological enemies, did she choose to resurrect a centuries-old sect, one which, by all accounts, had existed for little over a decade?

Webster, as well as being an anti-Semitic fantasist, was a staunch royalist. Prior to her career as a conspiracist, she had written a number of books about the French Revolution, including a romantic novel, always siding with the aristocracy. During her research, she had come across the works of the two men who were at the root of the whole Illuminati legend. One, a displaced ex-Jesuit priest writing at the time of the French Revolution, introduced the idea of the Illuminati to continental Europe, and passed the baton to an – otherwise esteemed – Scottish scientist, who spread the word to the English-speaking world.

The Abbé Augustin de Barruel had been forced to flee France when the militant Catholic order known as the Society of Jesus, or Jesuits, had been dissolved by the French monarchy in the mid-18th century. When the explosive events of the French Revolution unfolded, Barruel, like many others, searched for answers, and a cause. As a royalist he was unlikely to blame a profligate court for the masses' uprising and instead, in *Memoirs Illustrating the History of Jacobinism*, an exhaustive four-volume account, published in 1798–9, he set about establishing the identity of the agitators. Among the culprits – enlightened *philosophes*, revolutionary Jacobins and Freemasons – Barruel traced the origins of these seditious ideologies back to a defunct philosophical group in an obscure provincial town – the Illuminati. Its founder, Adam Weishaupt was:

... an odious phenomenon in nature, an Atheist void of remorse, a profound hypocrite, destitute of those superior talents which lead to the vindication of truth, he is possessed of all that energy and ardour in vice which generates conspirators for impiety and anarchy.

Were it not for Barruel the story of the Illuminati would have ended almost as soon as it began, when it was outlawed in 1788 by government decree. But the Illuminati story was too good for Barruel to pass up: these (foreign) philosophers, to Barruel's eye, seemed to advocate the ideologies of the radical French *philosophes* in spades – yet also appeared to have connections with mystical, pre-Christian (for which extrapolate anti-Christian) sects. Even better for Barruel, as the Illuminati no longer existed, they couldn't come forward to refute his claims. In terms of the Illuminati story, he had established the group's reputation, sowing the seeds for a myth that would take on a life of its own.

Concurrent with Barruel's obsession with the alleged role of the secret societies in the French Revolution, Scottish scientist John Robison was examining the evidence from the other side of the channel, and came to the same conclusion, laying the blame squarely at the feet of the Illuminati. However, Robison approached the Illuminati story from a position of Protestant rectitude. His *Proofs of a Conspiracy* of 1798 positively bristles with moral condemnation:

Their first and immediate aim is to get the possession of riches, power, and influence, without industry; and, to accomplish this, they want to abolish Christianity; and then dissolute manners and universal profligacy will procure them the adherents of all the wicked, and enable them to overturn all the civil governments of Europe; after which they will think of farther conquests, and extend their operations to the other quarters of the globe, till they have reduced mankind to the state of one indistinguishable chaotic mass.

Robison's words reached the newly formed United States in the autumn of 1798, a time of considerable political turmoil. Revolutionary events in France had impressed the country deeply, with allegiances to both sides split down party lines. Conservatives feared that whatever ungodly influence had brought down the French monarchy would spread to American shores, and the arrival of Robison's text only served to underline their concerns. From the conservative standpoint, the French Revolution was the result of the Enlightenment gone mad, and it was the spread of these revolutionary ideas that had incited an unruly populace to topple the established order. Even though the US had itself been forged from revolution, and was founded on the democratic principles that seemed to have had such a pernicious effect in France, conservatives feared that these foundations were still vulnerable to seditious influences. For just over a year, the imagined dangers of an Illuminati-provoked revolution were kept in the public eye through a series of sermons by a handful of conservative New England clergymen. Of course, the Illuminati had never set foot on American shores; they had ceased to exist a decade previously. But for conservatives they embodied the seductive dangers of freethinking, of excessive rationalism and, worst of all, for the clergy, deism. Essentially, the Illuminati scare was the first recorded example in the US of a campaign against the decline in family values. Given how briefly the fears reigned, and how quickly they subsided, it is easy to underestimate their influence, but at their height even George Washington was convinced of the seriousness of the situation, writing to a member of the clergy in 1798: "It was not my intention to doubt that the doctrines of the

Illuminati, and the principles of Jacobinism, had not spread in the United States. On the contrary, no one is more fully satisfied of this fact than I am."

This is the story of how the Illuminati fears developed, and were rediscovered and invented, from Barruel, to Webster, to Welch to the present. But what about the actual, historical Illuminati? Who were they and what were their aims? Although there have been a number of sects and groups whose name derives from the idea of illumination – the 16th-century Alumbrados of Spain, the mystical Illuminés in southern France in the 18th century to name but a few – the actual Bavarian Illuminati was founded in 1776 by university professor Adam Weishaupt in Ingolstadt in Bavaria. The aims of the Order of the Illuminati were to study and spread the principles of the Enlightenment in a deeply conservative and traditional part of Europe. Secrecy was crucial to its survival: neither church nor crown would have countenanced the group's anti-clerical and anti-monarchist ideas. Weishaupt actively sought to promote a system of education independent of the domineering influence of the Catholic Church prevalent at the time, and believed that "Hidden schools of wisdom are the means which will one day set men free from their bonds".

At its height the Illuminati numbered 2,500, with members across Europe, including some of the period's leading thinkers, such as Goethe. Yet just 12 years after the group's founding, it was disbanded by a governmental edict outlawing all secret organizations, and the Illuminati ceased to exist.

And yet, for nearly 250 years references to the Illuminati and its alleged influence on major world events have continued to resurface. Weishaupt himself is arguably among the most maligned figures in history, with his aims distorted beyond all recognition, until, if he is remembered at all, it is as the embodiment of evil, "A Human Devil" according to one early

20th-century conspiracy theorist. Even in his own day Weishaupt was accused of all manner of crimes – procuration, poisoning and heresy – and was forced to live the rest of his life in exile. And yet, when publishing a defence of his order, he continued to emphasize its philanthropic aims, painting a picture of a world of universal brotherhood, one which aspired to the highest moral principles. In *An Improved System of the Illuminati* of 1787, he described the ideal candidate for the Order of the Illuminati as:

> [W] hoever is the friend and brother of the unfortunate; who-ever has a heart capable of love and friendship; whoever is steadfast in adversity, unwearied in the carrying out of what-ever has been once engaged in, undaunted in the overcom-ing of difficulties; whoever does not mock and despise the weak; ... whoever shuns idleness; ... whoever, when truth and virtue are in question, despising the approbation of the multitude, is sufficiently courageous to follow the dictates of his own heart – such a one is a proper candidate.

But his defence did not include an apology. Unrepentant to the end, he wrote: "I am proud to be known to the world as the founder of the Illuminati."

So, from philosophers, to republicans, to revolutionaries, anarchists, communists or the Antichrist, who are the Illuminati? This book traces the development of their identity, real or imagined, from Weishaupt's founding of the order to present-day theories. It looks at how perceptions and fears of the Illuminati have resurfaced, quite improbably, over more than two centuries, and have now come entirely loose from their his-torical moorings. The book begins by examining the activities of Weishaupt's Illuminati, and whether there was any truth in the accusations levelled against them. It then goes on to look at how the order's reputation spread to France during the Revolution, and onto the US at the end of the 18th century, and its effect on the political discourse of the day. The trail runs cold for the best part of a century, until it is revived in the early 20th century by the writings of Nesta Webster in the 1920s. Subsequent chapters look at how Webster's model for conspiracy theories was later picked up by the extreme right, and used to further the cause of anti-communism in the 1960s and New World Order fears in the 1990s. The final chapters look at how the Illuminati story was embellished by the left, first ironically, in the works of counterculturalists such as Robert Anton Wilson in the 1970s, and then in earnest by New Age and UFO theorists. Ultimately, however, what is most revealing about following the evolution of the myth is what it says about our own anxieties. Looking at history through the refracted prism of the Illuminati reveals much about the nature of fear itself.

Chapter One: European Secret Societies and the Origins of the Illuminati

A courier on his way to Paris from Frankfurt on a summer's night in 1785 found himself caught in a torrential downpour. He fought through the rain, desperately seeking shelter as the storm thundered overhead. He would never reach his destination – a violent flash of lightning cracked through the sky and struck him dead. Among his belongings was found correspondence from several members of the Bavarian Illuminati. Concealed in the lining of his clothing was further documentation about the organization and their plans to bring about revolution in Europe. The Illuminati, among other secret societies, had recently become the focus of a government edict outlawing clandestine organizations. And although they had not been mentioned by name, their atheistic, radical philosophies made them deeply unpopular with the Bavarian government. The death of the courier, reportedly on his way to deliver dispatches to another Illuminati cell, had clearly been the result of divine retribution; the monarchy's decision was vindicated by the Holy Father himself.

Some versions of the story claim the unfortunate courier was murdered, the documents planted on his body. Others that he and his horse were charred to coal, but that the saddlebags carrying the documents remained strangely untouched. Contemporary accounts have no record of this episode, but later commentators on the Illuminati myth lay great store by it. And why not? Although apocryphal, the story encapsulates a lot of the Illuminati legend in a nutshell: the midnight intrigue, the clandestine correspondence, the plans for revolution – and the evidence that God was not on their side. This last point would have resonated deeply with the citizens of Bavaria at the time, who, at the height of the Enlightenment in Europe, were caught in a Church-dominated timewarp.

The intellectual glow of 18th-century Bavaria was far less bright than that of its Protestant neighbours and the revolutionary ideas of the Enlightenment sweeping the rest of the continent made few inroads in the electorate. In Catholic Bavaria there were few aspects of public and social life in which the Church, in the form of the Society of Jesus, did not exert its power. Centuries of Jesuit-run education had resulted in a country that was intellectually stagnant and mired in superstition.

In an era which saw radical reform in the relationship between Church and State elsewhere in Europe, Bavaria's court was avowedly Catholic. All holders of government office, including those in educational establishments, were made to swear their belief in the Immaculate Conception and their allegiance to the Church, and, true to the ideals of the Counter-Reformation, any suggestion of Protestantism was dealt with swiftly and mercilessly.

The militant Catholic order of the Jesuits had successfully established schools throughout Catholic Europe and had been firmly in control of Bavarian education since the late 16th century. By the 1630s all educational institutes were run by the Jesuits, including the universities they had founded in Ingolstadt and Munich. And although the celebrated Jesuit education had initially been equal, if not superior, to that of its Protestant neighbours, by the late 18th century it had ossified into a stale method of learning by rote. The curriculum was rigid and allowed no deviation from the Church's dictates, which manifested itself in the most rigorous censorship. Educated Bavarians were aware of the new ideas sweeping the rest of Europe; however, they were equally aware that they had no access to the books that revealed them.

But it was not enough to clamp down on signs of Protestantism; the Church needed concrete reaffirmation of the the public's faith, and so religious festivals and rituals were reintroduced. Where the Church was unbending in education, it was considerably more lax when it came to worship. By the late 18th century, acts of devotion had been stripped of their more onerous elements and evolved into public celebrations. Pilgrimages, for example, could be taken by carriage, and saints' days required the most cursory church-going before elaborate feasting. With many rites now devoid of meaning, superstition and myth arose in their place; peasants buried effigies to protect their fields from frost, and offerings were placed on altars to ensure plentiful harvests. This attitude had a more sinister side: with superstition went a fear of sorcery, and between 1750 and 1756, two young girls were beheaded and burnt as witches.

It is against this background of superstition and intellectual suffocation that the Order of the Illuminati was created. This group, which has been blamed for every calamity, natural or manufactured – from the French Revolution onwards, that has been linked to the Order of the Assassins of ancient Persia and the heretics of medieval Spain, as well as alchemists and satanists – was developed, in part, as a group to disseminate learning. Stifled within the constricting intellectual climate of Bavaria, Weishaupt and his peers were driven by an awareness that a revolution of ideas was taking place elsewhere on the continent. It is unlikely that the order would have developed in quite the same way, if at all, in a more enlightened country. Yet its founder, Adam Weishaupt, was not only motivated by the thirst for enlightened thought. Without a doubt, he was also driven by a profound anti-clericism, aimed specifically at the Jesuits.

Adam Weishaupt, born in 1748 in Ingolstadt, was himself a product of a Jesuit education. Upon the death of his father, a professor at the university in Ingolstadt, Weishaupt's education was overseen by his godfather, the powerful Baron von Ickstatt. As a result of his patronage, the young Weishaupt was educated at a Jesuit college. Although this experience was to make a lasting, negative impression – Weishaupt was never known to refer to the Jesuits with anything other than contempt – some aspects of the society were later adopted wholesale in the formation of Weishaupt's order.

At age 15 Weishaupt, too, attended the university and, despite the Church's best efforts, by all accounts was able to find access to the works of the French enlightened philosophers. Certainly by this time he had earned a reputation as a brilliant, if radical, thinker with a correspondingly difficult personality – arrogant, confrontational, and with an unwavering sense of righteousness. By the time he had finished his studies and was offered a teaching post at the university, his relentless questioning of Jesuit doctrine and teaching methods were well known, which in that Jesuit-dominated environment did not endear him to his colleagues. Here his connections with von Ickstatt would once again bear fruit, and his unpopularity did not prevent the rapid advance of his career. More controversial, however, was his appointment to the chair of canon law, a position that, until then, had been held only by Jesuits. Politicking and intrigue ensued, and Weishaupt's salary was withheld when he took the post. Weishaupt reacted by spreading gossip and rumour, which only fuelled his colleagues' distrust.

The most comprehensive account of the Bavarian Illuminati was written by René Le Forestier and it remains unrivalled to this day. Much of the detail about Illuminati ritual and correspondence comes from his doctoral thesis of 1915. He relates how around the mid-1770s Weishaupt began to think about creating his own secret society. Whether this was before or after his first brief, unsatisfactory brush with the Freemasons is uncertain, but aspects of Freemasonry would play their part in the development of Weishaupt's society. If Weishaupt was moti-vated to form his society in response to what he saw as Jesuit intrigue and control of the university, he was also inspired by a desire to create a forum for learning and educated discussion, and a genuine belief in egalitarianism. Weishaupt wrote about his desire to establish "reading societies and subscription libraries", adhering to Rousseau's dictum that "reason should be the religion of man". His copious writings return repeatedly to the theme that Illuminism would entail "enlightening under-standing" with the ultimate aim being nothing less than "the happiness of the human race". However, when the aims of the order were made public in the late 1770s, questions were immediately raised about the lengths Weishaupt was prepared to go in his quest to spread Enlightenment. His much quoted mission statement is a gift to conspiracists: "Remember that the end justifies the means, and the wise ought to take all the means to do good which the wicked take to do evil." The debate con-tinues to this day.

Weishaupt's desire to create a secret society was not in itself suspicious or necessarily malign. The late 18th century was a golden age of social groups, secret and otherwise, and positively jostled with garrulous meetings of like-minded people in coffee houses, clubs and salons. Those who were drawn to intrigue and secrecy could join the Freemasons with relative ease. All that was required of their members was a moderate level of literacy and the ability to pay the group's fees, meaning that, in theory, merchants could rub shoulders with magistrates, labourers with lords. For a while in the mid-1770s the court of Munich was kept entertained by its flourishing secret "friendship" society, based on the chivalrous associations that were popular in France. The highest members of the court, including Max III Joseph, the Elector, belonged; all wore what were essentially friendship rings and swore allegiance to fidelity, sincerity and everlasting love. On the other side of the Atlantic, Benjamin Franklin sought to create a mutual aid society for young unattached men. His racily titled "Free and Easy Society" was a misnomer; far from being a raucous drinking group, the aim of Franklin's society was to give young men a framework for doing good deeds and providing mutual support in business ventures. An oath of sobriety, modesty and intellectual endeavour was expected of its members.

In this context, the origins of Weishaupt's secret society were potentially no more sinister than organizing a reading group for Bavarian merchants, albeit with more elaborate rituals than the usual lending library. In 1774 Weishaupt was introduced to Freemasonry by a visitor to the university. Intrigued, Weishaupt pumped his acquaintance for as much information about the organization as he was free to divulge, filling in the blanks where his source could not provide the details. When Weishaupt attempted to join a lodge in Nuremberg, his imagination went into overdrive and he became convinced that its members had him under surveillance at Ingolstadt as a test of his suitability. The persecution complex that made him so resentful of his Jesuit colleagues seemed to translate into eagerness where it related to the Masons, and he was keen to measure up, looking forward to his initiation and planning to carry out his duties with the diligence and exactitude of the pedant that he was. His enthusiasm would soon turn to disappointment though: the lodge's dues were difficult to meet on a professor's salary, living expenses in Nuremberg were much higher than in Ingolstadt and, most distressingly, the much-vaunted secrets of Freemasonry seemed to be freely available in many books. The element of secrecy being the main attraction, Weishaupt's initial flirtation with Freemasonry ended abruptly, but the desire to form his own society became more firmly entrenched.

Around the same time, an Ingolstadt military officer founded his own secret society devoted to studying the secrets of alchemy. Weishaupt was again recruited, but his rationalist, scientific mind recoiled at the idea that the cream of young Bavarian intelligentsia would be distracted by the fruitless pursuit of the philosopher's stone. Whether or not this was the final push needed, Weishaupt hastily founded his own society, initially called the Order of the Perfectibilists, and later to be called the Order of the Illuminati.

If Weishaupt had stuck with the original name of Perfectibilists, or called his group the Order of the Rationalist Bavarian Students, or something equally literal, his group might have slowly sunk into obscurity after it was disbanded in 1784. One aspect of its myth seems to have grown from its name, as it became, and continues to be, linked in the popular imagination with any and every group that has ever aspired to "illumination". And although the creation of a myth was part of Weishaupt's plan, certainly in terms of recruiting members, like all myths it was to take on a life of its own.

Weishaupt described his ultimate aim for the association as the "speedy prospect of universal happiness, in a state of liberty and moral equality, freed from the obstacles which subordination, rank, and riches, continually throw in our way" (Robison, *Proofs of a Conspiracy*, p64). And the means of achieving this? A form of rational Enlightenment thought that he described as "illumination", and therefore "The proficients in this order are … justly named the Illuminated." Considering the malign reptutation the Illuminati subsequently were to acquire, Adam Weishaupt's mission statement seems strangely modern, appealing as it does to the idea of taking individual responsibility to attain personal fulfilment:

And of all illumination which human reason can give, none
is comparable to the discovery of what we are, our nature,
our obligations, what happiness we are capable of, and what
are the means of attaining it.

(Robison, p65)

In May 1776 Weishaupt founded his order, initially with only
five members. Although subsequently these original members
were alleged to have included the Englishman Francis Dashwood
(of the notorious Hellfire Club), the Marquis de Sade (seemingly
between prison sentences and slumming it with a provincial
Bavarian professor) and a Rothschild, the reality was more pro-
saic, and comprised Weishaupt and five law students from the
university (one of whom was so lazy and contributed so little to
the organization that he was soon thrown out of the group).
Despite the group's small number, from the outset Weishaupt
used the principles of secrecy that would come to dominate the
organization and would be interpreted in a much more sinister
light by its critics through the ages. Of the original group, for
example, only two were aware of the whole story of the order's
aims and origins. Weishaupt had a firm grasp of human nature
when he used these elements of secrecy and concealment as a
means of attracting members to the group:

Of all the means I know to lead men, the most effectual is a
concealed mystery. The hankering of the mind is irresistible;
and if once a man has taken it into his head that there is a
mystery in a thing, it is impossible to get it out, either by
argument or experience.

(Robison, p129)

But what were these aims, and what was there to be secretive about? One of Weishaupt's principal aims was to create a

library, first in Munich and then elsewhere in Bavaria, containing all the books that Catholic, Jesuit-dominated Bavaria denied its students. Many of these books were freely available in the rest of the enlightened continent: the newest scientific texts (considered heretical by the Church), or works by the French *philosophes*, with their potentially dangerous advocacy of equality and democracy, were widely circulated beyond the confines of Bavaria. Weishaupt's ideology, too, would have been entirely familiar to his enlightened contemporaries. Weishaupt promoted the study of science as a discipline to be employed for the good of mankind, not for mystical reasons or individual gain, so alchemy or metaphysics was not on the Illuminati agenda, whereas the study of chemistry or physics was.

However, Weishaupt's aims were not entirely selfless. By educating and influencing his young charges (and they were young: men between 18 and 30 were considered the prime recruits for the order, while Weishaupt himself advocated members as young as 15), he aimed to bring about reform in all aspects of society, in education, government and religion. And he would also be able to more widely disseminate his other message: anti-Jesuitism.

Weishaupt had been at odds with his Jesuit colleagues since his arrival at Ingolstadt. By all accounts Weishaupt himself was a difficult individual, who managed to alienate those in authority and then complain he was the victim of a conspiracy. At the university he styled himself as the voice of reason and progress fighting the obscurantism of the Church. Weishaupt's resentment centred on what he perceived to be his colleagues' hindrance of his plans for modernization, with, on several occasions, debates raging over the books selected for the university library. The fact that the Jesuit order had been dissolved by government decree in 1773 did little to assuage Weishaupt's suspicions that his colleagues were in league against him, and in this he was not alone. During the late 18th century vehement, anti-Jesuitism was still present in much of Europe.

After centuries of power and prestige among the Catholic countries of Europe, the suppression of the Jesuit order was swift. From 1759 suspicions against the Jesuits had resulted in their progressive expulsion across Catholic Europe, beginning with Portugal and its colonies, followed by France in 1764 and Spain in 1767. By 1773, under Pope Clement XIV, the order was dissolved completely. At a stroke, it lost its missions, universities and churches, leaving 22,000 of its number adrift, without position or obvious livelihood. For many of its critics, the idea that the Society of Jesus had simply disbanded was unthinkable; that it had ceased to exist incredible, and it led to fears that the order had gone underground, that a clandestine regrouping would lead to a re-creation of the order elsewhere. The fact that the enlightened Frederick II of Prussia and Catherine II of Russia offered refuge to many of the ex-Jesuits in the form of teaching positions added to popular suspicion. Clearly their numbers were reassembling, with the protection of the crowns of Europe.

Enlightened, Protestant Europe had a history of anti-Jesuitism that stretched back much earlier than its present incarnation. The Society of Jesus had been conceived as a militant Catholic order in the 16th century, by Ignatius of Loyola, to expand the power of the Church and was viewed with suspicion since its inception. Rumours abounded, linking the order with assassination plots of heads of state, of planning to overthrow the French government, and of involvement in the Gunpowder Plot. A 17th-century forgery purporting to reveal the secrets of the order was wildly popular and went into several reprints. Its accusations of corruption and embezzlement entered the popular imagination, and for many the Jesuits took on the role of bogeyman, responsible for everything from fleecing widows of their fortunes to performing black magic. Even among the educated, the Church was seen as backward, as a hindrance to political and intellectual development. Voltaire, although himself educated by the Jesuits, was typical of the *philosophes* in his criticism of the established Church, and the Jesuits in particular. He saw the Jesuits as the perpetrators of superstition and bigotry, and the agents focussing distrust and hatred of marginal figures in society, such as Jews, under the guise of heretics. The entry in Diderot's *Encyclopedia* encapsulates the conspiratorial thinking about the order, from both the intelligentsia and in the popular imagination, linking them to the attempted murders of monarchs, of all manner of venal sin, and of magic and mysticism. Diderot is unstinting in his condemnation, taking issue with the Jesuits' secrecy ("At all times they have kept their constitutions a mystery ... For important matters, they write ... in cypher") and their duplicity ("the men...are all made by oath to be spies and denouncers of one another"). Their founder is dismissed pithily: "Decorated with the title Knight of Jesus Christ and the Virgin Mary, he set about teaching, preaching, and converting men with zeal, ignorance, and success." Such was the suspicion against the order that even Pope Clement XIV believed the Jesuits were plotting his murder, and so imprisoned their leader, Lorenzo Ricci. When the pope died in 1774 rumours abounded that the Jesuits had poisoned him.

Unbeknownst to them, the Jesuits played a crucial role in the creation of the Illuminati, and not simply in the latter's desire to undermine them. Weishaupt modelled his method for study and organization on many Jesuit methods, particularly in the pyramidal structure, and his encouragement of members' spying on one another. And later, when rumours of dastardly Illuminati plots were common currency in Europe and beyond, they would bear a striking resemblance to these earlier fears of Jesuit plots (many of which, it must be said, the Illuminati were themselves guilty of spreading).

From the outset, Weishaupt planned his secret society as a complex structure involving different levels of study, each overseen by an immediate superior. Slowly, his ideas of enlightened egalitarianism would be revealed to his disciples, who, as they acquired knowledge, would ascend the ranks of the organization, each in turn then responsible for the education of their own recruits. Weishaupt's aim was to recruit among the students of Ingolstadt, slowly acquiring more disciples as suitable members were vetted and invited to join the order. If, at its height, the order was rumoured to number 2,500 (and there is good reason to believe this was exaggerated) for the first two years of its existence, the dreaded Illuminati, the scourge of governments, of the established Church and of the civilized world, numbered only 12.

It is a truism that the key aspect of secret societies that intrigues us most but leaves them open to so much misinterpretation is their secrecy. By their very nature not much is known about them. For the first few years, the Illuminati, on the other hand, seem to have left a paper trail covering half of Ingolstadt, documenting every aspect of the group's plans. Part of its disciples' duties were to document their studies, submitting papers to their superiors, who in turn wrote reports on their pupils' progress. These reports were submitted up and down the hierarchy, with reports and comments submitted back and forth, seemingly *ad infinitum*. Revolutionary or not, Weishaupt certainly had the makings of a petty bureaucrat. Later, when the order was banned by government decree, this excessive documentation would prove its downfall.

Many of Weishaupt's letters from this time attest to the type of member the Illuminati were hoping to recruit, looking for the brightest and the noblest, both in character and by birth – powerful members of society who could eventually be placed to influence aspects of political, religious and educational life:

By this plan we shall direct all mankind. In this manner, and by the simplest means, we shall set all in motion and in flames. The occupations must be so allotted and contrived, that we may, in secret, influence all political transactions.... Who would have thought, that a professor at Ingolstadt was to become the teacher of the professors of Gottingen and of the greatest men in Germany?

Spartacus (Weishaupt) to Cato (Zwack), 1780

Members were given new names by their superiors (eg., in the early stages, Weishaupt) usually with classical allusions. Much has been made of Weishaupt's choice of Spartacus – after the Roman slave who led the rebellion – as his pseudonym. Other names of the founder members included Tiberius and Ajax, and later Cato, who was to become Weishaupt's right-hand man. (Ajax, on the other hand, was asked to leave the group in disgrace when he neglected his recruitment duties in favour of pursuing a young lady in Munich.)

The first years of the Illuminati were characterized by excessive paperwork and a need to recruit new members. At first Weishaupt had organized the order along the lines of English Freemasonry, using three levels of grade: Novice, Minerval and Minerval Illuminé, or Master. The first, Novice stage, could last anywhere from one to three years, depending on the age of the novice, although in theory it was indefinite, and advancement depended on the quality of the novice's studies. Once invited to join, the novice was given his *nom de guerre* by his superiors, which would also indicate the theme his studies might take: "Tiberius", for example, might be required to research the history of his namesake. These studies were accompanied by detailed documentation, all handed in to his superior, and accompanied further studies relating to the novice's particular subject area (eg arts or sciences). The novice met weekly with his superior (or fortnightly if away, although this again was supplemented by copious amounts of correspondence) to discuss the development of his studies. So far, joining the Illuminati sounds about as threatening as a first-year degree course.

But this was not the only duty the novice was expected to perform. The novice ascended the ranks by recruiting his own disciples, whose studies he in turn would supervise. At this stage Weishaupt was concerned with the exclusivity of his order (although this would change in a few years when numbers remained stagnant). Potential recruits were approached with tact and discretion; too much information divulged too soon could be potentially damaging to the group, and so candidates were sounded out over a period of time until members were confident they shared a similar philosophy. Weishaupt was looking for young men from good families initially, with the idea that they would be more receptive to his ideas, and more likely to carry them in to places of authority when they took up positions in the establishment later. Later, Weishaupt's Illuminati confrère Baron Knigge would criticize this method as being too slow, requiring generations for the Illuminati philosophy to infiltrate society at any significant level. For now, though, the provincial law professor had to make do with recruits in his immediate environment, who tended to be students. Contrary to later myths, the Illuminati were looking for candidates of good character; no one suspected of gossiping (for obvious reasons), lying, cheating or general debauchery was to be considered. Nor were monks ("Ex-Jesuits must be avoided like the plague", Weishaupt instructed), members of other secret societies or, at first, women, allowed to join. One of the many crimes levelled against the Illuminati by later critics would be their plans to recruit women (the virtuous to insinuate their way into polite society; the less virtuous for general merriment and carousing). As will become clear later on, this, like most accusations of the group, says more about the group's critics than it does about the order itself. Likewise, the group's anti-clericism, which it shared with the *philosophes* and other enlightened thinkers, would be reinterpreted as heathenism and then satanism, but in fact Weishaupt made a point of recruiting Christians.

Once a novice had successfully recruited a new member, he would become a mentor, responsible for overseeing the studies of his new disciple. The mentor would now receive a new level of information, among which were the rules governing his own behaviour in this new position. One of the cardinal rules for a mentor was characteristic of the group as a whole: Weishaupt demanded the utmost secrecy, not just between members and the general public, but between members themselves, explaining: "One must speak sometimes in one way, sometimes in another, so that our real purpose should remain impenetrable to our inferiors." Weishaupt intentionally organized the group so that, apart from himself, few, if any, members were privy to the set up of the whole organization. Novices only knew the name of their immediate superior, and were kept wholly ignorant of who might be above them, and so on up the chain. When novices themselves became mentors, they were sworn never to divulge the name of their immediate superior, and so on, meaning no member was ever sure where he was placed in the pyramid.

Further safeguards were put in place to ensure secrecy. Lower orders could not discuss the most insignificant details among themselves, or with higher orders until permitted to do so. Nor could lower orders keep any correspondence relating to the group in their possession. Upon receiving a letter from their superior, for example, they were instructed to return the original with their answer. Weishaupt devised a coded alphabet to relay more controversial information, and members were instructed to keep documents in a locked box, labelled, in case of the owner's death, with instructions to give the box to another Illuminati member. These safeguards did not ensure the group's secrets were kept out of the public eye when the Elector of Bavaria outlawed the group, but they must have kept the members busy at the time, and perpetuated the group's sense of importance.

At the earliest stages, the novice would be free to leave the order whenever he chose, as long as he swore not to reveal any of its secrets. This was relayed in threatening language suggesting he would have a great deal to fear if he did so, but this is no different from oaths required from many secret societies and, indeed, fraternity houses up and down the United States. If the novice chose to stay within the order, and to take on his studies and role as initiate, he swore fidelity to the group, forsaking all personal aims for the good of his fellow Illuminati. Members were obliged to fill in detailed questionnaires pertaining to their family background, with particular attention paid to what books were in their possession. Members also swore unfailing obedience to their superiors (which, again, makes those suspicious of the group nervous of its intentions), but safeguards were in place – by way of the inevitable form filling – which allowed the novice to submit a secret monthly report on the behaviour of his mentor, who in turn would be expected to report on his report.

The next stage, the Minerval, involved an initiation ceremony, the kind that sends conspiracists into a frenzy of excitement, but that appears to adhere so closely to the unwritten rules governing the behaviour of clandestine groups that it seems almost laughable. For this, the initiant would be taken to a secluded spot, perhaps a forest at midnight or a room illuminated only by moonlight, overseen by the symbols of Minerva, such as an owl. Here, he would swear an oath of allegiance, and a sword was pressed to his bare chest as a symbol of what he could expect if he were to betray the group, accompanied by further threats of vengeance. Now, welcomed into the higher level, the Minerval could look forward to more rigorous studies (with a choice of specialization, again strangely like a degree course) as well as a vast increase in his administrative duties, with reports both on his disciple's progress, and comments on his superior's comportment.

For all Weishaupt's emphasis on fidelity to the group and brotherly love, the underlying message was that members were essentially kept in check by spying; they were required to report on the behaviour of others, and in turn were aware that other members would be reporting on them, without ever being sure who these other members might be, or how high up in the order they were placed. As Weishaupt wrote to Knigge in the 1780s:

> Every person shall be made to spy on one another and all around him; friends, relations, enemies, those who are indifferent – all without exception shall be the object of his inquiries; he shall attempt to discover their strong side and their weak, their passions, their prejudices, their connections, above all their actions – in a word, the most detailed information about them.

For the first few years, however, could this have mattered? Eighteen months after its inauguration the group still numbered only 12, most of whom were based in Ingolstadt. Recruitment was initially slow, and the order was beset by money problems. Weishaupt's dream to create a library was costly and most of the group's funds were diverted into seeking out the books needed to stock it. Members were sent to retrieve volumes from Protestant Germany and elsewhere; the banned books of the notorious Illuminati library contained ideas current and widely circulated on the rest of the continent. In that respect, Weishaupt was providing a service to his fellow Illuminati, allowing them access to the latest developments in philosophy and the sciences. Bavaria's intellectual stagnation backfired; if its censorship had been less draconian, the Illuminati may not have formed at all. Almost tragically, when Weishaupt was to recruit Baron Knigge, the latter revealed that the intensive Illuminati studies were no more sophisticated than that of the average school child in Protestant Germany. But there was another aspect to the library. Alongside the scientific and philosophical treatises were titles pertaining to world religions, including the Jesuits, as Weishaupt believed the more information he could accrue the more likely he could combat them. This aspect of the library no doubt contributed to later accusations of mysticism and black magic, although that was not the intended purpose.

For the first few years, while the order was slow to recruit new members, Weishaupt tried all manner of ways to boost the Illuminati coffers. Copious letters to "Cato", Xaviar Zwack, a government lawyer recruited later in 1776 and soon supplanting the fickle Ajax as Weishaupt's loyal adjunct, reveal these to be strangely naive.

No scheme to raise money seemed beneath Weishaupt's consideration. Members were exhorted to seek out wealthy recruits, even offering advancement up the Illuminati hierarchy in exchange for cash. The library was plundered for lesser books or multiple copies, with the idea of selling them, and it was even suggested that if members were truly loyal to the order they would put personal considerations aside and marry into money for the good of the group. Needless to say none of these schemes had a lasting effect on the Illuminati finances, and the group remained insignificant until it moved into its second phase, with the recruitment of Baron Knigge in 1780.

The urbane and worldly Baron Knigge came from an old

family in Hanover. Widely read in the works of the *philosophes*, and himself a playwright of note, Knigge had had a successful career at the royal court before running through his fortune and incurring the jealousy of his fellow courtiers. He retired to Frankfurt to live frugally on what was left of his money. In many ways he was a secret society groupie, seeking out the latest esoterica in the way that today's celebrities pick and discard mystical religions or faddish diets. As a young man he had been involved in the Freemasons but never progressed beyond the level of apprentice, probably because his superiors found him too indiscreet and inclined to gossip. Aware he was unlikely to progress through the ranks by conventional means, Knigge instead read all he could about the order, befriending anyone who might reveal its secrets to him. Later, he took up with the Knights Templar, drawn to the group's mysticism and ceremony, and finally dabbled in the study of alchemy. Having made the tour of popular 18th-century secret pursuits (with a brief stop via the Rosicrucians) Knigge made another attempt to infiltrate the Masons, this time with the idea of orchestrating a massive re-organization of the group. When Weishaupt made contact with an invitation to join the Illuminati, Knigge leapt at the opportunity.

It was the meeting with Knigge that revealed the first phase of the Illuminati in its true colours – as a provincial study group whose secrets were no more esoteric or radical than the education of the average Protestant school child. But Knigge was well connected, and able to bring a coterie of influential friends to the order. Although some of these dropped out when they realized the nature of the group and the extent of the commitment required of them, Knigge persevered, lured by the promise of quick ascension up the ladder and Weishaupt's emphasis on his key interests: philosophy and science. Weishaupt's egalitarianism was put to the test in his dealings with Knigge, and clearly found wanting: evidently, power and connections would advance a member more quickly than diligence and study. In a very short time Knigge was on his way to reaching the highest order of the Illuminati.

Here Weishaupt found he was a victim of his own success. While the order remained small, Weishaupt was able to keep his disciples in a state of ignorance regarding their position within the group, and what they might need to do to advance up the ladder to attain the next level of Illuminati wisdom. The truth was that at this stage there wasn't a great deal of wisdom to impart, no esoteric secrets to reveal. After the Minerval ceremony by moonlight, Weishaupt hadn't thought through to the next level (no one had achieved it but him). With Knigge, this had to change, and it had to change fast. If the secrets of the Illuminati were revealed to entail no more than a stuffed owl and a frat-boy oath, it would lose all credibility and the few members it had.

This led to one of the many contradictions in the order, and also was to provide further ammunition for those who wanted to castigate the group. In several letters to Zwack around this time, Weishaupt relates some of his ideas for this new phase of the Illuminati. This arch anti-cleric, motivated equally by anti-Jesuitism and the quest for enlightened thought, admits to Zwack the undeniable power of Catholic ritual, with its incense and incantations, to bind men to their faith. Why not, he mused, draw inspiration from this to develop their own rituals. To this end he looked back to much earlier religions. The Masons incorporated aspects of Ancient Greek cults into their ceremonies; Weishaupt needed to find another avenue and looked to Ancient Persia, Zoroaster and the cult of fire. This new development meant that Weishaupt could claim, retrospectively, that fire was the symbolic aim of the Illuminated. The new, higher grades would reflect these origins in some way, with names incorporating references to fire or the ancient Persians. To attain these levels, initiates would need to study physics and even electricity, thus combining elements of enlightened thought with the ancient mysteries. Several centuries later, Weishaupt's decision to incorporate arcane, ancient ritual into the Illuminati structure was used as supposed evidence of the order's pre-Christian antecedents. It was in fact, as genuine as a pantomime, tacked on to existing (equally fabricated) ritual to increase membership. Working out the actual detail was onerous though, and Weishaupt appeared to struggle with the concept, when another tack was taken, that of aligning the order with the Masons.

During the 18th century opinions about the Masons varied wildly. Some saw them as no more than debauched gentlemen's clubs, others as pseudo-mystical establishments known for arcane rituals, while still others considered them centres for discussing enlightened thought. By the end of the century, however, all these reputations would be eclipsed when they became synonymous with revolution and the Jacobins. The true origins of Freemasonry are unclear, obscured by the self-aggrandizing, romanticizing myths of the Masons themselves, and further conjecture by those critical of the Brotherhood. But the first lodges appear to have originated in England, where they may have developed from medieval guilds, and later spread to continental Europe, finding favour particularly in enlightened, Protestant countries. English lodges were based on three degrees, that of apprentice, fellow-craft and master, and, certainly in the 18th century, seemed to be based on the idea of an egalitarian, intellectual social club, accepting all religions and members at all levels of the social scale. Freemasonry on the continent developed in a different direction. In the 18th century, one school of thought traced the Masons back to the Knights Templar, who were persecuted and destroyed by the French king Philippe IV in the 14th century. This theory claims that some of the Templars were allowed to escape France, where they fled to Scotland and created the Scottish Freemasons. In any event, the Scottish system, which strongly influenced the continental lodges, incorporated more grades and emphasized its Templar antecedents. German Freemasonry followed this trend, incorporating seven grades that clearly heralded the order's allegiance, with titles such as Scottish Knight and Templar.

Eighteenth-century German Freemasonry was something of a fad among the worldly and fashionable. It was a pan-European organization, and its international flavour found favour in the Prussian court, which suffered somewhat of an inferiority complex when it came to culture and looked abroad for its artistic expression, with Mozart operas sung in Italian, and French spoken at court. Among notable Prussian Masons were Crown Prince Frederick himself, as well as cultural titans such as Mozart and Goethe. Perhaps as a backlash against the age of reason, or as a precursor to the *Sturm und Drang* of German Romanticism, German Masonry focussed on the mystical aspects of the craft; ceremony played a large part in the lodges, and drew on the Templars and Crusades for its imagery, involving elaborate costumes with crosses and helmets. Two aspects of German Masonry were to resurface in the Illuminati, and were to allow the Illuminati in turn to influence Masonry: unwavering obedience to the group, and the principle of the "unknown superiors", in which no member ever knew the entire set up of the organization, where he was placed in the hierarchy, and who was positioned at the very top.

By the 1770s, however, German Freemasonry was in crisis. Its leader, Baron Karl Gotthelf von Hund had died without revealing the secrets of the organization, leaving the lodges without direction. The Templar connection seemed to have evolved into no more than elaborate play-acting, and the secretive nature of the group made it prey to charlatans, as no one knew who was a superior – enterprising fraudsters could infiltrate lodges by claiming to know the true secrets of the group. Worse still, rumours abounded that the outlawed Jesuits had joined the Masons with the idea of regrouping.

It was to this situation that Weishaupt and Knigge brought their next phase of the Illuminati. With German Freemasonry directionless and the Illuminati needing to boost its numbers, the idea came to Weishaupt to infiltrate the Masons. With secrecy still paramount, this would allow Weishaupt to create an order within an order, with members unaware of who belonged to what (and indeed, where they themselves fit in the proceedings), to poach the Masonic membership (which included some very influential and high-ranking members) and, finally, to resolve the issues of higher Illuminati grades. Knigge, who had always been drawn to the mystical aspects of the secret societies, was instrumental in establishing these new grades, and gave them names such as Priest, Reigning Priest, Grand Magus and Man-King; progression up these ranks became so inextricably linked with the Masons that it was impossible to attain a higher level without being a member of both.

While this development seemed to solve many of the Illuminati's problems, all was far from well between Weishaupt and Knigge. Knigge had quickly scaled the heights of the Illuminati structure, and sat at its pinnacle with Weishaupt, yet they were fundamentally different in their approach to the organization and its aims. Weishaupt still felt that recruitment should happen slowly, with possible members approached over a period of time and vetted for their suitability. Knigge was all for numbers, and proved his point by, according to his reckoning, recruiting 500 members in 1780. This backfired, however, as according to Illuminati regulations, he was to be personally responsible for overseeing their studies and duties within the group. Other aspects of Knigge's approach were troubling to

Weishaupt, namely the pseudo-religious rites and rituals that were becoming part of the initiation into higher orders. For a group that had been organized to discuss enlightened philosophy and scientific developments, and to fight the obscurantism of Jesuitism, this was completely antithetical, as it appeared to be actively encouraging the superstition and ignorance it had been formed to combat.

Membership continued to grow and, these differences aside, the alliance with Freemasonry, measured purely in numbers, was a resounding success. In 1779 the order had spread from Bavaria to Germany and Austria, then to France, Italy and Switzerland. By 1783 the Illuminati had a presence in Bohemia, and by the next year in Hungary. Sources for actual numbers are unreliable, but at its height membership was reported at anywhere between 600 and 2,500, and included such luminaries as Goethe, Mozart and Schiller, members of the nobility, as well as (according to rumour) Joseph II of Austria.

By 1783 this success was threatened as relations between Knigge and Weishaupt worsened. Knigge wrote to Zwack in January of that year: "It is the Jesuitry of Weishaupt that causes all our divisions, it is the despotism that he exercises over men perhaps less rich than himself in imagination, in ruses, in cunning... I declare that nothing can put me on the same footing with Spartacus as that on which I was at first... I leave him to blow himself and his Order into the air." In 1784, Knigge, after threatening to reveal many of the group's secrets, parted company with Weishaupt. Many of the new members did not take their oaths of secrecy in any way seriously. Details about the group were leaked to the public, which led to suspicions about its motives and, further, wildly embroidered rumour. Allegations that Joseph II might have been a member gained ground, and led to fears that the Illuminati were involved in a plot to annexe Bavaria with Austria. The Illuminati were accused of corrupting youths, of being traitors to the crown and of political conspiracy. In June of that year, the Elector Karl Theodore decreed the first of the government edicts forbidding the creation of all secret societies without government approval.

The Illuminati were not mentioned by name, and the feeling might have been at the time that if they were to keep a low profile, the issue would blow over. In any event, the members did not appear to take it seriously. A second edict in March 1784 proved them wrong, and specifically outlawed the Illuminati. Measures taken against the group were much more serious: papers were seized, and members arrested, with amnesty being offered to those prepared to provide information against the group. Weishaupt, whether having taken measure of the way the wind was blowing, or purely by luck, had by this time already fled Bavaria. Yet another ferocious argument with the university over his choice of books for the library had proved insoluble, and he left for the safety of Gotha where he continued to write copious, inflamed pamphlets against the upholders of obscurantism and enemies of Enlightenment. His absence only fuelled the anti-Illuminati feeling in Bavaria, however, with wild accusations raised against him as former members were interrogated.

The witch hunt had barely begun, and would gather momentum the following year, when in October 1786 the authorities seized documents, including letters from Weishaupt, from the lodgings of a former Illuminati member that were later published in the popular press. The scandal snowballed, and even respectable newspapers, responding to the public's eager consumption of lurid Illuminati details, printed new allegations and debates on a regular basis. Among these were reports that the documents contained instructions for making secret inks and poisons; for creating drugs for procuring abortions; for devising a locked box that would explode when forced open, as well as sensationalist details about the power of superior members over their initiates. The public lapped it up, which opened the flood-gates for more scandal, conjecture, rumour and intrigue. Weishaupt was forced to publish a defence of the Illuminati that year, among which was an admission that "My general plan is good, though in the detail there may be faults". Knigge, two years later, added his own. But there was no turning back: public and government opinion had so turned against secret societies, and the Illuminati in particular, that there was no way the group could continue to exist. By 1784 the group had completely dis-banded and Weishaupt continued to live in exile in Gotha.

The Illuminati is dead; long live the Illuminati. The group may have ceased, but rumours about it did not, and they spread from Bavaria to the rest of Germany and beyond. In 1790 over 50 books were published about the order, and readers' views still filled the letters pages of the newspapers on a daily basis. Mythologies surrounding it took on a life of their own, far more powerful than anything the group ever achieved in its short, actual life. One of the interesting aspects of the Illuminati myth is how it provides a template for later conspiratorial thinking; how the pattern of the public's reaction to its particular bogey-man remains the same, though the face of the alleged enemy may change. Fears of the spectre of the Illuminati in 18th-century Bavaria ran parallel with other contemporary fears, fed into them and ultimately absorbed them, so that, by the end of the decade, in the public's mind the Illuminati came to stand for everything that Weishaupt originally sought to combat. Anti-Illuminati feeling grew alongside and was fired by anti-Jesuitism, and the two became inexorably, inextricably combined.

Many believed that the Illuminati continued to flourish, and that they had, like the Jesuits before them, only been forced under ground. This extra layer of clandestine behaviour only made them seem more perfidious and sinister, and their lack of public presence, i.e., their very absence, was used as concrete proof of their underground activities. This argument is a continuing, persistent thread running through the history of the Illuminati myth, and is used by conspiracists such as John Robison and the Abbé Barruel in the 18th century, through to Nesta Webster and Lady Queenborough in the 20th.

One key issue in the Illuminati debate at the time was the confusion among the public of the nature of the different secret societies. By the 1780s, in addition to the Templars and the Illuminati, gregarious Bavarians with a penchant for secrecy and ceremony could join the Rosicrucians, the Asiatic Brothers or the African Builders, not to mention the different branches of Freemasonry, including the English, Swedish and French orders. While the aims of these groups may have differed, many shared the "Strict Observance" system, with the hierarchy of "unknown superiors"; this shadowy arrangement demanded to be seen as conspiratorial and sinister, and if one society was seen to be suspect, all were viewed in the same light and, ultimately, seen as the same organization – an attitude which continues today. Thus, the philosophical "enlightened" Illuminati are conflated with the mystical Rosicrucians, the esoteric alchemists, the Knights Templars etc. For the general public, the fact that other groups were still thriving was enough to prove that the Illuminati must also be. Some groups were quick to exploit this confusion, and tried to turn it to their advantage. The Rosicrucians, trying to distance their group from the anti-Illuminati smears, spread their own rumours that the Illuminati still existed in the guise of the Masons.

And if Bavaria was now suspicious of all secret societies, uninterested in separating fact from fiction or differentiating between any of the societies, it was equally undergoing a wave of anti-enlightenment thought. Some have seen the anti-Illuminati fears of this time as a symptom of a greater swell of opinion against philosophy, one which would climax post-1789 with the inextricable association of Enlightenment principles with revolution. In Germany, from the 1770s, this view was already gathering momentum, and manifested itself on one side in the rise of Romanticism and on the other in plans to create organizations to re-instill Christian values and combat rationalism. Ironically, these organizations were to take the form of secret societies; such was the prevalence of clandestine groups at the time, it seemed the obvious route.

The professed aims and ideologies of the Illuminati were, without a doubt, radical, and particularly so in tradition-bound Bavaria. But what was so interesting is the way in which their ideas, so in step with the philosophies of the French Enlightenment thinkers, were interpreted to their most extreme conclusion (and continue to be so). In Bavaria, the Illuminati's anti-clericism was not exclusive to the group, as has been seen in the general atmosphere of anti-Jesuitism of the time. Nor were the Illuminati avowedly atheist, sharing, as they did with the Masons, a deism which saw God as "The Grand Architect" of the universe. Yet this stance was to become associated in popular myth with the furthest extremes of anti-clericism, manifesting itself as its polar opposite, Satanism. Likewise, the Illuminati's anti-monarchism was taken to mean the complete destruction of all known governments, yet theirs was not the only group questioning hereditary rule and the divine right of kings: such ideas were current across the Atlantic in the United States and were equally prevalent in the Protestant countries of Europe. This wave of anti-enlightenment thought makes sense in the context of 18th-century Bavaria, whose tradition-bound society depended on an unquestioning allegiance to the authority of Church and monarchy, and therefore had most to lose by the spread of enlightenment philosophies that questioned such authority. The Illuminati, as Bavaria's homegrown embodiment of the Enlightenment, were to suffer the backlash, which to Weishaupt revealed the very conservatism and narrowmindedness he had been trying to combat, as he later wrote:

> The persecution of the Illuminati in Bavaria is perhaps in this century that event which will rouse humanity to indignation, if it becomes known in greater detail. It is the most complete victory of injustice, stupidity, malice, libel, Jesuitism and clerical intolerance over human reason.

Yet, at the same time, while the Illuminati were the victims of anti-enlightened thought, their aims were also conflated with the mysticism of other secret societies. This aspect of the Illuminati myth has been particularly persistent and, certainly from the early 20th century, seems to have overtaken the notion of the Illuminati as arch rationalists. Part of this may have been a result of etymology. When Weishaupt changed his group's name from the Order of the Perfectibilistes to the Illuminati, he gave later conspiracists the apparent link they needed to trace his order back through medieval Spain to ancient Arabia. The 16th-century Spanish Alumbrados were a group of mystics who sought communion, or "illumination", directly from God without the intermediary of Church ritual. Relentlessly persecuted by the Inquisition, the sect was almost immediately confused with other supposed "heretics", including one Ignatius Loyola, founder of the Jesuits. Loyola was arrested on suspicion of sympathizing with the group, and although he escaped with a warning, the association remained: for many this connection only proved the deep-rooted heresies of the Bavarian Illuminati. Later, in the early 17th century, the descendants of the Alumbrados spread to France, where they became known as the Illuminés. The movement was short lived, and its followers were quickly arrested. Nearly a century later, another obscure mystical sect with the same name surfaced in Southern France, and seems to have persisted until 1794; these Illuminés would add to the conspiracy theories circulating about the causes of the French Revolution, but had no connection with Weishaupt.

The alleged association with the Order of the Assassins is more dramatic, and thus more enduring and widespread, incorporating as it does the more lurid elements of mind-control, drug use and murder. This 11th-century Islamic sect terrorized the Muslim world with a campaign of violence and murder. Its members were noted for their ruthlessness and unquestioning obedience to their spiritual leader, known in the West as the "Old Man of the Mountain". Members allegedly regularly used hashish to reach a trance-like, "illuminated" state during which they committed their crimes, and also as a means by their leaders to ensure their members' commitment. "Assassin" is allegedly derived from "Hashashin" and also from the word for "keeper of the secrets". According to legend, the sect was based on the famous pyramidal structure, including the use of "unknown superiors"; for conspiracists this is a gift indeed, seen as positive proof that the Assassins were the precursor to the Illuminati. Even better for the myth-makers, the sect was said to use an extraordinary method of recruitment. Likely conscripts were intoxicated and kidnapped, then transported to a luxurious palace with beautiful gardens. Upon waking in this earthly paradise, they were allowed to enjoy their surroundings for several days, before being drugged again and returned to their original home. Thus primed, the future Assassin would be promised a place in paradise in exchange for his unwavering allegiance to his superiors. When the Illuminati myth resurfaced in the 20th century it became inextricably intertwined with all other "illluminated" myths. Ultimately, they all fed into one another, and are used to reinforce the veracity of each one; for example, the Assassin link has led to claims that Weishaupt himself regularly consumed hashish to reach a state of illumination, and that, by association, the fealty (and deadliness) of his members are not in doubt.

In 12 short years the Illuminati had gone from what was arguably a provincial study group, to, in the public mind, the scourge of western civilization. At no time was there concrete evidence that the Illuminati were the devastatingly well organized, well oiled machine they themselves claimed and were believed to be: from the outset rumour, fuelled by the press and the group's own writings, contributed to the myth.

And yet, in little over a decade, during this first wave of anti-Illuminati feeling, the key elements of that myth were already in place and had taken root. During a period which saw a flourishing of secret societies for a diverse range of interests, from the philanthropic or social to the mystical or philosophical, there was a sea change of public opinion about the nature of all secret groups. Secrecy was now undoubtedly suspect, associated with sedition in all its forms and to its furthest extremes: groups with political agendas must be anarchic; those with a spiritual or mystical aspect, satanic. Furthermore, this element of secrecy united all groups in the public's mind, attributing to them a common, sinister agenda, which incorporated all of society's worst fears. This is clearly seen in the idea of the Illuminati's library of banned books. Once the myth had taken on a life of its own, the imagined content of the books simply reflected whatever ideas society feared the most – whether anarchy, heresy (in the form of satanism or a "pagan" religion) or some vast unknowable evil. The fact that the rest of Europe was reading the same material was never raised, and the validity or not of censoring the material never questioned.

As the Illuminati myth became the repository for society's fears, so the perception of the order developed and transmuted into the very opposite of the original group's intentions, incorporating, often simultaneously, conflicting meanings. Thus in Bavaria at the height of fears of an underground plot by the Jesuits, the Illuminati came to stand for both an arch-rationalism, battling against the obscurantism of the Jesuits, as well as the Jesuits themselves. For those fearing the influence of this pervasive, omniscient group, there is no contradiction in this. Nor would there be when the Illuminati myth spread to the rest of Europe, and its message of rebellion was reinterpreted as the cause behind the French Revolution, working simultaneously in league with and against the aristocracy to overthrow the monarchy.

Chapter Two: Fears in Enlightenment Europe

On the morning of December 27th, 1798, the celebrated magician Count Cagliostro – society darling and conjurer to kings – was seized from his bed by the pope's soldiers and dragged in chains through the streets of Rome to the Castel Sant'Angelo. His rooms were ransacked and his beautiful wife Lorenza was escorted to a local convent. Among his belongings were papers foretelling the prophecy that the present pope, Pius VI, would be the last, and a strange array of objects, including a pair of crossed swords and a peculiarly flexible, anatomically correct female doll. News of his arrest swept the city and beyond, reaching the farthest corners of Europe: "Cagliostro has been arrested for trying to introduce the sect of the Illuminati to Rome."

Eight days later the magician was hauled before the Inquisition. He was subject to no less than 43 gruelling sessions of interrogation, during which time he was accused of the crimes of blasphemy, charlatanism, forgery, slander and fraud – even of forcing his beloved wife into prostitution. Yet these were nothing compared to the most serious of the accusations against him – his role in the French Revolution, and his participation in Freemasonry.

Only a few month's earlier, life for the count had been very different; Cagliostro had held Europe in the palm of his hand. He had been celebrated as a healer and mystic, and welcomed into the most privileged of salons. The society beauties who had hung on his every word would not have recognized him as he knelt, broken, before the Inquisition, awaiting news of his sentence, hooded and in chains. On April 7th, 1791 he was sentenced "to life imprisonment, to be served in a fortress, where the prisoner shall be closely guarded, with no hope of pardon" (Gervaso, *Cagliostro*, p225). A new law would confirm a previous edict banning all secret societies, particularly the Freemasons "and the other one which is commonly called Illuminati".

News of the verdict stunned Cagliostro's followers across Europe; the sentence seemed far in excess of the severity of his crimes. But the Europe of 1791 was very different from the one in which Cagliostro had made his name, and any secret activity alarmed the authorities.

The cataclysmic events of the French Revolution were of such a scale and of a violence never seen before, and their significance reverberated beyond the borders of France. When the events that had begun with the storming of the Bastille reached their bloody climax with the September Massacres of 1792 and the execution of the royal family the following year, the initial euphoria turned into terror. All of Europe looked toward France with anxiety. How could such a thing have happened, and what was stopping it from spreading to neighbouring countries?

With the revolution came such a radically new political landscape that it demanded a new understanding of the world. Old certainties were no longer; the very foundations of the civilized world had clearly no significance in the face of this powerful new force. With the toppling of the *ancien régime* came a radical shift in perception, and as familiar categories were destroyed and had yet to be replaced, conventional explanations for such extraordinary developments were increasingly seen to be inadequate. For the absolutist rulers of Europe, the idea that the French Revolution could have been a result of the French monarchy's deep unpopularity and flawed leadership would have meant accepting the need to put their own houses in order. For others, the conventional explanation for the cause of the revolution, that the people of France had risen spontaneously and of their own volition to protest an extravagant and morally bankrupt monarchy, just didn't seem plausible.

To understand the unthinkable a new explanation had to be found. The one that filled the vacuum was both an oversimplification and an elaborately constructed myth: the secret societies. As the revolution progressed, the secret society plot myth would become ever more convoluted and implausible, taking in such disparate and unlikely causes as a centuries-old vendetta, sorcery, satanism and, of course, the Illuminati. As the claims grew, the logic required to accept them became increasingly tortuous, and conspiracy theorists had to undergo ever greater imaginative leaps in their attempt to account for this vast web of plotting and intrigue.

Suspicions of Masonic involvement in the revolution did not initially require vast leaps of faith. Some of the revolution's most prominent figures, such as General Lafayette and the Comte de Mirabeau, were Masons. The Duke d'Orléans, great-great-great grandson of Louis XIII and cousin of the current king, Louis XVI, was made Grand Master of the French lodges in 1773. According to his detractors the Duke, later to style himself Philippe Egalité, had the most to gain from the revolution and the execution of his cousin: the French crown itself. What could be more plausible than that the Grand Master should summon all the strength at his command – that of the French Masonic brotherhood – to topple the monarchy? But this theory was only a small link in the vast conspiratorial chain forged at this time. According to one popular theory, the causes behind the revolution went much, much further back, and began with the Knights Templar.

The Templars were a band of warrior monks – crusading knights who had taken monastic vows – who had formed in the 12th century to protect pilgrims en route to the Holy Land.

Initially dependent solely on alms from pilgrims, their fortunes changed over the centuries. Papal protection had made them exempt from tithes and taxes, which vastly improved their finances, and from their original eight members they had grown to be a powerful organization. Whether because of their wealth, their power, or because of the secret nature of their oaths of allegiance, by 1307 they had fallen foul of King Philippe of France, who arrested their members, and imprisoned their Grand Master, Jacques de Molay. Accused of heresy, the Knights, including de Molay, "confessed" under public torture – an ordeal which many did not survive. De Molay was less fortunate, and spent the next seven years subject to brutal interrogation, trying, without success, to clear the name of the Templars. According to legend, as de Molay awaited execution in the Bastille, he set up four lodges of the Templars, who were sworn to avenge his death by destroying the papacy and the kings of France. After his execution the Templars were alleged to have gone underground, resurfacing in Masonic lodges, where they re-established themselves under the guise of the Scottish rites. A 1792 book, Le Tombeau de Jacques de Molay, attributed the revolution to descendants of the Templars. For many adherents of the Templar myth, the fact that the revolution "began" with the storming of the Bastille was no coincidence, but a symbolic act of retribution for the death of de Molay. Later, rumours circulated that at the execution of Louis XVI, members of the crowd cried out de Molay's name.

The secret society myth of the French Revolution has all the elements of conspiracy theory that continue to this day, and one of the most significant is the simple conflation of all secret societies with one another. According to this viewpoint, any clandestine activity is both suspect and connected to any other clandestine activity. Thus if one group falls under suspicion, all are tarred with the same brush. In no time, the Templars were connected with the Masons, the Masons with the revolutionary Jacobin clubs, and the Jacobins with the Illuminati, so that any and all groups were inextricably connected. The explanations for these connections became ever more convoluted, but created no less an impression for that. For a society in turmoil, such explanations were seductive, attributing blame firmly to a small group of insurgents, yet making them part of a conspiracy so vast that none could have seen it coming. But far from being the result of a conspiracy that extended back over centuries and continents, the origins of the secret society myths of the French Revolution can be attributed to a few key figures.

In the last quarter of the 18th century, France, the birthplace of the *philosophes* and the *encyclopédistes*, was simultaneously enjoying a conflicting trend, a mania for all things mystical and inexplicable. The hypnotist Anton Mesmer, ridiculed in much of Europe, had made a deep impression on the ladies of high Parisian society, establishing himself in sumptuous apartments, which were open to spectators of his marvellous feats of "animal magnetism" or mesmerism. Séances, spiritualism and alchemy all had their devotees among high society. Such was the prevalence of quacks and charlatans among the idle classes that one commentator on the revolution, the Abbé Fiard, devoted no fewer than three books to proving that magicians and sorcerers had caused the revolution. Certainly many dubious figures had the ear of Marie-Antoinette, which did not help her cause among a hostile populace.

Of these charlatans and conmen, none was as charismatic, and audacious, as the figure known as Count Cagliostro, among whose many accomplishments was to be the first to allege direct links between the Illuminati and the revolution. Born Giuseppe Balsamo in Palermo, Italy, Cagliostro's title seems, like most of the events of his life, to have been his own invention. Leaving Palermo at the earliest opportunity, he is believed to have travelled extensively in the East, where he was taught the secrets of alchemy and the occult. He spent some time in London, where he was initiated as a Mason, and where he developed his own version of the Craft – Egyptian Freemasonry. This version involved elaborate rites and ceremonies, incorporating exotic imagery drawn from his travels in the East and purporting to reveal to its members the secrets of oriental mysticism. His vagabond career took him through the courts of Europe, where his brand of mystical chicanery gained him access to the most influential of inner circles. A favourite of Louis XVI, he held "magic" suppers where he performed feats of psychic healing, held séances, and hypnotized willing participants, funding his extravagant life through the sale of dubious potions and "elixirs of eternal youth". He was one of the key players in the notorious Affair of the Necklace, an elaborate con involving purloined jewels and false identities which discredited the hapless Marie-Antoinette, and for which he spent six months in prison – an environment with which he was not unfamiliar. Fleeing France for Italy, he was arrested by the Inquisition for heresy, occultism and fraud, among other crimes, and was imprisoned in the Castel Sant'Angelo in Rome.

Prior to his arrest, Cagliostro's activities had made him notorious throughout Europe, and any news or gossip about the flamboyant figure was seized upon by an eager public. Newspapers across the continent were aware of this and this latest development in his colourful life would only guarantee more sales. So Cagliostro's confessions to the Inquisition made headlines; their actual veracity had little or no importance to those who reported them. From his side, they are unparalleled as a fanciful attempt to save his life and to perpetuate his own myth. These confessions, gleefully reported throughout Europe, involved exaggerated descriptions of his own (largely imagined) revolutionary activities and involvement with secret societies

such as the Illuminati. They have never had historical corroboration, either at the time or subsequently, yet when his biography, based largely on these confessions, was published in 1791
it was seen as proof for much of the Illuminati myths and sowed
the seeds for later, more elaborate anti-Illuminati literature.

During his trial, Cagliostro gained a lot of mileage from his
Masonic past, emphasizing his connections with the Templars,
the Strict Observance lodges and the Illuminati. He claimed
to have been introduced to the secrets of Masonry and
the Illuminati by the mysterious figure known as "der
Wundermann", the Comte de Saint-Germain, variously
described as a diplomat, spy, occultist and alchemist. Compared
to the Comte's powers of self-invention, Cagliostro was a mere
novice. This adventurer of unknown background spoke most
European languages but none with a native accent. Accounts of
his life claim sightings at various key interludes throughout the
18th century, appearing first in London in 1745 where he
befriended the Prince of Wales, then at the court of Louis XV as
a favourite of Madame Pompadour, and then later in Russia to
witness the coup that saw Catherine replace Peter the Great.
Familiar to all of Europe, but known by none, the Comte is
believed to have possessed the philosopher's stone and the
secrets of eternal life – throughout his long life legend has it he
never looked older than 40. Cagliostro would have been aware
of the power of such a notorious character in the self-mytholo-
gizing that was his confessions, and he presented a richly
embroidered tale of his initiation into the Illuminati by the
Comte, involving underground grottoes, sealed boxes and blood
oaths:

> An iron box filled with papers was opened. The introducers
> took from it a manuscript book [which] on the first page...
> read: "We, Grand Masters of the Templars..." then followed

a form of oath, whose exact words I cannot recall, but which invoked the destruction of all tyrants. The oath, written in blood, was attested by eleven signatures as well as my own... They were the names of the twelve Grand Masters of the Illuminati...from the little I managed to read, I gathered that the first move would be to strike against France, and after France against Italy, beginning with Rome.

(qtd Gervaso, *Cagliostro*, p92)

He wove elaborate tales relating the Illuminati's schemes to infiltrate positions of power all over Europe, starting by over-throwing the French monarchy, and eventually installing one of their own as pope. In order to achieve this, Cagliostro claimed that the Illuminati had deposited money throughout Europe under the auspices of the Masons and with the help of the Rothschilds.

Although this claim has never had historical confirmation, the reference to the Rothschilds was picked up in the 20th cen-tury by conspiracists such as Nesta Webster and used as spuri-ous "evidence" of a supposed Jewish conspiracy. And although many of the Illuminati's papers, confiscated by the Bavarian gov-ernment, had been published by this time, none corroborated Cagliostro's confessions.

Initially sentenced to death, Cagliostro's sentence was trans-muted to life imprisonment. The reasons for this are not known, but contributed to the belief that he had powerful friends behind him – such as the Masons or Illuminati – whose influence extended as far as the papacy. After 16 months in the Castel Sant'Angelo, suffering from hallucinations brought on by syphilis, the wretched man was moved to the San Leo Fortress, where he was incarcerated in an underground cell, 3m by 4m, and guarded day and night until his death in 1795. For years, sto-ries persisted that he had escaped and had been spotted throughout Europe, Russia and the US. It would take a decree by Napoleon attesting to his death to put the rumours to rest.

News of Cagliostro's trial reached France with the publication in 1791 of *Life and Deeds of Joseph Balsamo, so-called Comte Cagliostro*. Such was Cagliostro's notoriety that the book was an immediate success, yet the publishers, perhaps not trusting that Cagliostro's name alone would sell the text, appeared to tailor their translation to the French market. The French version focusses less on the facts of Cagliostro's life as a whole than on his colourful accounts of Egyptian Masonry, complete with pseudo-spiritualism and elaborate ritual devised specifically to titillate its young women members. This only served to further confuse the role of the Masons and perpetuate the Illuminati myth, and although the book was not the first to take an anti-Masonic position, it certainly helped to reinforce fears among those who already suspected the secret societies of orchestrating events behind the scenes.

One detail of particular interest to the French public was Cagliostro's claim that he had knowledge of a new secret society formed in Paris in 1786, with the aim of destroying the Catholic Church. Among the founders of this group were supposedly such high-ranking members of society as a bishop, three foreign ambassadors and a figure described as a "prince". Although there is no proof that such a society ever existed, or who its members might have been, anti-revolutionaries found it useful to see the Illuminati behind the unnamed secret society, and the Duke d'Orléans in the role of conspirator. The aristocratic Duke, while extremely popular among le *peuple* for his wholehearted embracing of revolutionary ideals and active participation in key events in the revolution, was viewed with less enthusiasm by royalists. Those who suspected the secret societies had a hand in the revolutionary upheaval were more than ready to accept that the Duke was involved in such underhand subterfuge. In the words of one anti-Illuminati writer:

> I cannot proceed in the narration without defiling the page
> with the detested name of Orléans, stained with everything
> that can degrade or disgrace human nature. He only wanted
> Illumination, to shew him in a system all the opinions, dis-
> positions, and principles which filled his own wicked heart
> .... This contemptible being was illuminated by Mirabeau, and
> has shown himself the most zealous disciple of the Order.
> (Robison, *Proofs of a Conspiracy*, p216)

Philippe, Duke d'Orléans was a notorious libertine who scan-
dalized French society long before he took up the revolutionary
mantle of liberty, equality and fraternity. As a young man his
carriage was frequently seen careening through the streets of
Paris, heedless of the welfare of any pedestrian unfortunate
enough to fall beneath its wheels. Enjoying to the full all that
his privileged life bestowed on him, the Duke quickly ran
through the family fortune. Threatened with destitution, he took
the unprecedented step of installing a series of shops and stalls
in his extensive gardens, creating, in effect, a perpetual carni-
val on the d'Orléans grounds, populated, as one critic sniffed,
"by the most common and perverse" crowd that the capital had
to offer. Although he was a cousin of Louis XVI, a long-standing
hatred of Marie-Antoinette meant that the Duke was not often
at court; instead, he travelled to London where he met the Prince
of Wales (the future George IV) and was impressed by English
government and parliament. By 1789 he was putting his democratic principles into action and had become involved in the
events of the revolution, even being elected president of the
National Assembly (a position he turned down). Although an
aristocrat, the people adored him: his bust, carried through the
crowd swarming the fallen Bastille, was met with cheers. (The

same cannot be said of finance minister Jacques Necker. His bust was pelted with rocks and destroyed by the same crowd.) By 1792 the Duke had renounced the d'Orléans name and styled himself "Citizen Egalité"; his gardens, formerly the Palais-Royal, were renamed "le Jardin de la Révolution".

But the following year Philippe Egalité suffered the fate of so many of his revolutionary compatriots and was executed on November 6th, 1793 as a traitor of the revolution. A hedonist to the last, on the morning of his execution he is reported to have breakfasted copiously with friends, drunk an entire bottle of champagne, and dressed immaculately for his journey to the guillotine.

A minor figure in conventional histories of the revolution, the Duke d'Orléans was elevated to the role of arch-plotter by some conspiracy writers because of his involvement with the Masons. (A persistent plot theory, begun by the royalist writer Galart de Montjoie, a contemporary of the Duke, and repeated by conspiracy writers today, is that the Duke orchestrated the revolution personally by hoarding grain, singlehandedly causing a famine among the general populace that led to rebellion.) The Duke explained his involvement in Freemasonry as follows: "At a time when no one could have foreseen our revolution, I attached myself to Freemasonry, which offered a kind of image of equality, just as I attached myself to the parlements, which offered a kind of image of liberty. I have since given up the phantom for the reality."

It is worth noting that Philippe's defence of his involvement with Freemasonry was not in response to attacks by counter-revolutionaries, but in answer to criticism from his revolutionary compatriots; as proof of his revolutionary credentials he had to protest that his involvement with Freemasonry was simply the prelude to the real enactment of democratic ideals. Freemasonry, at the time of the French Revolution, was all things to all people, and as such was under attack from both left and right.

By the 1780s Freemasonry in France was well established; in the last 20 or so years, 300 new lodges had been created, making their presence commonplace. French Freemasonry was characterized by the mystical aspects of the so-called Scottish rites, caught up with ritual and ceremony, and although members addressed one another as "brother", this was more a semblance of egalitarianism than the real thing. Most members were from the upper classes and were keen to maintain an element of exclusivity. Despite paying lip service to democratic ideals, the high membership dues required by many lodges prohibited members of the working class from joining. The left, therefore, had reasons to be suspicious of the lodges for their aristocratic membership. In addition the reference to Scottish rites suggested to some a connection with the deposed Stuart kings, and raised the question about the loyalties of the lodges and their members. This was to be a recurring concern for anti-Masons on both sides of the political spectrum. With their oaths of fealty to Masonic brothers and affiliated lodges across Europe, where did the Masons' sympathies lie? Would they be first to the lodge, and only second to the state? This concern would surface again and again across Europe, with heads of state and the general populace alike haunted by the idea of a vast network of affiliated groups crossing national boundaries.

For the French right, fears of Masonic activity came from the opposite end of the political spectrum and were based on perceived Masonic involvement within the revolutionary Jacobin clubs. The Jacobin clubs had their origins in the Club Breton, founded in 1789 in Versailles by deputies to the Estates-General, originally from Brittany, but soon including deputies from all over France. When the National Assembly moved to Paris later that year, the club took up residence in the refectory of a

Dominican monastery (known in Paris as Jacobins for their address on the Rue St Jacques). The club was founded to seek allies outside the National Assembly for its republican views, and initially included moderates such as Mirabeau among its members. Soon, patriotic groups affiliated with the club were formed throughout France. By 1792 it was known as the Société des Jacobins, amis de la liberté et de l'egalité, and its initially moderate political stance became increasingly radical; before long the term Jacobin became synonymous with revolutionary. Initially, its members were from the professional or bourgeois classes due to its high subscription fees. The provincial clubs were more democratic, but the original Parisian club had more than its fair share of liberal aristocrats. And of the deputies who made up the original Club Breton, all were Masons.

However, the Jacobins, by 1792, no longer presented a united front, but had split into factions of moderates (to become the Girondins) and radicals (the Montagnards). The Girondins were put under house arrest and executed by their former ally Robespierre. The Jacobins also had outlawed Masonic lodges by 1792 – hardly the actions of a revolutionary group with Masonic sympathies. For the French right, and many supporters of the ancien régime, the fact that there was a Masonic presence in the Jacobin clubs only furthered the theory that the Masons were responsible for the revolution. If this were the case, then they were particularly inept revolutionaries, as the plot they had allegedly orchestrated inexorably turned against them. Many aristocratic Masons met their fate at the guillotine (including the Duke d'Orléans), while others, such as Lafayette, lost all popularity and influence. The unfortunate Duke de Cossé-Brissac, former Grand Master of the Templars, was lynched – if the revolution had been enacted to avenge Jacques de Molay, it had spun wildly out of control.

All along, the Masons' critics and adherents alike took pains to distinguish the roles of English and continental Masonry. In England, members included high-ranking members of the royal family – during the late 18th and early 19th centuries the Prince of Wales, Duke of Cumberland and Duke of Sussex were all Masons – so the chances of any revolutionary Jacobin tendencies were non-existent. At the height of the Terror, English Freemasons made a point of illustrating their royalist leanings by printing a picture of the Prince of Wales on the front of one of their magazines. Later, Masonic publications referred to the Duke d'Orléans' death by guillotine as the "forfeit for his crimes". If the continental lodges were considered hotbeds of egalitarian fervour, across the Channel they were decidedly royalist.

However, it is important to note that just as Freemasonry accepted members from all walks of life, Masons could also be found on different sides of the political spectrum, and even those who could be counted among the revolutionaries did not provide a united front. One revolutionary journalist and self-confessed Freemason, Nicolas de Bonneville, was under attack from both the Jacobins and the counter-revolutionaries. For the Jacobins, de Bonneville's publications contained too many references to the mystical and occult to be taken seriously; for the counter-revolutionaries his activities were dangerously subversive. De Bonneville's Masonic beliefs may have embraced aspects of the occult, but his revolutionary credentials were not in doubt: a close friend of Thomas Paine, he shared many of Paine's ideals, advocating them in his journals and translating Paine's *Age of Reason*.

In Continental Europe, by this time, the trappings of Masonic ritual had entered the popular imagination, and rumours abounded that Masonic imagery had infiltrated the revolution. During the September Massacres, it was alleged that Masonic signs were exchanged between jailer and prisoners; those who responded correctly were spared the guillotine. John Robison, who would be so influential in spreading Illuminati fears to the United States, repeated the picturesque claims that the president of the French National Assembly wore a hat identical to that of the Masonic Grand Master, and that municipal officers wore the same scarves as the Masonic apprentices. Other writers would take up the theme, seeing in the shape of the guillotine itself a reference to the Mason's set square. The very ethos of liberté, egalité and fraternité was seen as fundamentally Masonic, a slogan derived from Freemasonry's ritual. By the time these rumours had been repeated, and published, and repeated again, they had evolved into references to the Illuminati, with claims that the red Phrygian cap of the sans-culottes originated in Illuminati initiation ceremonies.

This potent combination of Templars and wizards, of Masonic activity at once mystical and revolutionary, might have remained in the realm of popular myth were it not for the work of one man, who is believed by many to be singlehandedly responsible for establishing the conspiracy template still followed to this day: the Jesuit – and one-time Mason – Abbé Augustin de Barruel. A prolific writer of religious pamphlets and moral tracts and a committed royalist, the Abbé Barruel's dubious "masterpiece", *Memoirs Illustrating the History of Jacobinism* , codified many of the theories surrounding the causes of the French Revolution into one huge, overarching plot, taking in along the way all of the usual suspects of the Enlightenment – the *philosophes*, the Masons, the *enyclopédistes* – and establishing them, ultimately, as mere puppets of the Illuminati. His *Memoirs* contain all the elements that are recognizable in conspiracy narratives today, including a seemingly endless accumulation of "facts" proving the existence of a sinister cabal responsible for world-changing events, as well as the timelessness of such a group, with evidence of its existence from antiquity to the present.

The controversial and misguided Abbé Barruel became a

Jesuit in 1756 and, like many of his fellow priests, worked as a teacher, initially in Toulouse. By 1762 the anti-Jesuit feeling that was growing all over Enlightenment Europe had risen to such an extent in France that he was to leave his homeland in self-imposed exile, and travelled throughout Europe, living for a while in Prague. He would not return to France until 1773, when the Jesuit order was suppressed. Upon his return he was employed for a while as a tutor to the children of an aristocratic family, but a quarrel with his employer soon ended this position. He had already had some success with the publication of a tribute to Louis XVI upon his ascension to the throne, and it was on the strength of this that he continued to pursue a literary career. These early works reveal the elements of the political outlook that would colour his notorious *Memoirs*. Although the paranoid thread that runs through the later work was not yet in evidence, the conservative *Année Litteraire* that he was involved in from 1779 is dedicated to debating the arguments of the *philosophes*. As the *philosophes*, led by Voltaire, were so vociferous in their attacks on the established Church, and the Jesuits in particular, it is unsurprising that a once-exiled, former Jesuit would rise to the challenge in print. In the next few years Barruel published more anti-*philosophes* material in *Les Helviennes*, his first major work, translated into several European languages and which brought him wider acclaim.

By this time Barruel was beginning to hit his stride and he found himself in the vanguard of polemical conservative journalists, writing anti-*philosophes* tracts in the monthly *Journal Ecclesiastique*. The events of the revolution provided plenty of fodder for his opinionated diatribe, which became increasingly vitriolic. By 1789 he had begun to identify some of the key causes of the revolution, attributing it to "the decline of public morals and the progress of the *philosophes*". What had not yet surfaced in his writings was a direct attack on the secret societies.

This was to change in the next few years.

The September Massacres of 1792 caused Barruel to take refuge in England in 1792, during which time he met, among others, Edmund Burke (whose *Reflections on the French Revolution* had been published two years earlier) and John Robison, the Scottish scientist whose *Proofs of a Conspiracy* would later feed into the vast secret society myth, albeit from a Protestant stand point. While in London, Barruel's pronouncements began to take on a more paranoid tone and all-encompassing reach, which would reach their apogee in the *Memoirs Illustrating the History of Jacobinism*.

The vast four-volume work was published in 1798–9 and met with immediate success throughout Europe. It was translated into nine languages, including English, German, Italian, Portuguese and Dutch, and an abridgement was published the next year. The French edition remained continuously in print until 1837 and it continues to have its supporters among right-wing conspiracist groups, such as the John Birch Society.

Barruel's *Memoirs* provided readers with an accessible, seemingly logical and exhaustively detailed account of the causes of the French Revolution, and it gained Barruel many admirers. Piling detail upon detail, "fact" upon "fact", Barruel aims to prove how the French Revolution was intentionally engineered by the secret societies – the Jacobins, the Freemasons and the Illuminati – and what the relationship was between these societies and the Enlightenment thinkers such as Voltaire, Diderot and the *philosophes*. In Barruel's mind, the anti-monarchy, anti-clergy *philosophes* were the direct descendants of the secret medieval guilds who made up the order of the Freemasons, and behind the Freemasons were the Illuminati.

The first two volumes do not present anything revelatory in terms of scapegoats: Barruel shines the spotlight on the usual suspects, the Enlightenment thinkers, whose alarming philosophy espoused, among other things, a breaking down of national boundaries, overthrowing the monarchy and establishing a democracy based on merit. Where Barruel's work becomes interesting, in terms of this plot theory, is in volumes three and four, where he traces the historical precedents for these philosophies, and comes to the conclusion that the Illuminati ultimately pull the strings:

> The secrets of the Lodges constitute the basis of the Revolution under the title of the Rights of Man. The first article declares man to be equal and free; that the principle of all sovereignty essentially resides in the people; and that law is nothing more than the expression of the general will. Such had been for nearly half a century the doctrines of Argenson, Montesquieu, Rousseau, and Voltaire. These principles of pride and revolt had long since been the ground-work of the mysteries of every class of Sophister, Occult Mason, or Illuminée; and now they decorate the title page of the revolutionary code.
> (Barruel, *Memoirs*, vol. 4, p397)

Barruel's work identifies what he sees as two forms of "illuminism", the atheistic and the theosophic. Weishaupt's secret society was an example of the first, fixated, as they seemed, on the destruction of the Church, Crown, and all public property. To achieve this, Barruel repeats the claim that the Freemasons of France were being manipulated by a malign group, and that, while there were many innocent Masons on the peripheries, the inner circle of elites was made up of the Illuminati masterminds. Barruel claims as many as 600,000 Masons were involved in this conspiracy with, at its centre, the usual revolutionary suspects, including Lafayette and the Duke d'Orléans.

It is worth mentioning here that some of Barruel's confusion can be attributed to a fairly straightforward misunderstanding, and that he was not alone among his contemporaries in confusing the terminology of two separate, diametrically opposed groups: the Bavarian Illuminati and the French Order of the Illuminés. As mentioned in the previous chapter, the Illuminés were a mystical sect in southern France, who had surfaced in the mid-17th century and may have descended from earlier "illuminized" sects, such as the Alumbrados of 16th-century Spain. Barruel, like many of his contemporaries, referred to a 1788 book by the Marquis de Luchet entitled *Essai sur la secte des Illuminés*. Luchet wrote his book as a criticism of the political influence of the mystical Rosicrucians on the Prussian court of Frederick William II, and used the term *Illuminés* to mean mystics of any description – theosophists, Rosicrucians, Martinists etc. Barruel was not alone in misattributing Luchet's allegations about the Rosicrucians to the Illuminati, which simply contributed to the general confusion about the different societies and their aims.

Barruel's book came at a time when a desperate need for answers and for an understanding of the inconceivable events of the revolution guaranteed him a receptive audience. The sheer scale of his book, and of the alleged conspiracy he claims to have revealed meant it was impossible to ignore, and the *Memoirs* were written about and discussed by leading literary and philosophical figures of the day. Political writer and English statesman Edmund Burke, in a letter later used as an endorsement by Barruel's English translator, wrote to Barruel on publication of the first two volumes on May 1st, 1797:

I have known myself personally five of your principal conspirators; and I can undertake to say from my own certain knowledge that, so far back as the year 1773, they were busy in the plot you have so well described, and in the manner, and on the principle you have so truly represented – to this

I can speak as a witness.

(qtd Roberts, *The Mythology of the Secret Societies*, p201)

In Burke's defence, at this time Barruel had not yet published the second two volumes, which became increasingly paranoid and hysterical. Here Barruel described the Illuminati as orchestrating "the most general, most astonishing, and most dreadful Conspiracy that ever existed", likening Adam Weishaupt to Satan ("an odious phenomenon in nature, an Atheist void of remorse") and referring to Knigge as a "genii, serving the King of Hell". Barruel's language, referring to heretics, vampires and Satan, was hard for many to swallow, and those who might have been sympathetic to his views rejected them with the publication of the last two volumes. Here he is clearly no longer in control of his vast, all-encompassing plot theory, and his arguments contain contradictory statements, attributing to the minister of finance Jacques Necker the role of both arch conspirator and pawn: the Rosicrucians were both enemies and allies of the Illuminati.

But not all of Barruel's readers necessarily accepted the message the writer was desperate to impart. Percy Bysshe Shelley read the book avidly, and recommended it to his friends: "Although it is half filled with the vilest and most unsupported falsehood it is a book worth reading" (qtd Roberts, p201). From its pages, Shelley found a growing admiration for the ideals of the Illuminati. (It is worth noting, and is no coincidence, that Mary Shelley's Victor Frankenstein studied at the University of Ingolstadt, a location symbolizing enlightenment and revolution in the sciences.) Thomas Jefferson was even more forthcoming in his condemnation, dismissing Barruel's arguments, in a letter to James Madison of 1800, as "the ravings of a Bedlamite" and claimed that the true nature of Barruel's fears "are that the craft [i.e., Freemasonry] would be endangered by the spreading of information, reason, and natural morality among men."

Barruel responded to his critics using many of the tactics of later conspiracist thinking, and which have haunting similarities to witchhunts of the 19th and 20th centuries, whether anti-Catholic, anti-Semitic or anti-communist. He defends his position in the preface to volume four, citing the fact of his critics' existence as proof of the Jacobin/Illuminati plot (an argument along the lines of "you think that because that's what the Jacobins want you to think"); if all else failed, Barruel simply accused his critics of being members of the Illuminati. In a series of letters defending his position against the philosopher Montesquieu, Barruel concludes that the philosopher is clearly an Illuminé for disagreeing with him. Interestingly, much the same argument was used against Barruel, as proof that the Illuminati could not exist: surely, if they were as powerful as Barruel suggested, they would not allow him to publish his vast tract denouncing their plans?

Barruel's reasons for fixating on the Illuminati as the symbol of everything that had gone wrong with the world as he understood it are not difficult to grasp: he was a royalist, anti-enlightenment, exiled ex-Jesuit. He had seen the execution of his king, the dissolution of his calling, and had lost his homeland, and if the ideas of the Enlightenment had caused these calamities, to his thinking they must have been perpetuated by someone. Unfortunately, his work cannot simply be filed away as an historical oddity. Not only was it extremely influential in its time, but it and the works it inspired have endured to the present day as incontestable proof of the extent of the Order of the Illuminati, and the vast scale of their influence. Today, the fact that the Abbé Barruel was a contemporary of the events he was writing about is used as proof of their veracity. One of the book's recent publishers markets it as an accurate historical document, and describes Barruel as "one of the few authors on the French Revolution to be specific in the people he names, the intrigues he recounts, and the supporting documentation he provides".

It is a moot point whether anyone today believes the accusations of an embittered ex-priest against the Illuminati. Where it does become problematic is when his works are picked up by extremist groups and used as supposed proof for the nefarious activities of their own bogeymen – in the 20th century references to the Illuminati began to be conflated with Jews, for example. The scattergun references to, for example, the Rothschilds, by self-preserving charlatans such as Cagliostro, are then picked up and used as "fact", rather than being seen in their historical context. In this light, the fact that "the ravings of a bedlamite" are marketed as historical truth is distinctly sinister.

Barruel himself did not initially make any reference to Judaism in his vast opus; at the time when he wrote the first edition, the Jewish community in France was marginalized and largely isolated, with no political presence. This was to change in 1791 when the French National Assembly ended all legal restrictions on Jews. For some this was seen as proof that the Jewish community benefited from the revolution, and thus must have played a part in its organization. Barruel was quick to accept this theory and added it to his paranoid mix; once the Conspiracy-Finder General endorsed such an idea it was widely accepted as truth, and by 1806 editions of the *Memoirs* were revised to incorporate this new twist. From this point on, Jews began to be seen as the ultimate power behind all secret societies, including the Illuminati and the Freemasons, and this rumour would lead ultimately to the creation in the early 20th century of *The Protocols of the Elders of Zion*, the notorious forged document purporting to outline secret Jewish rituals.

Contributing to this theory, both at the time and today, was the work of John Robison. Where Barruel's motives for embracing the Illuminati plot theory are reasonably straightforward, Robison's are much less so.

In all other respects an esteemed scientist, Robison is remembered today as the author of *Proofs of a Conspiracy against all the Religions and Governments of Europe Carried on in the Secret Meetings of the Freemasons, Illuminati, and Reading Societies, collected from Good Authorities* (1797). Robison's motives for writing this book are unclear. As a scientist he might have been expected to embrace the principles of the Enlightenment, rather than denounce them, and he did not seem to suffer the same irrational fears as the Abbé Barruel, but he evidently had his own prejudices. His background may not have prevented his mistakes, but it does bestow an apparent, and dangerous, respectability upon his theories, and upon those who have reasons for perpetuating them.

Scottish born and university educated, Robison travelled extensively throughout Europe and Canada before returning to Scotland where he was made Professor of Physics (known at the time as natural philosophy) at Edinburgh University. A distinguished scientist, he contributed various articles to the *Encyclopedia Britannica*, and in 1783 became general secretary of the Royal Society of Edinburgh, newly formed to further scientific knowledge.

Like many of his contemporaries, Robison was a Mason, and may have been prompted to write his book out of a need to differentiate "good" Freemasonry (ie, English Masonry) from its subversive brethren across the channel, which, in his view, had become dangerously preoccupied with elaborate ritual and political agitation. Robison's book, as histrionic and error-ridden as Barruel's, took as its starting point a similar premise, and aimed to prove how the revolutionary activity sweeping Europe in the 1790s, particularly the French Revolution, was the work of a small group of agitators: the Illuminati. Robison contributed to the increasingly popular theory that the Illuminati had simply gone underground after they had been banned by the Elector of Bavaria, which provided the cover they needed to carry out their revolutionary activities. His argument rested on the idea that such extraordinary revolutionary activity had to have been manipulated, and as proof of such a theory he attempted to provide links between the Illuminati and important revolutionary figures such as the nefarious Duke d'Orléans, Talleyrand and Mirabeau.

The Comte de Mirabeau was a wildly popular revolutionary figure and spokesman for the Third Estate, but until the events of 1789 he had led a privileged life of dissolution and scandal. Prodigiously intelligent, he was a larger-than-life character from the outset, born with a club foot and, reportedly, molars. A bout of small pox in his youth disfigured him further ("ugly as Satan", his own father described him), yet this did not seem to have had a detrimental effect on his romantic conquests. A serial adulterer, at one stage he was imprisoned – initially sentenced to death – for "crimes of seduction". As luck would have it, Mirabeau's jailer was a Mason, and not only was his sentence revoked, but he was granted special privileges.

Robison based his theories about Mirabeau's involvement with secret societies on three diplomatic visits that Mirabeau made to Berlin in 1786, and which Mirabeau wrote about in a book entitled *The Prussian Monarchy Under Frederick the Great*. In the book Mirabeau praises the Illuminati for their anti-Jesuit activities, yet seems to have been somewhat unclear about the various roles of the secret societies in Prussia, and at times he confuses the rationalist Illuminati with the mystical Rosicrucians. Although he was not alone in this confusion (as we have seen, in France the Bavarian Illuminati were frequently confused with the mystical French sect, the Illuminés), Robison believes this confusion to be intentional:

> He [Mirabeau], also, while at Berlin, published an Essai sur la
> Secte des Illuminés, one of the strangest and most impudent
> performances that ever appeared. He there describes a sect
> existing in Germany, called the Illuminated, and says, that
> they are the most absurd and gross fanatics imaginable,
> waging war with every appearance of Reason, and main-
> taining the most ridiculous superstitions. He gives some
> account of these, and of their rituals, ceremonies &c. as if he
> had seen them all. His sect is a confused mixture of Christian
> superstitions, Rosicrucian nonsense, and everything that can
> raise contempt and hatred. But no such society ever existed,
> and Mirabeau confided in his own powers of deception in
> order to screen from observation those who were known to
> be Illuminati, and to hinder the rulers from attending to their
> real machinations .... He knew perfectly well that the
> Illuminati were of a stamp diametrically opposite; for he was
> Illuminated ... long before.
>
> (Robison, *Proofs of a Conspiracy*, pp212/3)

Robison then set out to prove that Mirabeau, thus initiated,
brought the radical ideas of the Illuminati to the Paris lodges,
where he recruited figures such as Talleyrand, and where the
seeds of revolution were sown – a story that continues to be
adopted as fact by conspiracy theorists to this day.

This story was based on a meeting in Berlin in 1786 between
Mirabeau and an ex-Illuminatus and radical, Jacob Mauvillon,
during which time Mauvillon allegedly indoctrinated Mirabeau
in the ways of the Illuminati with the express purpose of
Mirabeau taking them to the French lodges. Robison's book not
only condemns the perceived radical activities of the continental Masons in the strongest terms, but his disgust for the

immoral lives of his villains rings with the censure of the Calvinist, attesting to Mirabeau's "profligacy, debauchery, gaming and impiety", claiming he was "destitute of decency in his vices" and that "[d]rinking was the only vice in which he did not indulge – his exhausted constitution did not permit it" (Robison, p214).

But the most pointed of his moral outrage is reserved for the profligate Duke d'Orléans, which may have been due, in part, to the Duke's position as Grand Master of the French lodges (Robison seems unaware of the fact the Duke relinquished the title in 1787); one can't help but suspect that Robison is keen to create a distance between his Masonic brothers in Britain and the degeneracy across the Channel. Robison is at great pains to explain that no such position exists in the English lodges, and that such an abuse of power as wielded by the Duke d'Orléans is therefore impossible in England: "In this country we have no conception of the authority of a National Grand Master. ...In the great cities of Germany, the inhabitants paid more respect to the Grand Master of the Masons than to their respective Princes. The authority of the D. of Orleans in France was still greater ...."

He then repeats scurrilous gossip, all of which goes toward reinforcing the Duke's reputation as a reprobate. He is described plotting with men disguised as women "among whom were Mirabeau ... and other deputies of the Republican party"; he is seen watching the protesting mob, but "skulking in a balcony behind his children", to do so. And finally, he is accused of procuring "[a]bove three hundred nymphs ... to meet and to illuminate the two batallions ... who were coming to Versailles for the protection of the Royal Family" (Robison, p217). This, Robison says, follows Weishaupt's example of exploiting his countrywomen for Illuminati purposes. Transvestitism, cowardice, pimping...we should expect nothing less of the

Illuminati, Robison seems to say.

Robison then presented an alarmist, hysterical interpretation of Enlightenment ideals, and used it as "evidence" of Illuminati manipulation of the French Revolution:

> Nothing can more convincingly demonstrate the early intentions of a party ... in France to overturn the constitution completely and plant a democracy or oligarchy on its ruins. ... The Illuminati ... accounted all Princes usurpers and tyrants, and all privileged orders as their abettors. They intended to establish a government ... where talents and character alone should lead to preferment. They meant to abolish the laws which protected property accumulated by long continued and successful industry .... They intended to establish universal Liberty and Equality, the imprescriptable Rights of Man .... And, as necessary preparations for all this, they intended to root out all religion and ordinary morality, and even to break the bonds of domestic life, by destroying the veneration for marriage-vows, and by taking the education of the children out of the hands of the parents. This was all that the Illuminati could teach, and THIS WAS PRECISELY WHAT FRANCE HAS DONE.
>
> (Robison, p215)

This much-quoted passage of Robison's clearly equates the ethos of the Illuminati with that of the Enlightenment, referring to the common aims of establishing a democracy based on merit and the unalienable rights of man. Such ideals would be more than familiar to the revolutionaries on the other side of the Atlantic in the United States. Yet to the old guard of Europe, these ideals were terrifying, threatening the social order with, as seen in France, cataclysmic results. For Robison, and those who shared his conservatism, concepts such as "liberty" and "equality" were wielded like threats, identified as both the motives for and the result of the destruction of "religion and ordinary morality".

Many of Robison's theories were influenced by the French *emigrés* who had fled the revolution, including the Abbé Barruel, and his writing in English brought these ideas to another audience, serving only to perpetuate the rumours that had been circulating. Another writer Robison quoted at length was the Austrian Leopold Hoffman, a former Mason and counter-revolutionary who had been writing feverish denunciations of secret societies since two years before the revolution. He made a healthy living stirring up antagonism against the Illuminati in particular and once the revolution was underway went to elaborate lengths to prove a connection between the Illuminati and the revolutionary Jacobin clubs.

Hoffman was motivated by personal animosity as much as a belief in the dangers of the secret societies. For some years he was engaged in a cat-and-mouse game with Adam Weishaupt's right-hand man, Baron Knigge, playing out in the newspapers accusations and counter-accusations of Illuminati activity in Bavaria. A consummate newspaperman as much as anything (and always with an eye to his next pay cheque), Hoffman was aware of the sales value of any Illuminati story, and went to great lengths to keep them in the forefront of the public's consciousness.

As "proof" of the Illuminati's activities, Hoffman was obliged to concoct increasingly elaborate plot scenarios, smearing anyone who crossed him along the way. He was no match for the witty and literary Knigge, who countered with elaborate parodies, using the conspiracists' own language to make fun of him. Knigge's satirical novel *Order of the Simpletons* lampoons writers such as Hoffman, whose conspiracy theories Knigge saw as responsible for engendering panic and suspicion, and of returning society to the pre-enlightened state of the Inquisition.

By this time terms such as Illuminati, Jacobin, or even Inquisition had become almost meaningless, and were bandied about as terms of approbation, intended to smear whoever did not subscribe to one's own world view. But Hoffman's theories had gained some ground among conservatives and counter-revolutionaries. They would take root with Robison and, when he had added to and developed them, they would positively flourish. If Robison's work were remembered simply as a personal response to the contemporary phenomenon of the French Revolution, it would serve as an historical artefact, as an illustration of contemporary fears and prejudices by a commentator across the Channel. But his text had far-reaching consequences.

Robison's claims that Illuminati cells had crossed the Atlantic to America had a great deal of influence in the nascent United States of the 1790s and would contribute to the establishment of the Alien and Sedition Act of 1798 and the Anti-Masonic Party in the late 1820s. By then Robison's influence had become so enmeshed in conspiracy thinking that his book was accepted as historic fact; for many conspiracists and extremist groups, such as the far-right John Birch Society, it is still quoted as truth today. The preface of the present edition describes Robison as "one of the leading intellectuals of his time" and claims that "the line from the Illuminati Order to the Communist Manifesto is straight and unbroken".

In just over 15 years, the short-lived Illuminati had gone from a provincial philosophy club with a membership of just five members to being seen as nothing less than the scourge of the civilized world. Since the Illuminati's demise in 1785 the western world has been more alert to its perceived activities than it ever had been during the group's existence, and this was due almost exclusively to the works of Barruel and Robison.

Thanks to Robison, a whole new audience would be introduced to and alarmed by the Illuminati myth: the newly formed United States.

Chapter Three: Illuminati Scares in 18th-century America

On May 9th, 1798, Rev. Jedidiah Morse addressed a congregation at the New North Church in Boston. Morse, a committed New England Calvinist, had, for most of the previous decade, been increasingly alarmed by what he saw as the nation's impiety and lack of respect for authority, particularly among the youth at the northeast's most respected educational establishments. He addressed the assembled with his concerns, and was unflinching in describing the extent of the rot that permeated the nascent United States and the pernicious source responsible:

> For more than twenty years past a society called the Illuminated has been in existence in Germany; its express aim is "to root out and abolish Christianity, and overthrow all civil government"; it approves of such atrocious principles as the right to commit self-murder and the promiscuous intercourse of the sexes, while it condemns the principles of patriotism and the right to accumulate private property; in the prosecution of its infamous propaganda it aims to enlist the discontented, to get control of all such cultural agencies as the schools, literary societies, newspapers, writers, booksellers and postmasters; it is bent upon insinuating its members into all positions of distinction and influence, whether literary, civil or religious.
>
> (qtd Stauffer, *New England and the Bavarian Illuminati*, pp233–4)

Morse's sermon ignited a slow-burning fire across New England. It would culminate in thunderous warnings from pulpits throughout the region and incendiary editorials for and against the minister's position. Morse's dire predictions even reached as far as George Washington and President John Adams, both of whom responded seriously to the allegations. The US was finding its way as a country. Having thrown off the chains of one oppressor its citizens felt vulnerable to the machinations of potential new foes – real or imaginary. Was Morse on to something? If so, how did a New England minister come to be aware of the dastardly ambitions of a European secret society?

Morse's sermon gave the Illuminati plot myth its first public airing in the US and kept Morse and his counterparts elsewhere in the region busy spreading the alarm for several years. (Vernon Stauffer's 1918 study of this period remains the most comprehensive history of the Illuminati scare, from which many of the sermons have been quoted.) Although this was the first time the spectre of the Illuminati was evoked as a threat against all that Americans held dear, it was not the first time the US had sought to rally itself against perceived enemies. And apart from Morse's explicit reference to the Illuminati, his sermon was typical of the politicized sermonizing New England church-goers expected from their conservative clergy.

Late 18th-century American politics were strongly influenced by the major event transforming Europe across the sea – the French Revolution. American attitudes toward the French Revolution were conflicting, and would become split along party lines. France had proved a worthy ally in the fight for independence from Great Britain and, initially, its revolution was greeted with the euphoria to be expected from a newly established republic. As events in France took their bloody toll, however, it caused introspection and anxiety about America's own revolutionary past, and provided a frightening vision of democracy run riot. Could America expect the same if its democratic principles were followed through to their logical conclusion?

Up until the 1790s the Federalist party in the US pretty much ran the show, with revolutionary hero George Washington at its head. But by 1791 divisions in the party were threatening its dominance. When Thomas Jefferson established the Democratic party in 1792, taking former Federalist James Madison with him, each party sought to rally the public's support. One method was by using the example of the French Revolution for their own ends. For the Federalists, it was expedient to promote an idea of a foreign enemy, one that posed a threat to American liberties. But until the French Revolution began its ghastly transformation into the Terror, they would have been hard-pressed to summon anti-French support. In the very early years of the decade, large swathes of the US were overcome by a pro-French fever. By the end of the century, the US would make a dramatic turnaround; from sympathizing with the French in the early part of the decade, Americans would swing to the opposite extreme, perceiving in France a deadly enemy, and, at the heart of that enemy, the work of the Illuminati.

A popular attitude among Americans at the time was that their own revolution had somehow provided France with a lead, showing the way to throw off tyranny. France's crumbling monarchy deserved to be toppled; that the authority of its Catholic Church – always suspect to a nation of Puritans – was dragged down with the crown was only to be applauded. Philadelphia, the most cosmopolitan of American cities and the most influenced by French culture, succumbed to wild displays of pro-French exuberance, including riotous singing of revolutionary songs, impassioned proclamations of *Liberté, Egalité* and *Fraternité*, and colourful displays of French flags and revolutionary insignia. Even the normally sober New Englanders were overcome with French zeal, with the Federalist minister David

Tappan, Professor of Divinity at Harvard, heralding the advent of the revolution in a 1793 sermon: "What a glorious revolution suddenly bursts upon our sight! What freedom of thought! What justness, energy, and grandeur of sentiment! … See tyranny both in Church and State tottering to its foundations!" (qtd May, *The Enlightenment in America*, p194). By 1794, he, along with the rest of the Federalist clergy, would have a dramatic change of heart, condemning the revolution and spreading rumours of Jacobin threats. But for the time being, America's excitement at events in France took over the nation.

When the French ambassador, Edmond Charles Genet – displaying his revolutionary credentials by styling himself "Citizen Genet" – arrived in Charleston from Paris in April 1793, he was greeted by rapturous crowds and public spectacles. This cosmopolitan young diplomat was only 30 when he arrived in the US, but his diplomatic career had not been uneventful: he had been employed by the Ministry of Foreign Affairs since an adolescent, and in his early 20s worked as secretary at the Russian Embassy at St Petersburg. His vociferous support of the French Revolution had not endeared him to the Russian court, however, and he had been summarily dismissed in 1792. No matter: in France he had made a name for himself among the Girondin faction, and it was with the full support of the French government that he was dispatched to negotiate with the Washington administration regarding America's financial debt to France, incurred during the war for independence.

Moving on to Philadelphia, Genet was met with even more adulation. Impassioned, stylish and urbane, Genet made headlines wherever he went, and his taste for the dramatic gesture delighted republicans, but made the Washington administration suspicious. True to his revolutionary principles, Genet did not hide his jubilation at the execution of Louis XVI in January 1793. For many in the US this marked the beginning of the end of their brief love affair with France. Louis had been a loyal ally in the colonists' fight for independence, and had provided valuable funding. The sorry state of France's financial affairs was not entirely unconnected with the American Revolution and many Americans were horrified by the death of the king. Those nearest to Genet, however, seem to have been swept along on a wild tide of enthusiasm. One rumour circulated that at one of the many banquets laid on for the young diplomat in Philadelphia shortly after the French king's death, Genet led the assembled company of Philadelphia's great and good in a carousing celebration of the death of the monarch, culminating in the desecration of a roast suckling pig christened "Louis" by the revellers. Clearly matters were getting out of hand. As the revolution began its inexorable slide into the Terror, Philadelphia became sharply divided. While many abandoned their Francophilia, others embraced the revolution, going so far as to adopt the revolutionary calendar and the garb of the sans-culottes.

Genet, whether carried away by his reception, or self-aggrandizing by nature, over-stepped the boundaries of diplomatic protocol and behaved more like a head of state than one of its servants. When France declared war on Great Britain in February 1793, Washington responded with the Proclamation of Neutrality in April, forbidding any act that would involve the US in the situation in Europe. Genet apparently shrugged this off and, acting on his own initiative, issued licenses permitting the seizure of British ships by American privateers, at a stroke invalidating the idea of US neutrality. This, coupled with Genet's meddling in other foreign interests and a belief that he had the support of the people over their own president, led to the American government's demand for Genet's recall. Genet, reckless perhaps, but no fool, had no desire to return to France, where the Girondins' fall from grace had led them straight to the guillotine. He chose to live out the rest of his days in upstate New York, marrying the governor's daughter. His diplomatic career in the US had been brief, but would have lasting repercussions on Franco-American relations, and would play a significant part in the Illuminati plot conspiracy.

Many years later, in 1813, John Adams wrote to the Francophile Thomas Jefferson, urging him not to underestimate Genet's influence during this period, and the brief but very real fear that Genet would inspire the American people to revolution:

> You certainly never felt the Terrorism, excited by Genet, in 1793, when ten thousand People in the Streets of Philadelphia, day after day, threatened to drag Washington out of his House, and effect a Revolution in the Government, or compel it to declare War in favour of the French Revolution …. The coolest and the firmest Minds, even among the Quakers in Philadelphia, have given their Opinions to me, that nothing but the Yellow Fever … could have saved the United States from a total Revolution of Government.
>
> (qtd May, p244)

The idea that there were forces at large with the desire or ability to overthrow the American government was a haunting one, and these exuberant displays in support of France were not the only aspect that worried the Federalists. Coinciding with Genet's triumphant reception in Philadelphia was the rise of the political social clubs known as the Democratic societies.

These societies grew out of the general fashion for social clubs during the early to mid-1790s in the US and like other groups organized to discuss ideas – even the Illuminati – their opponents believed their numbers were far larger and their influence far greater than in reality. Essentially, in the way of many 18th-century societies across the Atlantic, these clubs were pro-Enlightenment, and devoted to discussing, among other things, the nature of democracy. However, in the US this wasn't just idle speculation; democratic principles were being enacted in reality, not just in theory. Still, the government didn't like the idea of a group of insurgents carrying out their own interpretation of democracy, which is what they feared of the Democratic societies. In Philadelphia, some clubs openly modelled themselves on the clubs of Paris, which is where the problems began. Although there had been a long tradition of organized social groups in the colonies ever since Benjamin Franklin organized his fraternal clubs in the 1720s, once the newest incarnations were equated with the rebel Jacobins abroad, all organizations became suspect. However, despite their opponents' worst fears, few if any of the groups met in secret; most were quite open about their membership and espoused the kind of egalitarianism familiar to all liberals today, advocating, for example, women's rights, the abolition of slavery and penal reform. However, in October 1794 the Democratic societies became allied with a rebel cause that would put them in an entirely different light – the Whiskey Rebellion.

An unpopular tax on whiskey, introduced by Alexander Hamilton in 1791, had provoked a series of increasingly violent confrontations between Pennsylvanian farmers and federal tax inspectors. Whiskey in that part of the country served, among other things, as a form of currency; to the farmers it seemed like a tax on their livelihood and came to symbolize the imbalance of wealth between the industrial northeast and agrarian west. Tax inspectors were met with a series of intimidating tactics: some were tarred and feathered and run out of town; others found roads impassably blocked by piles of manure or fallen trees. By the summer, matters came to a head. News came of Federalist sympathizers in the city of Pittsburgh, prepared to sell out the farmers to the government. Seven thousand rebel farmers prepared to march on the city.

Attempts at reaching a reconciliation delayed the march, and by the time the rebels eventually arrived in the city on August 1st, 1794, they had lost the taste for looting and pillaging. The situation was further diffused by the warm welcome extended by the canny citizens of Pittsburgh, who cheered the rebels' arrival, and even fed them as they swarmed the streets. By the end of the day, most of the farmers had left the city, having caused little damage. But the government had a different interpretation of events and, if publicly they sought to negotiate with the rebels, privately they prepared for war in the belief that the events in Pennsylvania were a domestic manifestation of the revolutions raging across Europe. In October, Washington led 13,000 militia across the Alleghenies to put an end to the insurrection.

George Washington was explicit in his belief that the rebellion had been instigated by what he described as "certain irregular meetings" between the farmers and a group of more organized agitators – the Democratic societies. His Address to Congress in November of that year made specific reference to these "self-created societies", a phrase that Federalists leapt on to mean anything from the Democratic societies to clandestine meetings of Jacobins. Federalist newspapers picked up the phrase, with an editorial in a Massachusetts paper warning that the Democratic societies were working secretly to "unhinge the whole order of government and introduce confusion, so that the union, the constitution, the laws, public order and private right would be all the sport of violence or chance." For a brief period in the autumn of 1794, secret political clubs were outlawed.

The pro-Federalist New England clergy were quick to draw the necessary conclusions from Washington's address. The Democratic-Republicans were problematic for the Calvinist New Englanders for numerous reasons: their cosmopolitanism and pro-French Enlightenment sympathies clearly aligned them with revolutionary ideals, those that would destroy the very fabric of American society. Democratic hero Thomas Jefferson had a long connection with France, having lived in Paris for five years as the US minister to France from 1784. His opponents sniffily referred to his "womanish attachment to France", at one swoop questioning where his loyalties lay, and conjuring, if only sub-liminally, an image of French effeteness in contrast to the moral rectitude of the Protestants of the United States. France was inextricably linked with revolution, and revolution, to the con-servative clergy, with deism. The publication in 1794 of Thomas Paine's *Age of Reason* made explicit what the New England clergy feared most, that revolution, followed to its natural conclusion, would result in the destruction of the Church. Paine wrote:

Soon after I had published the pamphlet, Common Sense, in America I saw the exceeding probability that a revolution in the system of government would be followed by a revolution in the system of religion. The adulterous connection of church and state, wherever it had taken place, whether Jewish, Christian or Turkish, had so effectually prohibited by pains and penalties, every discussion upon established creeds, and upon first principles of religion, that until the system of government should be changed those subjects could not be brought fairly and openly before the world; but that whenever this should be done a revolution in the system of religion would follow. Human inventions and priestcraft would be detected; and man would return to the pure, unmixed, unadulterated belief of one God and no more.

The pulpits of New England trembled. Deism to the conser-vative clergy, was at the heart of all revolution. Essentially a reac-tion against the superstitious nature of 18th-century faith, at the heart of deist philosophy was the idea that God had created the universe and the marvels of nature, but that He would not intervene in its running in the form of miracles and the like. Deists such as Thomas Paine, and many other of the founding fathers, believed that God's will was not enacted through supernatural signs or portents but through a series of immutable "natural laws". For the conservative clergy, however, this rejection of established doctrine was tantamount to sacrilege. And as far as they were concerned, once impiety had entered the hearts of Americans, revolution of all government would not be far behind. And many of the New England clergy were aware of a distinct irreverence creeping into society, particularly among the young. Having enjoyed considerable status supporting the colonists during the American Revolution, the clergy's position in society had since weakened. Church attendance was down, and the many issues that were pressing to a New England Calvinist were met with indifference by larger society. The Reverend David Tappan, Professor of Divinity at Harvard, preached in 1793 that "sceptical, deistical, and other loose and pernicious sentiments were infecting society". He blamed this on the vogue for European Enlightenment ideas among some sectors of American society: "A species of atheistical philosophy, which has of late reared its head in Europe, and which affects to be the offspring and the nurse of sound reason, science, and liberty, seems in danger of infecting some of the more sprightly and freethinking geniuses of America" (Stauffer, p88). Timothy Dwight, president of Yale, also saw the work of the Enlightenment by way of a liberal education behind the radical behaviour and decline in religious attendance of his students:

> Youths particularly, who had been liberally educated, and who with strong passions, and feeble principles, were votaries of sensuality and ambition, delighted with the

prospect of unrestrained gratification, and panting to be enrolled with men of fashion and splendour, became enamoured of these new doctrines. The tenor of opinion, and even of conversation, was to a considerable extent changed at once. Striplings, scarcely fledged, suddenly found that the world had been involved in general darkness, through the long procession of the preceding ages; and that the light of wisdom had just begun to dawn upon the human race.

The outcome of such an education led the young to an arrogant dismissal of the principles and beliefs of the past:

All the science, all the information, which had been acquired before the commencement of the last thirty or forty years, stood in their view for nothing... Religion they discovered on the one hand to be a vision of dotards and nurses, and on the other hand a system of fraud and trick, imposed by priestcraft for base purposes upon the ignorant multitude. Revelation they found was without authority, or evidence; and moral obligation a cobweb, which might indeed entangle flies, but by which creatures of a stronger wing nobly disdained to be confined.

(qtd Stauffer, pp85/6)

From the mid-1790s the clergy came out in staunch support of the Federalist government. At the time, individual sermons reached a much wider audience than the minister's own congregation: ministers might deliver the same sermon at different churches, and sermons were often published in the newspapers, or later as pamphlets. Thus the rousing words of a New England minister would have far wider implications than his immediate congregation, often reaching as far as the White House.

As fears of insurrection and a general wave of anti-French

feeling swept the northeast, the dangers this posed to America became a constant theme. David Tappan, in a sermon of February 1795, took the government's lead by emphasizing the link between secret societies at home and abroad:

> The destructive effects of them [secret political clubs] in France have been noticed in the preceding discourse. The unhappy influence in this country is sufficiently exemplified in that spirit of falsehood, of party and faction, which some of them, at least, assiduously and too successfully promote, and especially in the late dangerous and expensive western insurrection [ie, the Whiskey Rebellion], which may be evidently traced, in a great degree, to the inflammatory representations and proceedings of these clubs, their abettors and friends.

While the Federalist party welcomed the popular support of the clergy, to their opponents such partisanship was proof of the Church's lack of integrity. As political sermons were a prominent feature during the war for independence, the clergy perceived this criticism as yet further evidence of the growth in immorality and impiety, and of the influence of France, all of which contributed to turning Americans away from the Christian religion. A Connecticut paper of 1795 pointed explicitly to the Democrats' role in all this, describing theirs as "a crazy system of Anti-Christian politics" and stating:

> The French are mad in their pursuit of every phantom which disordered intellects can manage. Having set themselves free from all human control, they would gladly scale the ramparts of heaven, and dethrone ALMIGHTY JEHOVAH. Our own Democrats would do just so, if they dare.

As the decade progressed the divisions became only more marked. The Jay Treaty of 1796 between the US and Great Britain (rendering very favourable commercial rights to Britain) was deeply unpopular among the Democrats, who saw it as toadying to the British crown, selling out republican ideals and, in light of the relations between France and Britain, overtly hostile and damaging to Franco-US relations. Within the year these fears were realized, as hundreds of US ships were captured by French privateers. Reports of the harsh treatment meted out to US crews by the French heightened animosity, and fears of an impending war with France became a very real concern. Behind this lay a greater fear. Napoleon's meteoric rise in the aftermath of the French Revolution had seen France victorious in several campaigns in Italy (1796–7), and as it continued on its rampage across Europe, setting its sights on Britain, it seemed France would stop at nothing less than world domination. A lurid and popular pamphlet of the day, entitled *The Cannibals' Progress; or the Dreadful Horrors of the French Invasion*, ran to many editions. One edition warned in its preface: "The pamphlet should be owned by every man and read in every family. There they will find, from an authentic source, the consequence of being conquered by France... Murder, robbery, burning of towns, and the violation of female chastity, in forms too dreadful to relate, are among them."

As if the situation were not fraught enough, the following year, 1798, saw the publication in the US of John Robison's *Proofs of a Conspiracy*. The conspiracists' handbook had arrived.

Robison's book confirmed the worst fears of conservative Americans. Here was proof indeed, from a respected academic with a first-hand account of events in Europe, of the Jacobin conspiracy to overthrow government, church and all known institutions in every civilized country throughout the world. Here was the cause for the Enlightenment run riot, just as many

Americans suspected. What was new, and ominous, was Robison's claims that the group *behind* the group behind the revolution was the Illuminati. The effect was incendiary. The revelation struck deep at the heart of conservative America and the fear of the Illuminati came to dominate American life at the end of the 18th century. Robison's descriptions of the Illuminati's plans for world domination were reconfirmed by the publication later that year of the Abbé Barruel's monumental *Memoirs*.

> As the plague flies on the wings of the wind, so do their [ie, the Illuminati's] triumphant legions infect America. ... So numerous were the brethren in North America, that Philadelphia and Boston trembled, lest their rising constitution should be obliged to make way for that of the great club; and if for a time the brotherhood has been obliged to shrink back into their hiding places, they are still sufficiently numerous to raise collections and transmit them to the insurgents of Ireland; thus contributing toward that species of revolution which is the object of their ardent wishes in America.
>
> (Barruel, *Memoirs*, p271)

It was impossible to remain unaffected by the news, and for Morse and his colleagues it crystallized their suspicions about the deism infiltrating American society, about the pro-French Democrats and about the cosmopolitan, enlightened Jefferson, Paine et al. The Illuminati plot myth filled the need for answers as to how and why the democratic ideal had gone so wildly off course in France, and provided a rallying call to conservatives. Jedidiah Morse would devote the next several years of his life to spreading the word, and was remarkably successful in doing so.

Before he became preoccupied with the machinations of the Illuminati, Jedidiah Morse (among other accomplishments, the father of Samuel, the inventor of the telegraph) was one of New

England's best-known authors and respected clergymen. Just a year after graduating from Yale, he wrote one of the first popular books on US geography, *Geography Made Easy*, and later the influential and widely read *American Universal Geography*. Morse travelled ceaselessly to research and promote his work, and had seen more of the country than most of his fellow citizens. He may have disdained the "cosmopolitanism" of the opposition party, but Morse himself was no ignorant provincial. On the other hand, although he was minister at the New North Church in Boston from 1789, and it was here that he delivered his most renowned sermons, he was never comfortable in Boston social circles, complaining often in letters about the city's love of luxury and secular habits.

From the early years of the decade Morse and his colleagues had campaigned steadily against the dangers of secularism creeping into society, believing that the likes of Paine, Jefferson, and the recent tours of deist speaker Elihu Palmer, had inspired in the American people "uncleanness, Sabbath breaking and all the flood of iniquity which springs from these", with Jefferson "the arch-apostle of the cause of irreligion and free thought" (qtd Knight, ed., *Conspiracy Theories in American History*, p511). The devout John Adams had beaten Jefferson to the presidency in 1796, but vigilance was still required. President Adams himself declared in March 1798, on the occasion of the National Fast, that the country was "at present placed in a hazardous and difficult position". With the arrival of Robison's book, Morse was anxious to warn his countrymen of the deeper cause and on May 9th of that year Morse delivered the first of his Illuminati sermons, describing "a work written by a gentleman of literary eminence in Scotland, within the last year, and just reprinted in this country, entitled 'Proofs of a conspiracy...'". He explained:

I hold it a duty, my brethren, which I owe to God, to the cause of religion, to my country, and to you, at this time, to declare to you, thus honestly and faithfully, these truths. My only aim is to awaken in you and myself a due attention, at this alarming period, to our dearest interests. As a faithful watchman I would give you warning of your present danger.

This danger had begun abroad with the spread of Enlightenment ideals, and had led inexorably to bloody revolution:

By these awful events – this tremendous shaking among nations of the earth, God is doubtless accomplishing his promises, and fulfilling the prophecies. The wrath and violence of men against all government and religion, shall be made ultimately, in some way or another, to praise God. All corruptions, in religion and government, as dross must, sooner or later, be burnt up. The dreadful fire of *Illuminatism* may be permitted to rage and spread for this purpose.... But while we contemplate these awful events in this point of view, let us beware, in our expressions of approbation, of blending the end with the means. Because atheism and licentiousness are employed as instruments, by divine providence, to subvert and overthrow popery and despotism, it does not follow that atheism and licentiousness are in themselves good things, and worthy of our approbation .... We have reason to tremble for the safety of our political, as well as our religious ark. Attempts are being made, and are openly, as well as secretly, conducted, to undermine the foundations of both.

At the time of Morse's first Illuminati sermon the public's most pressing concern was the unfolding XYZ Affair, a series of diplomatic incidents that contributed to the deterioration of

Franco-US relations. His allusions to the perfidy of France were very much in keeping with the public mood, but mention of the Illuminati was almost premature – until the arrival of Robison's book later that year, no one had yet heard of them in the US. However, the theories would gain credence over the coming months and would become a persistent presence in public discourse in the northeast.

Just a few months later, on June 19th of that year, as part of its graduation ceremony, the senior class at Harvard was treated to a speech by David Tappan, warning of the dangers of self-indulgence and referring ominously to "a more recent system, which...has for its ostensible object the regeneration of an oppressed world to the blissful enjoyment of equal liberty". This "more recent system" was the Illuminati, and Tappan traced its lineage from Weishaupt to the French Revolution for the benefit of his students. Meanwhile, over at Yale, President Timothy Dwight continued to elaborate on his pet theme – the death of religion – by incorporating Robison's and Barruel's theories. Dwight was a highly respected member of New England society: erudite, cultured and deeply religious (he was known as "Pope Dwight"). When he made the dangers of the Illuminati the subject of his sermon on America's national day – July 4th – the country sat up and took notice. During this sermon he called attention to "the duty of Americans at the present crisis". The crisis mentioned "consists of two great and distinct parts: the preparation for the overthrow of the anti-Christian empire; and the embarkation of men in a professed and unusual opposition to God, and to his kingdom, accomplished by means of false doctrines, and impious teachers." These Godless men included the usual suspects – Voltaire and the *encyclopédistes* – but Dwight also revealed to the American public the alleged extent of the Illuminati's influence, referring – again clearly under the influence of Robison – to their success in perverting the original philanthropic aims of German and French Freemasonry to embrace "every novel, licentious and alarming opinion".

Dwight explained in his sermon:

Thus minds already tinged with philosophism were here speedily blackened with a deep and deadly dye; and those which came fresh and innocent to the scene of contamination became early and irremediably corrupted ... In these hot beds were sown the seeds of that astonishing Revolution, and all its dreadful appendages, which now spreads dismay and horror throughout half the globe.

(Timothy Dwight, "The Duty of Americans in the Present Crisis")

Dwight traced the Illuminati's dastardly path from Germany (where "public faith and morals have been unhinged", leading to the country's "total ruin"), through France, where their work was plain for all to see, on to England and Scotland. Most frightening to the American people, Dwight attested to secret papers in Germany that proved the Illuminati had been present in the US since the 1780s. Americans must stand vigilant, Dwight warned, and in his sermon made a direct comparison between revolutionary philosophies and the work of the Illuminati:

For what end shall we be connected with men of whom this is the character and conduct? Is it that we may assume the same character, and pursue the same conduct? Is it that our churches may become temples of reason, our Sabbath a decade, and our psalms of praise Marsellois [i.e., the revolutionary Marseillaise] hymns? ... Is it that we may see the Bible cast into a bonfire, the vessels of the sacramental supper borne by an ass in public procession, and our children, either wheeled or terrified, uniting in the mob, chanting mockeries against God, and hailing in the sounds of *Ça ira* the ruin of their religion and the loss of their souls? ... Shall we, my brethren, become partakers of these sins? Shall we introduce them into our government, our schools, our families? Shall our sons become the disciples of Voltaire, and the dragoons of Marat; or our daughters the concubines of the Illuminati?

The genie was out of the bottle and there was no turning back: from late summer 1798, the Illuminati plot was everywhere. Federalist orators throughout the northeast took up the cause, comfortably eliding the threat of the Illuminati with the activities of their political opponents, Jefferson's Democratic-Republicans.

Theodore Dwight, Timothy's brother, addressed the issue in a speech at Hartford, Connecticut, referring to "a set of men whose avowed subject ... was the destruction of all religion and government". Of these "modern Illuminati" he said: "I know not who belongs to the society in this country; but if I were to make proselytes to illuminatism in the United States; I should in the first place apply to Thomas Jefferson ... and [his] political associates."

At a stroke, the issue was now openly divided along party lines. In conservative New England, the newspapers were quick to pick up the theme, but among the clamour of fear-mongers were some dissenting voices. An editorial in the *Massachusetts Mercury* in July of that year demanded Robison's credentials: "at this distance, it is impossible to decide on the truth of his assertions, or the respectability of his testimonies", and questioned whether Morse et al. were wise to pin their arguments on only one source. After all, the piece argued, Robison had attacked that hero of the American Revolution, the "worthy La Fayette" and his book was clearly the work of "incorrigible prejudices". The piece concluded with the admonishment that Americans stand firm against becoming "the dupes of every tale which the prejudices or ignorance of Europeans may fabricate."

Morse, who had introduced the Illuminati plot myth, saw the article as a direct challenge and responded in a series of inconclusive articles that relied on the circular argument that he had the backing of his esteemed colleagues Dwight, Tappan et al., so no further justification was necessary. The publication in translation of volume three of Barruel's *Memoirs* that autumn aided believers in their cause, apparently providing independent corroboration of Robison's theories. In November, Morse renewed his appeal in his Thanksgiving sermon at Charlestown, Massachusetts, and asked his countrymen, not to join in thanks, but to unite in protecting their country from "foreign perils". The nature of these perils were expanded upon in the published version of the sermon, which included a 50-page appendix and extensive footnotes that made explicit reference to the Illuminati and their presence in the US:

> The probable existence of Illuminism in this country was asserted in my Fast Discourse of May last. The following fact, related by a very respectable divine, while it confirms what is above asserted, shows that my apprehensions were not without foundation .... In the northern parts of this state, as I am well informed, there has lately appeared, and still exists under a licentious leader, a company of beings who discard the principles of religion, and the other obligations of morality, trample on the bonds of matrimony, the separate rights of property, and the laws of civil society, spend the Sabbath in labour and diversion, as fancy dictates; and the nights in riotous excess and promiscuous concubinage, as lust impels.

In accusing this "company", Morse evokes the litany of mis-behaviour – deism, immorality, destruction of the marriage vows etc. – now prevalent among many Illuminati conspiracy theories at the time.

Morse's latest sermon reached all levels of society, and if it didn't of its own accord, Morse was not averse to self-promotion and sent copies to both President John Adams and former president George Washington. Early the following year he received a letter from Washington with the following endorsement of his sermon: "I have read it and the Appendix with pleasure, and wish that the latter, at least, could meet a more general circulation than it probably will have, for it contains important information, as little known, out of a small circle as the dissemination of it would be useful, if spread throughout the community."

Others were less convinced, and as the debate re-entered the public sphere, Morse's sermon was applauded and satirized in equal measure. While the Federalist papers printed articles describing Jefferson as "the real Jacobin, the very child of modern illumination, ... and the enemy of this country", those in support of Jefferson printed letters from Europe claiming that Robison's or Barruel's work had since been discredited there. The *Massachusetts Mercury* goaded Morse and his followers by drawing comparisons between the threatening behaviour of the Illuminati and a far more respected sect, the Quakers. Point by point, the editorial equated the Illuminati's philosophy with that of the Quakers – known throughout New England for their pacifism and quiet dignity – and at once rendering fears of the Illuminati absurd:

The Illuminati esteem all ecclesiastical establishments profane, irreligious and tyrannical; so do the Quakers. They hold also the obligations of brotherly love and universal benevolence. The Quakers not only profess these Atheistical principles, but actually reduce them to practice. The Illuminati hold the enormous doctrine of the Equality of mankind. So do these Quakers. They, like the Illuminati, have a general correspondence through all their meetings, delegates constantly moving, and one day, at every quarterly meeting, set apart for private business; and I engage to prove at the bar of any tribunal in the United States, that these Friends, these men so horribly distinguished for benevolence and philanthropy, (Ah! philanthropy!) have held, and do still hold a constant correspondence with their nefarious accomplices in Europe...

Thomas Jefferson, too, provided a counterpart to the growing hysteria. In a letter to James Madison of January 1800 his exasperation with the scare-mongering of the Abbé Barruel and Jedidiah Morse is tangible:

I have lately...got sight of the Abbé Barruel's "Antisocial Conspiracy", [i.e., volume three] which gives me the first idea I have ever had of what is meant by the Illuminatism against which "Illuminate Morse" ... and his ... associates have been making such a hue and cry. Barruel's own parts of the book are perfectly the ravings of a bedlamite. But he quotes largely from Wishaupt [sic] whom he considers the founder of what he calls the order....

Jefferson provides an alternate interpretation of Weishaupt's aims, seeing in his wish to spread the Illuminati's enlightened ideals not a sinister plan to take over the world, but a desire to educate:

Wishaupt seems to be an enthusiastic philanthropist. He is

among those ... who believe in the infinite perfectibility of man. He thinks he may in time be rendered so perfect that he will be able to govern himself in every circumstance, so as to injure none, to do all the good he can, to leave government no occasion to exercise their powers over him, and, of course, to render political government useless. This ... is what Robison, Barruel and Morse have called a conspiracy against all government.

Weishaupt's problems, Jefferson continued, were due to the fact he lived under a repressive government, necessitating that he work in secret, and then under the guise of the Masons. Had Weishaupt enjoyed the freedoms of the American life, Jefferson explained, he could have operated quite openly:

The means he proposes to effect this improvement of human nature are "to enlighten men, to correct their morals and inspire them with benevolence". As Wishaupt lived under the tyranny of a despot and priests, he knew that caution was necessary even in spreading information, and the principles of pure morality. He proposed, therefore, to lead the Free Masons to adopt this object .... This has given an air of mystery to his views, was the foundation of his banishment, the subversion of the Masonic Order, and is the colour for the ravings against him of Robison, Barruel, and Morse, whose real fears are that the craft would be endangered by the spreading of information, reason, and natural morality among men .... I believe you will think with me that if Wishaupt had written here, where no secrecy is necessary in our endeavours to render men wise and virtuous, he would not have thought of any secret machinery for that purpose.

Jefferson's was not the majority view, however, and in the heated, anxious atmosphere of the autumn and winter of 1798–9 the Illuminati scare continued to spread, at once contributing to and being influenced by an increasing xenophobia among the American people.

Over the course of the 1790s the east coast had suffered recurrent epidemics of yellow fever, a misunderstood and consequently deadly disease at the time. Port cities were especially vulnerable, as the disease seems to have spread through contact with trade ships from the West Indies. In the autumn of 1798 Philadelphia, Boston and New York were all ravaged by the disease, with contemporary accounts estimating the death toll at 10,000 (the number is since believed to have been roughly half that). At the sign of an outbreak, the sick were quarantined, with whole sections of the city shut off. In Philadelphia, citizens became afraid to report cases of the illness for fear they would be essentially locked up in their own homes, while in New York, officials congratulated themselves for confining the illness to areas largely populated by foreigners.

This, combined with the worsening relations with France contributed to an atmosphere of almost hysterical suspicion. Contributing to the alarms raised by the east coast clergy was the lingering effect of the diplomatic incident known as the XYZ Affair. In May 1798 President John Adams had sent a delegation to France to settle disputes relating to French raids on US ships, and America's financial debt to France. When the US committee arrived, Talleyrand, Minister for Foreign Relations, refused to meet them directly, and instead sent three agents to negotiate what was essentially a bribe before the meeting could take place. When Adams's men wrote back to the president describing the situation, the letters were made public, with the names of Talleyrand's agents replaced by the letters X, Y and Z. The Federalists played the situation for all it was worth, keeping it in the public eye as an example of the treachery of the French and by implication the Federalists' opponents at home, Jefferson's party. Beset by fears real and imagined, the east coast became prey to a series of wild, unsubstantiated rumours that autumn and winter. An anonymous letter sent to John Adams warned of a plot to burn Philadelphia; when the letter was made public, many of its citizens fled the city. Also in Philadelphia were rumours of an unnamed tailor single-handedly sewing hundreds of French army uniforms, clearly in anticipation of a French invasion. Around this time stories circulated about the so-called Tub Plot, which described how conspirators from France had smuggled secret documents detailing the overthrow of the US government in the false bottoms of two wooden tubs. There were lurid reports of the massacre of the entire crew of the US ship *Ocean* at the hands of the French. These stories had several things in common, but the most important was that they were completely fabricated. Eventually they would be discovered to have originated with the Federalists and would be discredited, but until then they were remarkably potent, contributing to an atmosphere of suspicion that culminated in the passing of the Alien and Sedition Acts in the autumn of 1798.

During this time Jedidiah Morse continued his anti-Illuminati crusade despite, or because of, vociferous criticism from the opposition party. As far as he was concerned, his views were endorsed by the president himself, whose speech on the occasion of the National Fast Day in 1799, although not referring directly to the Illuminati, called for Americans to be vigilant against foreign, subversive elements:

> The most precious interests of the people of the United States are still held in jeopardy by the hostile designs and insidious acts of a foreign nation, as well as by the dissemination among them of those principles, subversive of the

foundations of all religious, moral, and social obligations, that have produced incalculable mischief in other countries.

By early 1799 Morse came to possess evidence that he believed would silence his detractors, what he described as "an official authenticated list of the names, ages, places of nativity, professions, &c. of the officers and members of a Society of Illuminati, consisting of one hundred members, instituted in Virginia, by the Grand Orient [i.e., Masonic lodge] of France." He devoted his third, and what would be his last, Illuminati sermon to these revelations.

Basing his sermon on a letter he received purporting to document the activities since 1786 of the Masonic Wisdom lodge in Virginia, Morse details the nature of the enemy – not Americans, but foreigners ("the members are chiefly Emigrants from France and St. Domingo") – as well as the extent of their presence in the US, and their ultimate goal:

> We have in truth secret enemies, not a few scattered through our country; ... enemies whose professed design is to subvert and overturn our holy religion and our free and excellent government. And the pernicious fruits of their insidious and secret efforts, must be visible to every eye not obstinately closed or blinded by prejudice.

This sermon was the most sensational of all Morse's public speeches, and for the first time in the US makes a connection between the Illuminati and the Masonic lodges – but, like Robison, Morse goes to great lengths to distinguish between "good" Masons and bad or "false" Masons. The Wisdom lodge of Virginia was one of the latter, Morse asserted; he had it on good authority from reliable Masons that the Wisdom was not a genuine lodge at all, but an Illuminati cell. Extrapolating from the alleged number of members in Virginia, Morse estimated there must be something like 1,700 Illuminati members in the US.

This separate distinction between the Illuminati and the Freemasons was crucial if Morse hoped to retain any kind of support for his views. Freemasonry had had a strong presence in America since its earliest colonial days, and if Morse suggested that the Freemasons were somehow in league with the Illuminati he would lose all credibility, even among his most staunch Federalist advocates. Most of the founding fathers were Masons, including Benjamin Franklin, Thomas Jefferson and Samuel Adams; revolutionary hero John Paul Jones was a Mason, as was midnight rider Paul Revere. The nation's first president was well known to be a Mason and wore full Masonic regalia at the cornerstone ceremony of the US Capitol. Masonic imagery went into the designing of the Great Seal. Masons were inextricably bound into the fabric of the American establishment; they weren't planning to overthrow the government – they were the government.

The "false" Masons on the other hand, were dangerous, extensive, prolific; it was the duty of all Americans to guard against their influence or suffer the consequences. His sermon concluded:

That there are branches and considerably numerous too, of this infernal association in this country we have now full proof.... That they even boast that their plans are deeply and extensively laid, and cannot be defeated, that success is certain. If then, Americans, we do not ... act ..., we must expect to fall victim to the arts and arms of that nation, on the title page of whose laws, as well as on its own standards, is written the emphatic and descriptive motto HAVOC AND SPOIL AND RUIN ARE OUR GAIN.

The sermon caused an immediate sensation. Demand was such that on publication it was reprinted four times in quick succession. The Federalist papers threw their weight behind it and urged their readers to obtain a copy: "Every person who does not wish to be blind to his own destruction will undoubtedly furnish himself with the document; since it establishes beyond a doubt the existence of the infernal club in the very heart of our country." Sermons from Connecticut up to Maine picked up the theme, elaborating on the presence and aims of the "infernal club", the Illuminati. Morse entered into a vast correspondence with his numerous supporters, one of whom wrote from Connecticut to say that because of Morse "the facts in ... Robison and Barruel have got into every farmhouse".

The Democratic papers, fearing that Morse's sermon would sway public opinion irrevocably, went into overdrive, seeking by every way possible to discredit Morse and his allegations. They noted that all references to the Illuminati led, inevitably, back to France, and suspected the scare to be nothing more than a Federalist ploy to heighten antagonism against the French, and, by extension, turn the public away from the Democrats. The *Independent Chronicle* of Virginia asked why, if the danger was so great, Morse did not take his evidence – his "preposterous documents" – straight to the president. The *American Mercury* of Connecticut wrote in mock despair: "He will ... do more honour to himself and his profession, to return again to his old business 'of writing geography' and not thus attempt to agitate the public mind with such alarming discoveries of Illuminatism."

It did not take long for Morse's opponents to gain the upper hand. Just two short months after the sermon, at the height of Illuminati fever, Democratic papers revealed a situation that discredited the whole Illuminati myth, and would cause considerable embarrassment to Morse. Firstly, the source of Morse's "authenticated list" was discovered: arch-Federalist Oliver

Wolcott, confirming what the opposition had long suspected, that the Illuminati plot was a ploy by the Federalists to discredit their opponents, with Morse as the unwitting dupe. Even more damaging to Morse were the revelations in the *American Mercury*. The paper published a letter from a respected historian in Hamburg, one Professor Ebeling, who was in regular correspondence with many prominent Americans of the day – including Morse and Jefferson – and was a member of the Massachusetts Historical Society. Ebeling's letter described the work of John Robison from the European perspective, saying, essentially, that Robison's *Proofs of a Conspiracy* had been completely discredited in Europe, and that Robison himself was considered a very disreputable character, in deep financial debt, who had been expelled from his Masonic lodge. The Democratic papers crowed, with some accusing the Federalist clergy of mounting a campaign similar to the Salem Witch Trials.

Morse, horrified at having his main source revealed as a sham, tried to restore his reputation by a closer investigation of the Wisdom lodge in Virginia. There, too, he was unsuccessful. Entering into a correspondence with the congressman for Virginia, Josiah Parker, Morse discovered that although the majority of the lodge's members were French or of French origin, the congressman could vouch for the strength of their characters and their unblemished reputations. The Wisdom lodge was not a hotbed of radicalism but a gathering of upstanding Virginians. The Illuminati trail had vanished and Jedidiah Morse abandoned the crusade shortly after, as did the majority of the public.

The scare may have passed from the public's consciousness, but its repercussions were profound. It contributed to an atmosphere of frenzied distrust that led to the passing of the Alien and Sedition Acts in the summer of 1798, the most restrictive domestic security laws in the US to date. Starting with the

Naturalization Act in June, the length of residency required for citizenship was extended from five years to 14. This was followed by the Alien Act and Alien Enemies Act, which gave the president the power to imprison or deport, without trial, aliens considered "dangerous to the peace and safety of the United States" or those whom the government had reason to believe "are concerned in any treasonable or secret machinations against the government". The greatest impact was felt by the last act, the Sedition Act, which severely curtailed the freedom of the press – specifically the papers critical of the Adams administration. Under this act, stiff fines or up to two years' imprisonment would be imposed on those who "write, print, utter, publish, or shall cause or procure to be written, printed, uttered or published...any false, scandalous and malicious writing or writings against the government of the United States... with intent to defame the said government...or the said President...; or to excite against them the hatred of the good people of the United States." In reality, any paper expressing or printing an opinion critical of the government was in danger of having legal action taken against it. This, combined with the fact that most of the courts in the northeast were presided over by Federalist judges, led to wildly biased sentencing. Most of the opposition's newspapers were affected in some way; in all 25 people were arrested under the act, while others suffered from other forms of harassment, from beatings to private lawsuits. Ultimately, however, the act was wildly unsuccessful. Reports of Federalist persecution led to comparisons with the repressive British regime, and contributed to Thomas Jefferson's victory over Adams in the 1800 election.

The Illuminati fear was significant in other ways: its legacy would have lasting repercussions on the position of Freemasonry in the US. Although the original proponents of the Illuminati plot myth, Jedidiah Morse and his contemporaries, were careful to separate "genuine" Masonic lodges from any taint of Illuminati intrigue, once the equation of secret societies with conspiratorial thinking had been made it became impossible to disentangle them. Despite Freemasonry's respectable, even illustrious origins in the US, its reputation would go into sharp decline from the beginning of the 19th century, reaching its nadir with the establishment of the Anti-Masonic Party in 1826. This powerful political party established itself as a genuine opponent to America's two main parties – the first of America's third parties – and even had its own presidential candidate. Although the Anti-Masonic Party did not see out the 19th century, the reputation of the Freemasons never fully recovered.

However, this would not be the last the world would hear of the Illuminati. Although the term was now synonymous with secret conspiracies, the definition of such was transmutable. It could expand, adapt and distort to absorb and reflect society's current anxieties. For most of the 19th century, fears of the Illuminati lay dormant. They would resurface with a vengeance at the beginning of the 20th century, under the ugly guise of anti-Semitism.

Chapter Four: The Illuminati and the Rise of Anti-Semitism

We shall create and multiply free Masonic lodges in all the countries of the world, absorb into them all who may become or who are prominent in public activity, for in these lodges we shall find our principal intelligence office and means of influence. All these lodges we shall bring under one central administration, known to us alone and to all others absolutely unknown, which will be composed of our learned elders .... In these lodges we shall tie together the knowledge which binds together all revolutionary and liberal elements.

In 1920 a peculiar document began circulating throughout the cities of Western Europe. It purported to be the transcript of a secret meeting of "elders", describing a point-by-point plan to take over the world. They would do this by the means by now familiar to any student of conspiracy: by secretly establishing their members in positions of authority; by taking over educational establishments; by indoctrinating the young; and by the Illuminati standby of infiltrating Masonic lodges, and taking advantage of their powerful social connections. The quote above could very well have come from the writings of Adam Weishaupt; its reference to "one central administration... absolutely unknown" might have been modelled on Weishaupt's system of "unknown superiors", and its underlying philosophy of "the end justifies the means" could have been written by

Weishaupt himself. However, the document was nothing to do with Weishaupt, or the Illuminati. It was a forgery, and it was malignant. Its tone was threatening, hysterical even, and it seemed to offer proof of a threat to the western world that made earlier Illuminati plot scares look like the work of the boy scouts. It was called *The Protocols of the Elders of Zion*, and it unleashed upon the world a new and virulent form of anti-Semitism that would reach its conclusion in the Holocaust.

However, in the years immediately following World War I, the *Protocols* became inextricably linked with the Illuminati myth and shaped its modern-day incarnation, which persists even into the 21st century. After lying dormant for over 100 years, fears of the Illuminati threat proliferated, and fed into the contorted evolution of the *Protocols*; the resulting hateful propaganda reflected back onto the Illuminati story, *ad infinitum*, like two funhouse mirrors reflecting ever-more distorted images. It was during this period that certain myths were solidified: that of the link between Judaism and secret societies, and the idea that the Order of the Illuminati was several centuries – millennia, even – old.

The murky origins of the *Protocols* have left a soiled trail crisscrossing Europe, from France to Russia and back again. Historian Norman Cohn's *Warrant for Genocide* provides the definitive account of the complex history of the *Protocols*. He traces their beginnings to the alarmist Abbé Barruel, who, several years after the success of his infamous *Memoirs* was persuaded to revise his earlier theory to incorporate Jews into the list of revolutionary conspirators. His reason for doing so is itself the result of what is now known to be a forgery, a letter from one JB Simonini (a pseudonym), allegedly an army officer in Florence.

Among Barruel's original rogue's gallery of conspirators behind the French Revolution there was no mention of Jews. He pointed his finger at Jacobins, *philosophes* and *encyclopédistes*, "false" Masons who strayed from their rightful path, and, of course, the Illuminati – anyone, in fact, who appeared to challenge the status quo. His omission of the Jewish community was due to the fact that, as noted in chapter 2, at the time of writing his *Memoirs* at the end of the 18th century, Jews in France had very little influence: they numbered perhaps only 40,000 in the whole of the country, lived largely separate from the rest of society, and had no political presence. The revolution changed all this. With the new government came emancipation and new, unprecedented rights for the Jewish community – including full citizenship. In the eyes of conspiracy thinkers, France's Jews appeared to benefit directly from the revolution. Where the monarchy had fallen, the aristocracy had lost their ancestral lands, and the Church had been destroyed, the previously powerless Jews of France appeared to have come out on top. Once this notion was planted in the public's consciousness, it began to take root, and by the beginning of the 19th century it continued to flourish.

One occasion which brought the theory to public attention was Napoleon's meeting in 1806 with 71 prominent French Jews, a meeting that was, essentially, to reassure the emperor of the Jewish population's allegiance to France. Napoleon called this gathering the Great Sanhedrin, a name taken from the ancient Jewish court. To his critics, and to those who feared the power of this mysterious people, this name suggested that a secret Jewish government had existed for centuries, and had only now revealed itself in the successful aftermath of the revolution. To Napoleon's enemies, he was nothing less than the Antichrist, and in convening the Great Sanhedrin, was presenting himself as messiah to his Jewish citizens. *L'Ambigu*, a journal published in London for French *emigrés*, proclaimed: "It remains for us only to watch this Antichrist fight against the eternal decrees of God; that must be the last act of his diabolical existence." Across the continent, the Holy Synod of the Russian Orthodox Church warned: "Today he proposes to reunite the Jews, whom God's wrath has scattered over the earth, to urge them to proclaim a false messiah on his person" (both qtd Cohen, p80). In this heated atmosphere, the mysterious document that would become known as the Simonini letter found a ripe environment for contagion.

The letter was sent to the Abbé Barruel some time in 1806 to alert him to the presence of a much more powerful organization than even the ones he had unmasked. The letter describes this group as "the most formidable power, if one considers its great wealth and the protection it enjoys in almost all European countries" (qtd Cohen, p28). And who is this power? None other than "the Judaic sect". The writer then goes on to provide a lurid account of his experiences. With distinct echoes of Cagliostro's fabricated eye-witness accounts of Illuminati initiation ceremonies, the writer explains how, upon meeting a group of Jewish Piedmontese, he pretended to be Jewish himself and was thus initiated into the Jewish master plan of world domination. His new-found companions showed him "sums of gold and silver for distribution to those who embraced the cause". And not only that: they promised Simonini would be elevated to the rank of general in their invisible army if he would become a Freemason. He was then given weapons decorated with Masonic imagery. The "secrets" revealed to him were pure fantasy, whose origins supposedly stretched back to the 11th century. Among them were claims that the Old Man of the Mountain, the leader of the Assassins, who terrorized the Muslim world from the 11th to 13th centuries, was both Jewish and had founded the Illuminati. Therefore, according to "Simonini", all of the Illuminati's activities – their infiltration of Masonic lodges, of educational establishments, of government offices – could be attributed to the Jews. And this wasn't all: the letter claimed that in Italy, as many as 800 Catholic churches were in fact Jewish, as most of the clergy were only pretending to be Christian. The letter warned that, as Jews were accorded more rights, they would buy up more and more land throughout Europe until the Christian populace was dispossessed. The ultimate aim the letter revealed, however, was "that in less than a century, they would be masters of the world, ... they would abolish other sects and establish the rule of their own sect, ... they would turn Christian churches into so many synagogues and reduce the remaining Christians to absolute slavery" (qtd Cohn, p28).

This one document appears, single-handedly, to have introduced the idea of the Jewish-Masonic plot myth. Of all the hysterical and alarmist theories that had surfaced during and immediately after the French Revolution – fears of magicians and mesmerists, Templars, Masons and Martinists – this one was completely new. Its effect on the Abbé Barruel was electrifying: here, at last, was the final piece in the conspiracy puzzle. Barruel would have accepted the letter's claims that the Jews had benefited from the French Revolution; he could see evidence of this all around him. And as he had so indisputably proven that the Freemasons had orchestrated the revolution, clearly the groups were working in sympathy with one another – that is if they weren't, in fact, one and the same group. Little did it matter that in reality few Masonic lodges accepted Jewish members – Barruel reasoned that they might simply be hiding their true faith. As an organization that promoted the idea of the rights of man, his argument continued, the Masons clearly had set out to improve the lot of the Jews – why do so unless they were in fact helping their own? This idea gained currency with the wider public, to the extent that many became convinced Napoleon was a Jew for the same reasons: in the wake of his military successes the Jewish community seemed better off, with its ghettoes closed and its people emancipated.

For Barruel the Simonini letter introduced a whole new angle to his conspiracy theories. He grafted the Jewish plot myth onto his previous theories and, in light of this new insight, reassessed the role of the Knights Templar (who had also, he had proven, been directing events behind the scenes at the French Revolution). The Templars and Jews, Barruel suddenly saw, had been in partnership ever since the Templars' founding in the 12th century. It was *they*, together, who oversaw the Masonic lodges by way of a "supreme council of 21, of which nine were Jews". Above this nine was a secret group of three, unknown to the others, and above this, overseeing all, was a secretly elected Grand Master. This fantasy has direct parallels with the Illuminati's principle of the "unknown superiors", and has proven to be remarkably enduring. Over the centuries, as the secret plot myth expanded and distorted to incorporate what-ever might be the current bogey of the day, the idea of the hidden power, behind the hidden power – behind the hidden power – and so on, like an infinite number of Russian dolls, has been remarkably resilient.

Barruel also perpetuated the idea of a vast, shadowy net-work, claiming that this supreme council had no fixed head-quarters, but convened wherever and whenever heads of state met, and was always in the background, never drawing atten-tion to itself. Supposedly, its members accounted for their move-ments by claiming they were for study purposes, or to attend conferences (perhaps a jab at the *philosophes*, or evidence of sus-picion of education in general). Barruel seems to have modelled his Grand Master on what little he knew about the Old Man of the Mountain, claiming that he demanded unquestioning allegiance from his followers, who could expect death as a consequence of disobedience. Orders were relayed from the Grand Master by a network of Freemasons extending across the continent, Barruel explained:

[F]rom neighbour to neighbour and from hand to hand the orders are transmitted with incomparable speed, for these pedestrians are delayed neither by bad weather, nor by the mishaps that normally befall horsemen or carriages; a man on foot can always get along when he knows the country.... They stop neither to eat nor to sleep, for each one covers only two leagues. Fifteen pedestrians, replacing one another, can reach Orleans from Paris in nine hours, using short-cuts and above all never stopping.

   (qtd Cohn, p31)

This idea of an omnipresent network, with its legions of foot soldiers, untroubled by weaknesses such as hunger and fatigue, laid the groundwork for the notion of a shadowy cabal of almost supernatural abilities, and was a major development in the expansion of the original Illuminati myth. As the story develops, the idea of the supernatural omnipotence of the group increasingly takes hold, until, by the late 20th century, the final imaginative leap is made, and the Illuminati become extra terrestials (see chapter 7).

The author of the Simonini letter has never been established, but it was known to have been written by a member of the French political police to discredit Napoleon and his support of the Jews. Barruel was the targeted recipient because of his flourishing career in unmasking conspiracies. An endorsement from France's arch-conservative would bring the contents to the attention of the wider public, doing a lot of political damage in the process. In the short term the letter did not have the desired effect. Barruel's subsequent reappraisal of the role of the Jews in his tortured plot-driven worldview did not garner immediate public support; upon his death in 1820 his latest *oeuvre* went largely unnoticed, and would never have the success of his *Memoirs*. But it laid the groundwork for the genesis of the

Protocols, and many of the theories he developed were to be replayed – distorted and magnified – like some hellish *leitmotif* echoing down the century.

The genesis of the *Protocols* is a tortured one, and carries parallels with the development of the Illuminati myth in that, once the stories began to gather momentum, they became unstoppable, gathering layer upon layer of lies until their origins were unrecognizable. The difference was that the *Protocols* were fiction to begin with. Literally so: they first appear in a mid-19th-century novel published in Germany. To understand their role in 20th-century conspiracy-mongering, including the Illuminati myth, it is important to trace their development.

The influence of the Simonini letter did not immediately take off; for several decades the Jewish plot myth lay dormant, or percolated just below the surface, without major repercussions. It next resurfaced in Germany in the 1860s. Jews in Germany made up a tiny percentage of the population at this time – 1.2 percent – yet, as Norman Cohn notes, the rights accorded to German Jews under Napoleon provoked a violent backlash of anti-Semitism. By 1869, when Jews in northern Germany were being granted the same rights as the rest of the population, this antagonism reached fever pitch.

It was during this period in Germany that the novel *Biarritz* was published – under the bizarre pseudonym of Sir John Retcliff, although it was actually the work of Herman Goedsche, who was a failed postal clerk and committed anti-Semite. A thoroughly unpleasant piece of work, Goedsche also acted as a spy for the Prussian secret police. Goedsche was dismissed from the postal service for his role in forging documents used against Democratic leader Benedikt Waldeck in his trial for treason in 1849 (Waldeck was subsequently acquitted). At a loose end, Goedsche turned his hand to writing trashy novels, of which *Biarritz*, published in 1868, was a particularly lurid example. The plot and purpose of the book is of no interest; were it not for one infamous chapter, both it and its author would be forgotten. The chapter in question is "In the Jewish Cemetery in Prague", a horrific account of a midnight meeting of mysterious elders who, conveniently for the narrator – and the reader – are happy to discuss their plans for world domination loudly, and in public. (Groups secretly bent on world domination seem strangely lax about security.) The narrator slips through the gates of the cemetery as the clock strikes 11pm. One by one, out of the sepulchral gloom, come 13 shrouded figures, who each stop at a particular tomb to pray. At the stroke of midnight, with the arrival of the last figure, a hollow voice from deep within the tomb greets the figures as the 12 Tribes of Israel, with the last figure representing "the unfortunates and exiles" of the world. Each figure in turn approaches the tomb to report on their activities over the last century, which include the by-now familiar litany of nefarious doings: hoarding gold; manipulating the stock exchange, and through that, heads of state; undermining the Christian Church, etc. etc. The figures then agree to convene in another 100 years when their plans for world domination will have come to fruition. The narrator and sidekick spend the rest of the novel attempting to save the world from this dire fate.

This fantastical piece of horror fiction did not sink back into the obscurity it deserved; this specific chapter proved alarmingly popular and acquired a life of its own. It was reprinted as a stand-alone text and with breathtaking speed made its way across Europe. Just four years after its first publication, in 1872 in St Petersburg, it was published as a pamphlet with a preface stating that, although it was a work of fiction, it was based on historical fact. Like the current day equivalent of the urban myth or Internet hoax, it continued its way around Russia, with versions appearing in Moscow and Odessa, and then moved on to Prague. By the time it reached France, reprinted in 1881 in the journal *Le Contemporain,* all traces of its fictional origins had been forgotten – or conveniently erased. It was now published as a factual document; all the 12 speeches had been consolidated and attributed to one rabbi, and the eyewitness account was purportedly from a reputable aristocratic source – oddly, Sir John Readclif. The text was now known as "The Rabbi's Speech" and it was received as genuine. It proved alarmingly enduring, and acquired added twists and embellishments as it made its wretched way around Europe. As late as 1933 a Swedish version appeared whose preface mourned the sorry demise of the estimable Sir John Readclif, who paid with his life for revealing "The Rabbi's Speech".

The legacy of "The Rabbi's Speech" spread like a disease through Europe, and manifested itself in several ways: firstly, it reintroduced into the secret plot myth the element of magic and the supernatural that had been touched upon by Barruel just before his death, but had previously been forgotten since the Middle Ages. The idea that Jews held secret, magical knowledge gained currency, and the idea grew that this had been passed on to the Templars in the Middle Ages, who in turn had founded the Masons. Several books published in France around the time of *Biarritz* in the late 1860s elaborated on this theme. Since the revolution, the Catholic Church in France had been in bitter opposition to Freemasonry; with their republican, anti-clerical ideals, the Masonic lodges embodied all the Church feared. For devout Catholics, the step from criticism of the Church to outright devil worship was a short one. The Masons, clearly, were guilty of both. And the Jews were Masons. Thus this circular argument, like a snake eating its own tail, was established.

By the 1890s in France, a number of hoaxes were perpetuated among the more credulous French citizens about the magical powers of both groups. Leo Taxil, an inveterate hoaxer, spread several stories about the link between the Freemasons and satanism. Considerable mileage was gained from a story that the Grand Master of Freemasonry in the US had a telephone system operated by demons, allowing him to keep in touch with other lodges throughout the world. Taxil's purpose, ironically, was to draw attention to the Church's antagonism toward Freemasonry, by highlighting its willingness to believe anti-Masonic lies. In this he was wildly successful, and many of his ridiculous claims entered anti-Masonic lore – and are still cited today. (Any claim, for example, that the Masons worshipped at the altar of the goat-headed Baphomet can be traced back to Taxil.) In France in 1893, a book appeared whose title made the connection explicit: *La Franc-Maçonnerie, Synagogue de Satan* (*Freemasonry, Satan's Synagogue*). The author, a Monseigneur Meurin, was an archbishop in Mauritius. His worldview seems to have been strongly influenced by the Abbé Barruel; he certainly seems to have taken on the mantle of paranoid cleric as Barruel's natural successor. For Meurin, the issue is simple: "everything in Freemasonry is fundamentally Jewish, exclusively Jewish, passionately Jewish, from the beginning to the end" (qtd Cohen, p48). It was only a matter of time before "history will tell how revolutions of recent centuries originated in the Masonic sect under the supreme command of the Jews." And how and why were these revolutions started by the Freemasons? Because they were in control of the government! "The fact that all revolutions are made in the depths of Masonic back-lodges would be inexplicable, if we did not know that the ministries of all countries...are in the hands of Freemasons who in the last analysis are controlled by Jews."

For a country that had a very small Jewish population, the enthusiasm for these rumours and the speed with which they spread was remarkable. Rural France had the most rapacious appetite for stories such as these, and it was here that the population was least likely to have had any dealings with the Jewish community, confined as it largely was to Paris or other cities. Yet it was undoubtedly this fear of the unknown, and the rural suspicion of the city, that allowed the stories to take root.

If in France "The Rabbi's Speech" reinforced the belief in the supernatural powers of Freemasonry and Judaism, in Russia it manifested itself more brutally, and was used to fan the flames of the spate of pogroms that swept the country in the late 19th and early 20th centuries. Russia in the 19th century was centuries behind its neighbours to the west: bowing under the weight of the last of Europe's absolute monarchies, mired in superstition and slow to adopt the modernization enjoyed in the rest of Europe's capitals. It had essentially not progressed beyond the Middle Ages, and nothing illustrated this more clearly than its attitude to its Jewish communities. Russia's five million Jews represented about a third of the world's Jewish population. Since the Middle Ages, they had lived in the Pale of Settlement (a group of provinces in what is now Poland), subject to severe restrictions and state-sanctioned persecution under successive tsars. After a brief respite in the mid-19th century, in which conditions for Russia's Jews looked set to improve under Alexander II, his assassination in 1881 set the course back several centuries. His successors Alexander III, and later Nicholas II, were vehemently anti-Semitic. Alexander III positively encouraged the notion that his father's assassins were Jewish, and a wave of more than 200 pogroms in 1881 alone swept the southwest of the country. The arrival of "The Rabbi's Speech" helped to reinforce this view: here was additional proof, if proof were needed, from abroad, of the Jewish world conspiracy.

Nineteenth-century Russia had its own home-grown anti-Semitic literature, and "The Rabbi's Speech" simply reaffirmed what had been circulating for some time: the notion that the unknown was concomitant with the hidden, and was thus sinister. An 1869 book, *The Book of the Kahal*, exploits its readers' ignorance; the use of the unfamiliar Hebrew word "kahal" in itself seems ominous (although it simply means "community organization" and was, until 1844, legal in Russia). The author, Joseph Brafmann, a spy for the secret police, took the actual, innocuous, minutes from kahals throughout the country and wove them together to suggest there was a vast web of intrigue connecting the groups. The book's currency was such that it was circulated as an official government document, and made a particular impression on the secret police. Others got in on the act: a particularly unsavoury character, Hippolytus Lutostansky, a former Catholic priest defrocked for sordid crimes too numerous to mention, wrote a book reviving the medieval myth of the Christian blood sacrifice in Jewish ritual. He attempted to blackmail leading Jewish figures by demanding money in exchange for publicly renouncing the contents of his book, but failed. It was later used as evidence by the prosecution in the infamous Beiliss trial of 1913, in which a Jewish clerk, Mendel Beiliss, was accused of the ritual killing of a Christian boy. Another of Lutostansky's titles, *The Talmud and the Jews* introduced to Russia the notion of the Jewish-Masonic connection. This was a novelty: masonry had enjoyed a respectable, philanthropic reputation in Russia up until it was outlawed in the 1820s. As proof of these allegations, Lutostanksy reprinted "The Rabbi's Speech" in his book.

And so the sorry litany continued, with a stream of self-serving crooks contributing to a body of hate literature that piled lie upon twisted lie. The work of one paranoid fantasist, writing under the name Osman-Bey (real name variously described as Millinger or Millingen), an international swindler constantly under arrest for skipping bail, made a healthy living from his anti-Semitism. His heinous *World Conquest of the Jews* ran to seven editions in the late 19th century. In it, he repeated the usual falsehoods about ritual murder, and traced all world events back to the benevolent Alliance Israélite Universelle in Paris, a philanthropic organization devoted to education. This 19th-century organization was, he claimed, not only responsible for the French Revolution, but also for the assassination of Alexander II, working, with direct echoes of the Abbé Barruel's allegations, through an intricate and vast network of spies and agents across Europe and into Russia. The book's structure, a bogus eye witness account of a lecture by a secret Jewish government, provided a model for the infamous forgery, *The Protocols of the Elders of Zion*.

The *Protocols* first appeared in Russia in 1903, as a series of articles in a St Petersburg paper, *Znamya (The Banner)*. Its editor, P.A. Krushevan, was a notorious anti-Semite; only a few months previous to publishing the *Protocols* he had instigated the vicious pogrom in his home town of Kishinev near Bessarabia, which had resulted in 45 deaths and over 400 injuries. The editor described the articles as being a translation sent from the French; how they had made their way into his possession was never explained. The articles were initially published under the title "Minutes of the Meeting of the World Union of Freemasons and Elders of Zion". No sooner had they appeared than, like "The Rabbi's Speech" before them, they took on a life of their own. Soon they were collected and published in cheap pamphlet form, with titles such as "The Root of our Trouble" or "Enemies of the Human Race". One edition at the time, called "Extracts from the Protocols of the Freemasons", was clearly influenced by the Jewish-Masonic plot myths that had been circulating in France. These pamphlets were aimed at the rabble, published under the imprint of the Imperial Guard with the express intention of summoning popular support for burgeoning extremist right-wing groups.

The text reached a different audience in 1905, when it appeared appended to a book by the bogus mystic Sergey Nilus, entitled *The Great in the Small: Antichrist considered as an Imminent Political Possibility*. This book was specifically produced to appeal to the mystical leanings of Tsar Nicholas II and it succeeded: on the tsar's orders the book was quoted in sermons in all 368 of Moscow's churches. Several reprints followed until the final, revised edition appeared in 1917. Because of the timing, its significance was colossal. The *Protocols* were about to go global.

The *Protocols*, a scant 100 pages, are made up of 24 chapters, supposedly lectures – protocols – from a secret Jewish government highlighting their plans to take over the world, and describing the state of the world once this has been achieved. The introduction from a 1922 edition published in England carries distinct echoes of the Illuminati's method of unknown superiors, describing how the plot stretches back to antiquity, but has only ever been revealed in its entirety to a select few:

> According to the record of secret Jewish Zionism, Solomon and other Jewish learned men already, in 929 BC, thought out a scheme in theory for a peaceful conquest of the whole universe by Zion. As history developed, this scheme was worked out in detail and completed by men who were subsequently initiated into this question. These learned men decided by peaceful means to conquer the world for Zion with the slyness of the Symbolic Snake, whose head was to represent those who have been initiated into the plans of the Jewish administration and the body of the snake to represent the Jewish people – the administration was kept secret, even from the Jewish nation itself.

The tortuous, alarmist language and illogical arguments of the text that followed regurgitated the anti-Semitic lies current at the time, while adding some of its own. It made explicit, for example, a link between the Zionist plot and the forces of liberalism, which were proving a force to be reckoned with in the early 20th century. In this way it has distinct parallels with anti-Illuminati literature: a new ideology, potentially threatening to the status quo, must be the result of a small group of malignant individuals, rather than an indication of a larger, more complex social issue. If in the 18th century the notion of the Illuminati answered a need for a simple answer to the complex question of the French Revolution, the *Protocols* step into a similar breach in the 19th century. The *Protocols'* influence on the spread of anti-Semitism led to the revival and reconfiguration of Illuminati fears in the 1920s.

Nilus's final, revised version of the *Protocols* appeared in 1917 under the title *He is Near, at the Door... Here Comes the Antichrist and the Reign of the Devil on Earth*. It was this edition that ended up in the possession of the deposed tsarina, one of only three books (the others being the Bible and *War and Peace*) found among her personal effects after the royal family's assassination. This chance event seemed to prove the authenticity of the text and was to catapult the *Protocols* to a much wider audience. The tsarina's personal mythology contributed to this development and provided more fodder for the conspiracist: after her death, she was found to have scratched a small swastika into the window-frame of her house in exile. She was known to have used the swastika as a personal talisman and often wore it as a piece of jewellery. The tsarina was well known to have been a deeply superstitious woman and whatever personal significance the swastika may have held for her, by this time it was beginning to carry its contemporary meaning. For those Russians familiar with the symbol, the tsarina's swastika and copy of Nilus's book seemed to point toward proof of a Jewish plot for world domination.

The *Protocols* became a very useful tool in the armament of the White Russian forces to explain the rise of the Bolsheviks and the October Revolution. Copies were distributed to delegates at the Paris Peace Conference of 1919 and to government officials on both sides of the Atlantic, with the aim of winning foreign support for Russia's civil war. It is difficult to conceive today how such a pile of scabrous nonsense was given any serious consideration, but as the world still reeled from the aftershocks of World War I it was perhaps more vulnerable to accepting easy answers. In any event, in 1920 the *Protocols* were published throughout Europe in several languages and were taken seriously by many established publications. In the UK, the fact they were published by the reputable Eyre & Spottiswood – publishers to the king – seemed to give them a respectability they by no means deserved. In May 1920 *The Times* (London) asked, "What are these 'Protocols'? Are they authentic? If so, what malevolent assembly concocted these plans, and gloated over their exposition? ... Have we, by straining every fibre of our national body, escaped a 'Pax Germanica' only to fall into a 'Pax Judaeica'?" Not all publications were so easily persuaded. A week after *The Times* editorial the *Spectator* had the measure of the *Protocols*, describing the text as "a piece of malignant lunacy", the work of "a panic-stricken Muscovite of the old regime", and "brilliant in its moral perversity and intellectual depravity". The article rightly predicted the "enormous harm" the document could wreak if "swallowed by the unthinking" (all qtd Holms, *Anti-Semitism in British Society, 1876–1939*, p148).

Just over a year later, in August 1921, *The Times* retracted its earlier position, and printed an editorial devoted to admitting its error. One of its correspondents, Philip Graves, had come across a pamphlet whose tone was remarkably similar to the *Protocols*. By all accounts Graves had been given this pamphlet by an intermediary, who had obtained it from a former member of the *Okrhana* – the tsarist secret police. This document was in French, and was a satire on the government of Napoleon III by Maurice Joly, entitled *Dialogue aux enfers entre Montesquieu et Machiavel*. The text is a philosophical debate between Montesquieu, representing liberalism, and Machiavelli, who argues the case for despotism. The forger of the *Protocols* lifted much of Machiavelli's dialogue in its entirety and put it in the mouths of the "elders". Joly's construction was even used as a model for the *Protocols* – his text contains 25 "dialogues", the *Protocols* 24. But whoever plagiarized Joly's work wasn't too concerned with logic; some of Montesquieu's arguments for liberalism are also attributed to the elders which, as Norman Cohn points out, contributed to the theory that liberalism was a Jewish creation. References to contemporary events in Russia had been shoehorned into Joly's original dialogue to give the fabrication credibility for a Russian audience. But *The Times* correspondent had revealed the *Protocols* for what they were: a vicious smear on the part of the Russian secret police, and clumsily done at that, to promote and justify the wave of anti-Semitism sweeping Russia, and to drum up international support for its civil war. But the proverbial Pandora's box had been opened, and there was no turning back. The *Protocols* had spread too far, and garnered too many supporters for that. Their insidious web by this time was spreading to the US; the Nazis would make use of them in the 1930s, and they are still circulated in parts of the Arab world today. It beggars belief that, in the 21st century, there are still those who refuse to believe the text is a forgery.

In the UK, with the *Protocols* discredited, the document was only of interest to extremist groups and fantasists. No longer printed by reputable publishers, copies were circulated by the fascist Society of Britons or Lord Alfred Douglas's extreme right-wing journal, *Plain English*. An unexpected off-shoot was their role in invigorating the Illuminati myth which, in the aftermath of World War I, gained a whole new lease of life, and a whole new audience that persists to this day. Without this next phase in the development of the Illuminati myth, it is likely the trail would have run cold. With so many real threats facing the 20th-century world, why look to a – frankly ludicrous – theory about ancient secret societies? Amateur historian Nesta Webster believed she had the answer, and it was her work that was instrumental in reviving the story. In terms of her contribution to the Illuminati myth, she was the Abbé Barruel of her day, and she was to provide the link between 18th-century Illuminati beliefs and those of the present day.

Webster was from a well-to-do family. As a child, her life was one of comfort and privilege (the title of her autobiography, *Spacious Days*, attests to this feeling of ease and leisure) and was spent in a stately home populated by an extensive domestic staff. As a young woman she moved in quite exalted circles and dabbled in many of the fashionable "alternative" interests of the time – spiritualism, mysticism, telepathy. None other than Edward VII's own palmist had predicted Webster's marriage to Arthur Webster, a member of the Burmese police whom she met in India on one of her extensive and leisurely travels. She began her writing career on returning to England, beginning with romantic novels, among which was the *Chevalier des Boufflers*, subtitled "A Romance of the French Revolution". Perhaps it was the exposure to the faddish spiritualism of the day, perhaps evidence of the fecund imagination that would obliterate all semblance of reason in later works, but it was while researching this book that Webster began to feel an intense connection with the period she was writing about, becoming convinced that she had lived as an 18th-century French aristocrat, and had ended her life on the guillotine. During a trip to Paris she recalled an overwhelming sensation of fear, and of vivid images of the city streets running with blood. From here it was a short step to writing a revisionist history of the revolution – *The French Revolution: A Study in Democracy* – and there she found her niche, writing over the course of her 30-year career seven revisionist history titles and numerous articles for extreme right-wing journals of the inter-war period such as the *Morning Post* and the *Patriot*. For a time (1924–7) she was a member of the British Fascist party, and although her ideas certainly accorded with the prevailing mood of the party, she would chart her own eccentric course through the murky waters of conspiracy theory. While her compatriots were intent on sniffing out the Jewish conspiracy as revealed by the *Protocols*, she, and she alone, was convinced of the real perpetrators: the descendants of Adam Weishaupt.

French Revolution, published in 1919, established Webster's worldview. Her over-identification with 18th-century French aristocracy led her to see the revolution as the symbol of man's fall from grace; all that had gone wrong with the modern world could be traced back to the execution of Louis XVI. From her vantage point, the demise of the traditional social order (that is, the decline of the upper classes at the end of World War I) was simply a continuation of the chain of events that had been set in motion in 1789. Referring to the works of Barruel and Robison, seen through the mist of her own occult interests and anti-Semitism, she would go on to concoct a rich stew of a conspiracy theory, incorporating ancient and modern secret societies, magic and mass-hypnotism. But as Webster describes in *French Revolution*, the catalyst to this intrigue was obvious, and for the first time in nearly a century, the name of the Illuminati was back in print:

The lodges of the German Freemasons and Illuminati were thus the source whence emanated all those anarchic schemes which culminated in the Terror, and it was at a great meeting of the Freemasons in Frankfurt-am-Main, three years before the French Revolution began, that the deaths of Louis XVI and Gustavus III of Sweden were first planned.

(Webster, *French Revolution*, p21)

Some reviews of the day revealed Webster's unorthodox research methods in *French Revolution*. The *Spectator* in 1921 wrote "...whenever she was making a point of importance she quoted the actual words of the actors in the drama" – that is to say, she made them up. Nonetheless, she did have her contemporary champions: Lord Kitchener described her as "the country's fore-most opponent of subversion". Her next books were devoted to expanding her theories at great length, with little regard for his-torical fact, and included *World Revolution: The Plot Against Civilisation* (1921), *Secret Societies and Subversive Movements* (1924) and *The Socialist Network* (1926).

All these titles travel the same road, tracing an uninterrupted line through every major world event and upheaval back to the legacy of the Illuminati. The first editions of *The Socialist Network* and *World Revolution* even provide separate charts tucked inside the back covers, which trace the genealogy of every left-wing group in Europe back to Adam Weishaupt, like a handy cut-out-and-keep guide to anarcho-socialism. *World Revolution* tracks the Illuminati's progress from 1789 to the rise of Bolshevism, taking in along the way the United Irishmen, the Revolution of 1848 and the Franco-Prussian war. Bringing her readers up to the present day, she asks: "But now we come to the further question – who are the modern Illluminati, the authors of the plot?" (*World Revolution*, p293.) And here she turns to the *Protocols* for answers.

Webster has little doubt about the authenticity of the *Protocols*, but only in so far as the text illustrates the extent of the Illuminati's master plan:

Now to any one familiar with the language of Secret Societies the ideas set forth in the *Protocols* are not new; on the con-trary many pages have a strange ring of familiarity. To the present writer the thought that occurred on every page was: "Where have I read that before?" And by degrees the conviction grew: "But this is simply Illuminism!" So striking, indeed, are certain analogies not only between the code of Weishaupt and the *Protocols*, but between the *Protocols* and later Secret Societies, continuations of the Illuminati, that a continuity of ideas throughout the movement becomes apparent.

(*World Revolution*, p296)

When referring to John Robison and the Abbé Barruel for the source of Adam Weishaupt's writings, Webster highlights the similarities between the *Protocols* and the aims of the Illuminati. Weishaupt's "end justifies the means" philosophy reappears in the *Protocols* ("In making our plans we must pay attention not so much to what is good and moral, as to what is necessary and profitable"), as does the necessity for spying on members, and for infiltrating universities and Masonic lodges. The ideas in the *Protocols* tick the conspiracists' checklist point for point – to a suspicious degree. At one stage Webster comes close to admitting the truth of the *Protocols*; that the reason they so closely conform to the notion of a secret world conspiracy is because they were forged by someone who wanted them to appear that way:

One possibility immediately suggests itself. Might they [ie, the *Protocols*] not be a forgery compounded by someone versed in the lore of Secret Societies? Supposing Nilus to have been a student of the subject and also, as he was known to be, a pronounced anti-Semite, it would not have been difficult for him to reconstruct the programme of World Revolution from earlier models.

(*World Revolution*, p305)

No sooner is this idea suggested than she swerves away from it, claiming that when she argued the idea in a newspaper article it only met "with resentment" and that the "advocates of

Jewry" merely "fell back on absurd explanations that the *Protocols* were an invention of the Russian secret police". Then, with the looking glass logic that comes so naturally to the revisionist, she concluded: "The truth is, then, that the *Protocols* have never been refuted, and the futility of the so-called refutations ... have done more to convince the public of their authenticity than all the anti-Semite writings put together" (*World Revolution*, p305). This topsy-turvy logic is a favourite ruse. Webster is not the first to use the argument that the very fact of lack of evidence about the Illuminati is proof of their existence (Barruel used a similar tactic): "The great care of the Illuminati after the publication of their secret writings was to persuade the whole of Germany that their Order no longer existed" (*World Revolution*, p79). In this world, the Illuminati take their cue from the devil himself, who they say played his greatest trick by convincing the world he didn't exist.

Despite writing at a time when fascism was on the rise in the UK, Webster's work was not wildly influential in the mainstream. The foreword to *World Revolution* attests, with a note of puzzlement, to the fact that *French Revolution's* impact was not that great: "The Socialist press was completely silent, whilst hostile reviews in the general press contented themselves with saying the work was 'biased'." The Illuminati/secret society interpretation of world history was clearly a step too far, even at such a time of uncertainty as when Webster was writing. But Webster was not entirely alone in her theories: she had – and alarmingly, continues to have – enough of a readership to require several editions. *Secret Societies and Subversive Movements* was reprinted eight times, with the most recent in 1964. And although her eccentric course separated her from the common or garden fascists in the British Fascist party, she was not unique, but seems to have been one of a breed of upper-middle-class, lady-like loose cannons. Although she did not acknowledge it, she had a precedent in Una Pope-Hennessy, who, nearly a decade before publication of Webster's *French Revolution* wrote *Secret Societies and the French Revolution*, which revives the Templar-Masonic-Illuminati plot myth. Contemporaneous with Webster was Edith Starr Miller, known as Lady Queenborough. Her *Occult Theocracy* (self-published in the early 1930s) covers by now familiar ground, and reaches the same conclusions as Webster's *Secret Societies* – that the world is threatened by a Jewish-Masonic-Illuminati-satanic (add your bogeyman here) plot to destroy the status quo by overthrowing Christianity. But whereas Edith Starr Miller was clear that the Illuminati were but a branch of the Jewish world conspiracy, stating "Illuminism represented the efforts of the heads of the powerful Jewish Kahal [sic] which has ever striven for the attainment of political, financial, economic and moral world domination" (qtd Barkun, *A Culture of Conspiracy*, p49), Webster is not always sure who is leading whom, and throws all possibilities into the mix, putting forward the curious theory of a German-Jewish alliance:

If, then, one inner circle exists, composed of Illuminati animated by a purely destructive purpose it is conceivable that they might find support in those Germans who desire to disintegrate the countries of the Allies with a view to future conquests, and in those Jews who hope to establish their empire on the ruins of Christian civilization – hence the superb organization and the immense financial resources at the disposal of the world's revolutionaries.

On the other hand, it may be that the hidden centre of direction consists in a circle of Jews located in the background of the Grand Orient [ie, continental Freemasonry], or perhaps, like the early nineteenth-century Illuminati, located nowhere but working in accord and using both Pan-Germans and

Gentile Illuminati as their tools.
    (qtd Barkun, p49)

Little is known about Edith Miller Starr; her book was only ever published privately and would have had a limited readership during her lifetime. But along with Webster, she is one of the most often-quoted "authorities" on the Illuminati conspiracy today. In this parallel world of pseudo-scholarship, writers such as Webster and Starr, drawing on the likes of Barruel and Robison, use the familiar conspiracists' trick of repeating – continually – allegation as fact, myth and fabrication as history. In this world Robison and Barruel were "learned men, candid men ... who had a reverence for truth and religion" (*Secret Societies and Subversive Movements*, viii). Today, a recently published book by a respectable mainstream publisher quotes liberally from Webster as an authoritative reference, citing her "impressive number of contemporary sources" (Marrs, *Rule by Secrecy*, p222). And it is from a similar strain of lunatic logic that a piece of propaganda such as the *Protocols* can be born from Goedsche's pulp fiction and Joly's liberal tract. Once enough sources have made reference to one another, they collude in creating an entirely erroneous impression of fact. In the 1920s *The Times* may have realized its error about the *Protocols*, but on the other side of the Atlantic their influence was only just beginning. And they had as their advocate one of the world's most powerful men.

A 1922 edition of the *Protocols* includes a new introduction with the following endorsement: "The only statement I care to make about the *Protocols* is that they fit in with what is going on now. They are sixteen years old, and they have fitted the current situation up to this time." Then, in case the reader missed the point, the introduction concludes: "THEY FIT IT NOW." And who was the emphatic author of such a claim? Automobile magnate Henry Ford.

Along with the affordable automobile, Ford was instrumental in introducing the *Protocols* to the US. Ford's anti-Semitism is perhaps now less well-known than his industrial successes, but during the period immediately following World War I he used his considerable influence to publish a series of anti-Semitic diatribes in his weekly journal, the *Dearborn Independent*. Despite (or because of) his extraordinary success in industry, Ford liked to present himself as a plain-speaking man of the people. His widely quoted maxim, "All the world needs for the guidance of its life could be written on two pages of a child's copy book", first printed in the journal, struck a chord with his public, and this wilful ignorance earned his paper a circulation upwards of 500,000. When the *Protocols* first came to Ford's attention in 1919, they accorded so completely with his worldview that he used them as the basis for article after article, revealing the extent of the Jewish influence on US life. Titles such as "How the Jews in the US Conceal their Strength" or "The Scope of Jewish Dictatorship in the US" left the reader in no doubt of the extent of the menace as perceived by Ford: the by-now common allegations of Jewish control of the world's financial institutions was joined by convoluted arguments proving Jewish involvement in the labour unions, the media, Hollywood and even baseball ("Jewish Gamblers Corrupt American Baseball"). The mainstays of the roaring twenties – alcohol and jazz – were, according to Ford, nothing but a Jewish plot to undermine the American way of life: "Jewish Jazz Becomes our National Music". These articles, 91 in all, and running to nearly 1,000 pages of vindictive hate, were published by Ford as *The International Jew: The World's Foremost Problem*. Shortly after publication nearly half a million copies were in circulation in the US, and the book was subsequently translated into 16 languages. In Germany, it was received with great fanfare, and Ford became something of a hero, with his biography a best seller and his life-size portrait in pride of place next to Hitler's desk.

Ford's vile theories did not exist in a vacuum; the extent of his readership attests to this. They fed into and were influenced by several waves of paranoia emanating across the country in the 1920s – fears of foreigners, foreign ideologies, foreign religions – which, in some quarters, manifested themselves as fears of secret societies, and of the Illuminati in particular. In common with Nesta Webster was a feeling that the Jews were the dupes of the Illuminati (who were spreading anti-Semitic propaganda to divert attention from their real activities) or that the Illuminati were a cover for the Jewish cabal. William Guy Carr, who spent his life writing books on the Illuminati conspiracy, with titles such as *Pawns in the Game* and *Red Fog Over America*, believed that the conspiracy was so old, and such a threat to Christianity that even Christ was aware of it: "The same conspiracy Christ exposed and condemned is going on today." Henry Ford restricted himself to the history of the US and was of the opinion that the secret societies were a diversionary tactic on the part of the Jews, not vice versa:

> Twice in the history of the United States people have been aroused by a sense of strange influences operating in their affairs [in the late 1790s and during the Anti-Masonic Party in the 1820s and 1830s] and each time the real power behind these influences was able to divert suspicion to the Freemasons... Books were written, sermons preached, newspapers took up the search, but none of the observers saw the Jewish influence there.

Although he does not name them outright, Ford's description of French 'pseudo-Masonry' is a clear reference to the Illuminati:

A pseudo-Masonry, of French origin, given to atheistic and revolutionary purposes, strongly patronized by Jews, was the disturbing element, but all that the public was able to see was the Masonic similitude and not the Jewish hand.

(Henry Ford, *The International Jew*, vol II pp 186–7)

Ford would later publish a retraction of his views in every major US newspaper, claiming he was unaware of the contents of his own journal. But his protestations rang hollow: evidence suggested he continued his anti-Semitic propaganda through his factories, employing his foremen to distribute leaflets and to perpetuate the idea of a Jewish-communist plot in order to damage the power of the unions.

Running parallel to Ford's allegations were those of Gerald B Winrod, a Kansas evangelist who, in the 1930s, would become infamous for his support of fascism (to the extent that when he ran as State Senator for Kansas, protestors campaigned to "Keep Nazism out of Kansas"). In the 1920s, however, he formed a fundamentalist organization, Defenders of the Christian Faith, whose credo was "Back to the Bible" and whose aim was to combat liberals – whether theological or political. His journal, the *Defender* was established soon after, and allowed Winrod to sound off at his chosen targets; in the 1930s this would include President Roosevelt, whom he considered a patsy of the twin scourges of communism and Judaism. Winrod's fundamentalism extended, post-Scopes trial, to seeking to drive Darwinism from the schools; his slogan "monkey men means monkey morals" (Ribuffo, *The Old Christian Right*, p90) is characteristic of his methods, that is approaching political issues from a moral standpoint. Much of the *Defender* is written at a fever pitch of moral outrage: with repeated references to "contamination", "vice", "filth" and "poison". His aim was to combat what he described as the encroaching "moral sag" of the US, and the

Protocols were a convenient weapon in this battle.

Although there is some suggestion that Winrod did not believe in the authenticity of the *Protocols*, he was happy to exploit them as a confirmation of his worldview, and in so doing resurrected the spectre of the Illuminati, but with new permutations in the story. Using the *Protocols* as supposed "proof", Winrod traced a link from the Illuminati to the Jesuits, and the Jesuits to the Jews, in one seething morass of paranoia. If proof were needed that the Illuminati myth is endlessly accommodating and flexible enough to incorporate the latest crackpot theory, Winrod's interpretation could be held up as evidence. According to Winrod, Jesuit founder Ignatius Loyola was a Jew, Weishaupt was an active Jesuit (although historically he was known to be anything but), and they were all in cahoots to destroy Protestantism.

The idea of a conspiracy by the Illuminati was particularly useful in Winrod's campaign against the decline in American morality: in Adam Weishaupt Winrod had found the embodiment of "moral sag". Weishaupt's revolutionary credo even included the threat to the sanctity of marriage – a notion that Winrod upheld as the saving grace of the American way of life. His unambiguously titled pamphlet, *Adam Weishaupt, a Human Devil*, is unequivocal in its mission, and traces the modern world's ills back to the ideas of the Bavarian professor. Here the Illuminati story takes off in yet another direction, particularly in the US, as Winrod introduces the idea of the Illuminati as the link between communism and Judaism. In *Adam Weishaupt* he proclaims "A study of the Illuminati will show where all the modern ideas of Bolshevism originated"; for example, Marx "edited his teachings" from Weishaupt before coming to the resounding conclusion that "*Modern Communism and old Jewish Illuminism* are one and the same thing".

Unfortunately, Winrod was not a solitary lunatic whose

alarms fell on deaf ears: in the early 1930s the *Defender* sold in the region of 20,000 copies; from the mid-1930s to the outbreak of World War II it reached 100,000. His readership was greatest among, if not exclusively restricted to, the rural poor in America's Bible Belt – Protestant fundamentalists in the south and midwest who had probably never met a Jewish person, but who associated Judaism with the threat of immigration, with dangerous urban influences and with left-wing politics. This last element would play an increasingly important role in the next stage of the Illuminati myth, when the US experienced its 'red scares' after each of the two world wars, and the Cold War era brought the fear of communism to the forefront of US politics.

Chapter Five: Reds under the Bed (with the Illuminati)

But the Communist movement is only a tool of the total conspiracy. As secret as the Communist activities and organizations generally appear, they are part of an open book compared to the secrecy enveloping some higher degree of this diabolic force. The extrinsic evidence is strong and convincing that by the beginning of the Twentieth Century there had evolved an inner core of conspiratorial power, able to direct and control subversive activities which were worldwide in their reach, incredibly cunning and ruthless in their nature, and brilliantly farsighted and patient in their strategy.

(Robert Welch, "The Truth in Time")

On December 9th, 1958, businessman Robert Welch invited 11 contemporaries, those he considered "public spirited and patriotic men", to attend a two-day seminar in America's heartland – Indianapolis, Indiana – during which he described his fears for the future of the US. Welch essentially lectured for two days straight. By no means a charismatic speaker, he delivered his dire warning in an adenoidal monotone, rarely looking up from his seemingly endless reams of notes except to adjust his glasses or necktie. He frequently gasped, gulped for air, or noisily cleared his throat, but did not waver from his central remit: that the US was in immediate danger of a communist takeover. His guests had been invited to join him in what was nothing less than a crusade against communism. In an era defined by its anti-communist hysteria, Welch was not a lone voice in sounding an alarm. But over time his contribution would distinguish itself by its unique take on the nature of the threat: for as Welch's theories developed, he would come to identify the Illuminati at the heart of the plot. In doing so, he revived a myth that, by the end of World War II, had largely been forgotten. By the mid-1960s he had extended the Illuminati story, bringing it into the Cold War era and, eventually, incorporating it into fears about the New World Order.

Robert Welch had been born on a cotton farm in North Carolina, a descendant of farmers and Baptist preachers. But he was no ignorant farm boy. His college-educated parents – his mother, especially – had tutored Welch and his five siblings at home, due to the lack of good schools in their rural community. Welch clearly thrived in this environment; by the age of 12 he was attending the University of North Carolina and by 17 had earned his BA, prompting the local papers to describe him as "the boy wonder". Leaving his home state, he briefly attended the US Naval Academy in Maryland before heading further north to Harvard to study law. Law School was not a success; why is open to conjecture, but Welch himself claimed he left due to the liberalism of his professors. Nonetheless, it is hard not to suppose a causal connection between these circumstances and his later conspiracy theories concerning the power of the "Eastern elite", and their relationship with the shadowy group he would identify as the "Insiders".

After a number of false starts in different business ventures, Welch made a success in his brother's confectionery firm, rising to the position of vice-president. During this time he travelled extensively across the country, and sat on several boards, including a local bank, the Harvard Brewing Company in

Massachusetts and the conservative National Association of Manufacturers. His business ventures brought him extensive contacts throughout the country: like-minded, right-leaning entrepreneurs and owners of small businesses who were wary of the merest whiff of socialism. Welch's interest in politics grew. Twice he travelled to the UK to experience first-hand the workings of a socialist government. He became increasingly active in Republican circles in Massachusetts, an enterprise doomed to failure in that most Democratic of states. By 1958 he had become disillusioned with conventional politics and was straying toward the murkier waters of extremism, siding with the red-baiting Senator Joseph McCarthy and twice addressing public gatherings of the Friends of Joseph McCarthy. His fellow Republicans, he was beginning to feel, were ignoring the bigger picture; if they accepted the idea of a red conspiracy in the US, it was only as a tactical means to defeat their Democratic rivals. Welch, on the other hand, was beginning to believe the rot went beyond that, and even began to suspect an infiltration of communists in his own party. He began to branch out on his own.

Even for an era that came to be defined by its paranoia, Welch stood head and shoulders above the rest, which was saying something, to put it mildly. The early years of the Cold War had seen America's anxieties about the threat of communism ratcheted up to an hysterical degree. The work of the House of Un-American Activities Committee and Senator Joseph McCarthey were both the instrument and the symbol of these fears. The HUAC had been established in 1945, the progeny of the earlier House Special Committee to Investigate Un-American Activities; a temporary committee was established in 1938 to investigate "the extent, character, and objects of un-American propaganda activities in the United States". Whereas the earlier committee had been formed to investigate the activities of pro-Nazi groups, by 1940 it began to focus on communist activities. With the end of the war, this focus became increasingly high profile, and in 1947 the HUAC was brought firmly centre stage with its infamous investigation into the alleged communist infiltration of Hollywood – long known as a centre of liberalism – in what became known as the Hollywood 10 case. The "Hollywood 10" comprised ten writers and directors, among them Ring Lardner, Lester Cole and Samuel Ornitz, who were questioned in court over their alleged involvement in subversive organizations. They refused to testify and all were sentenced to a year's imprisonment for contempt of Congress. Upon their release they were all blacklisted from working in the Hollywood film industry and sought careers further afield – in New York, Mexico or Europe. By the early 1950s, the use of the blacklist as a threat or punishment was in full force. The HUAC returned to Hollywood to root out the merest whiff of subversion. Hundreds more were blacklisted, while others "named names" to keep their jobs. It was an environment of fear and suspicion that allowed Welch's agenda to flourish.

Always a prolific writer, since the early 1950s Welch had been elaborating his political views in several right-wing tracts, including a 1952 pamphlet entitled *May God Forgive Us*, in which he alleged that the current administration under Democrat Harry Truman (elected for his second term in 1949) was deliberately shaping government policy "to favor the Communist advance." As proof of this he referred to the Truman–MacArthur controversy during the Korean War in 1951, in which General MacArthur, commander of UN troops, publicly criticized the president's decision not to use nuclear weapons. Truman dismissed MacArthur for insubordination, a move that Welch interpreted as evidence of the president's communist sympathies. By 1956 Welch was writing and editing a small circulation right-wing journal, *One Man's Opinion*, which two years later was to be renamed *American Opinion*. His most controversial work at this stage, however, was a private document, which he described as a "letter", initially circulated only to friends and like-minded acquaintances. *The Politician* (also known as the notorious *Black Book*) was a 60,000 word no-holds-barred polemic on the extent of communist influence on US politics. And this influence went straight to the top: in the "Communist dominated" Truman administration, according to Welch, "Truman was passively *used* by the Communists, with his knowledge and acquiescence, as the price he consciously paid for their making him President." But about current, Republican, president Eisenhower (who was elected in 1953), Welch was more direct still: "My firm belief that Dwight Eisenhower is a dedicated, conscious agent of the Communist conspiracy is based on an accumulation of detailed evidence so extensive and so palpable that it seems to me to put this conviction beyond any reasonable doubt. There is only one word to describe his purposes and actions. That word is 'treason'." This criticism of irreproachable and beloved World War II hero Ike, former Supreme-Commander of the Allied Forces, was beyond the pale. When the book was later published in 1963, after Eisenhower had been replaced by Kennedy as President in 1961, this was amended to say that Eisenhower had been "consciously serving the Communist conspiracy, for all his adult life" (qtd Lipset and Raab, *The Politics of Unreason*, p25).

In order to alert his fellow Americans to this insidious danger, in 1958 Welch formed what was to become known as the John Birch Society. His invitation to the 11 "public spirited and patriotic men" to attend his seminar was just the beginning. Over the course of the two days, he outlined the extent of the communist infiltration of the US, and the means to combat it. The transcript of that seminar became known as the *Blue Book*, and members would read the words of their society's founder with the avidity of the Bible. Welch also employed the rhetoric of the evangelist, describing the ideological conflict between the

US and communism as "a *worldwide* battle, the first in history, between light and darkness, between freedom and slavery; between the spirit of Christianity and the spirit of the anti-Christ for the souls and the bodies of men" (*Blue Book*, pp10–11).

Welch began his seminar, and thus the *Blue Book*, by exhorting its readers to "Look at the Score". (Keeping score became a regular event with the JBS, with Welch publishing annual "score cards" analysing the levels of communist presence in different countries around the world. At the height of the Vietnam War, Welch placed communist infiltration in the US at about 60 to 80 percent, believing the war was an intentional ruse by the US government to perpetuate communism.) The *Blue Book*'s "score" tallied current levels of communism against Lenin's plan for a world takeover, and "quotes" Lenin as describing the future scenario as follows: "First we will take Eastern Europe. Next, the mass of Asia. Then we shall circle the last bastion of capitalism, the United States of America. We shall not have to attack; it will fall like overripe fruit into our hands" (*Blue Book*, p2). The ease with which the world will fall to communism is a constant refrain: elsewhere, Welch warns that "...the Communists will be able to take Western Europe by telephone within the next two or more years if they consider it strategically wise to do so" (*Blue Book*, p10). The danger lay in the cunning and secrecy of communist tactics: "One of the hardest things for the ordinary decent American to realize is that a Communist looks and acts just like anybody else, only more so; or that anybody he, the ordinary decent American, happens to know personally, could possibly be a Communist" (*Blue Book*, p92). Welch's strategy was to "organize fronts – little fronts, big fronts, permanent fronts, all kinds of fronts" to educate the American people in rooting out communism.

To establish his society, Welch had chosen his initial recruits with care; his work with the National Association of

Manufacturers and the Republican party had enabled him to make extensive contacts across the US in the fields of business, commerce and politics. His guests were far from being incredulous or unworldly – on the contrary, many were ideally placed to question the veracity of Welch's claims. Among the assembled successful businessmen was also a law professor from the University of Illinois, a former personal aide of General MacArthur, and President Eisenhower's first commissioner of internal revenue.

Although Welch's guests were sympathetic to his anti-communist ideology, they were surprised by the global reach of the threat. Welch left them in no doubt that this was the case, describing a slow takeover of Europe, an insidious creep, as country by country, the communist scourge threatened to take over the world: "Unless we can reverse forces which now seem inexorable in their movement, you have only a few more years before the country in which you live will become four separate provinces in a worldwide Communist dominion ruled by police-state methods from the Kremlin. The map for their division and administration is already drawn" (*Blue Book*, p9).

Welch hit a collective nerve, and continued to worry away at it, successfully spreading his doctrine across the US. He followed up this initial seminar with another 28 in various parts of the country. In just two years, by 1960, the John Birch Society had 18,000 members, and chapters in 34 states. By 1965 the society had reached its peak, with an estimated 80,000 to 100,000 members. Its philosophy of right-wing self-determination – "our short-range purpose, our long-range purpose, and our lasting purpose, is to promote less government, more responsibility, and a better world" (*Blue Book*, p139) – clearly struck a chord with many conservative Americans.

But who was John Birch? Four years before the foundation of the society, Welch had written a biography of a Baptist missionary, one John Birch, who would become for Welch a symbol of the US government's role in the Cold War. The son of Georgia farmers, Birch had travelled to China in 1940 to work as a missionary. When war broke out between the US and Japan in 1941, Birch became a captain in the army. In circumstances that are still unclear, 10 days after the end of the war Birch was killed by the communist Chinese; he was awarded a posthumous medal for bravery. Welch became convinced that Birch had been deliberately murdered by the Chinese, with the collusion of the US government, who had kept the truth from Birch's family. For Welch, Birch represented the ideal American: a committed Christian of good, honest country folk, who died in the service of his country. Welch claimed to see "in the story of one American boy, the ordeal of his age" (qtd Broyles, *The John Birch Society*, p16). It is too late to ask whether or not John Birch would have liked to be forever more associated with an extreme right-wing group; along with Welch's *Blue Book*, members of the JBS were encouraged to read Birch's biography to refamiliarize themselves with the values he represented. But the real personality behind the society was not John Birch. As all its members knew, it was Robert Welch. And he was in many ways just another manifestation of personality-led red scares in the US.

Welch was tapping into a long tradition of populist American fears of communism. Twentieth-century America had already experienced several "red scares" by the time Robert Welch arrived on the scene. One followed the end of World War I, from 1919–21, when fears that the Bolshevik revolution might be the start of a worldwide upheaval that would spread to the US and, more recently, between 1947 and 1955 when the activities of Senator McCarthy were so all-consuming that his name came to define the era. But the personal crusade of McCarthy had been preceded by the activities of an earlier individual: in the 1930s, another wave of popular anti-communism had been drummed up by a radio broadcaster from Michigan, who at the height of his popularity is believed to have had more than 30 million listeners worldwide. He was a Catholic priest, Father Charles Coughlin, and he made it his personal mission to rid the US of communist influence in whatever guise.

In 1926, Coughlin was appointed to a diocese in a working-class suburb of Detroit. It was an underprivileged area, with little to distinguish it apart from a thriving chapter of the violently racist and anti-Semitic Ku Klux Klan. The few Catholic families living there were very much outnumbered, and often found themselves the target of intimidating Klan activities. To counteract this, Coughlin began broadcasting his sermons on a weekly radio programme, called *The Golden Hour of the Little Flower* after his church, the Shrine of the Little Flower. Radio was a new medium in 1926 and Coughlin was a natural on the airwaves. Within a year his local programme was being broadcast coast to coast, and he was receiving mail in such numbers (around 4,000 letters a week) that he had to hire full-time secretarial support. One contemporary described him as "without doubt one of the greatest voices of the twentieth century" possessing a mesmerizing quality and "a voice made for promises" (Bennet, *The Party of Fear*, p254). Week after week listeners tuned in in droves and by 1929 his audience numbered millions. With the Wall Street Crash that year, Coughlin must have offered his listeners succour from the hardships of the reality around them. Perhaps that charismatic, mellifluous voice provided an hour's respite from the realities of devastating unemployment and crushing poverty of the Depression years. His themes spoke to the ordinary person, exploring, for example, the origins of anti-Catholic bigotry in the US and other social injustices. As the Depression took its toll on the country (from 1930 to 1933 unemployment tripled, until, at the height of the Depression, the US saw over a quarter of its workforce unemployed), his sermons became increasingly political, and his popularity reached new heights. When Coughlin disparaged President Herbert Hoover as "the Holy Ghost of the Rich, the Protective Angel of Wall Street" (qtd Bennet, p254), 80,000 listeners wrote in. By 1931, however, his broadcasts were becoming too controversial for the mainstream network and he was in danger of being dropped. When he referred to his constitutionally enshrined right to freedom of speech, the result was a torrent of written support from his listeners. Shying away from controversy, his broadcaster CBS dropped the programme, but by this time Coughlin was so successful, he simply set up his own network.

Coughlin's success was due to his apparent championing of the ordinary citizen against big business, the East Coast elite and Wall Street interests. His listeners were largely working-class Catholic Americans whose religion and ethnicity had marked them out as targets for persecution in the US. One aspect of Coughlin's success was that he gave his listeners their own targets for grievances, figures such as "the Wall Street attorney", "the erudition of Harvard and Yale" or "the bankers with their hunting estates in Scotland" (qtd Bennet, p259). Unfortunately, he was not content to limit his ire to the Eastern elite (who, quite frankly, were impervious to the criticism) but soon moved onto more ideologically suspect ground. Left-wing ideologies came increasingly under attack, as he became convinced of an international Jewish-communist conspiracy.

Coughlin's broadcasts in 1932 had been unreservedly pro-Franklin Delano Roosevelt, to the extent that the priest was convinced his radio programme was instrumental in Roosevelt's presidential win over Herbert Hoover in 1933. Coughlin's infatuation with Roosevelt continued into the early months of the presidency, and he wrote countless letters offering unsolicited advice, even dictating letters on air for his listeners to send. Coughlin's enthusiasm was unrequited and, when it became obvious Roosevelt had no intention of offering him a key role in his administration, nor of acknowledging his input in any way, Coughlin's broadcasts soured. His criticism was as unreserved as his praise had been, booming over the airwaves, "Today I humbly stand before the American public to admit I was in error. Despite all the promises…[t]he slogan 'Roosevelt or Ruin' must now be altered to 'Roosevelt and Ruin'" (qtd Bennet, p257).

By the mid-1930s, Coughlin's broadcasts were becoming increasingly vitriolic. He began to accuse the president ("Franklin Double-Crossing Roosevelt") of betraying the American people with his New Deal, which had done so much to relieve the worst of the Depression, but which Coughlin now claimed was nothing less than communism: "Well we all know who we're voting for if we vote for Mr Roosevelt…the Communists " (qtd Bennet, p262). When his campaign for his listeners to back him against the president failed, his position swung ever more to the extreme right. Whereas before he could be seen as the champion of the common man, his language was now openly fascist, hysterically anti-communist and vehemently anti-Semitic. *Social Justice*, the journal he had founded in the early 1930s, reprinted *The Protocols of the Elders of Zion* in 1938; when challenged Coughlin claimed that the document was an accurate reflection of world events.

Yet even before Coughlin's broadcasts had taken an overtly paranoid turn, there is evidence that he was beginning to formulate his conspiratorial worldview. Without engaging in full-blown Illuminati mythologies, he was nonetheless convinced that communism was the creation of Adam Weishaupt, whose anti-clericism was responsible for, among other things, communist godlessness. In 1931 he wrote:

What is this thing called Communism? According to its founder, Adam Weishaupt, from whom Karl Marx drew his

inspiration, Communism is necessarily identified with atheism... Following his master, Karl Marx emphasized the fact
that "religion is the opium of the people". This accounts for
the fact that every form of religion has been practically
banned in Russia.

(qtd Lipset, *By the Sweat of thy Brow*, 1931, p181)

Coughlin was, of course, not the first to have seen Adam
Weishaupt behind the spread of communism. Nesta Webster's
all-encompassing conspiratorial view placed the Illuminati as
the masterminds behind every significant world event, upheaval,
or ideology since the French Revolution, so it will come as no
surprise that she saw Weishaupt as the prime mover behind
communism:

... in the Communist Manifesto of Marx, we find again all the
points of Weishaupt – abolition of poverty, inheritance, marriage, and all morality, of patriotism and all religion. Is it not
obvious that the plan has been handed down to the succeeding groups of Socialists and Anarchists by the secret
societies which had carried on the traditions of the
Illuminati?

(Webster, *World Revolution*, p188)

Coughlin never went so far as to refer to the Illuminati conspiracy by name, but he was explicit in his belief in a Masonic
world plot, denouncing in a broadcast in 1936, "a plot which has
been slowly woven with the active support of international
Masonry" and describing the "enemies [of] Americans and
Catholics" as "Masonry, high finance and Communism". This triumvirate of suspects is a common thread running through
extreme right-wing 20th-century thought: whether or not the
Illuminati are explicitly referred to by name, the Illuminati myth

informs the nature of the plot belief. From Coughlin's references to Weishaupt and Freemasonry, through McCarthy's use of imagery of infiltration and contamination, culminating in Robert Welch's coining of the "Insiders" to represent the perpetrators of the master conspiracy, the Illuminati myth runs parallel to or is directly replicated in 20th-century conspiracy thinking.

Coughlin's increasingly extremist position horrified Church authorities, who tried to distance themselves from the renegade priest and emphasize the distinction between official Church doctrine and Coughlin's personal views. Although many of his original listeners had abandoned the priest by this time, the smaller numbers of committed xenophobes who remained were unaware that Coughlin's views were not endorsed by the Church. From the late 1930s Coughlin's archbishop had fought to silence the priest; he succeeded in 1940 when Coughlin's radio pro-gramme was taken off the air. Two years later, the extreme views published in his journal *Social Justice* were found to be in breach of the Espionage Act of 1942 and the paper folded. Coughlin, who had long campaigned against alleged anti-American activities found the tables turned when he was accused of the same. He retreated into retirement and obscurity, but the legacy of his campaigns remained. When Senator Joseph McCarthy ushered in the second red scare in the 1950s, he appealed to a similar demographic.

During World War II, the US's alliance with the Soviet Union against the Axis powers had done a great deal to reduce fears of communist subversion in the US, but with the new political landscape of the post-war world came a resurgence of the old suspicions. Winston Churchill's reference in 1946 to the "Iron Curtain" that had descended across Europe made explicit the ideological differences dividing the continent. By the late 1940s and early 1950s, the successful spread of communism across Eastern Europe had re-ignited old fears, and the language of subterfuge, infiltration and attack re-entered the political vocabulary. It was in such a climate that the Illuminati myth could so easily take hold and flourish. Once again, the country's central institutions – its churches, schools, and government – would be described as under attack from a faceless enemy, one that so closely resembled the average American (in many ways was the average American) that detection was almost impossible. "Fifth columnists," warned Texas Congressman Martin Dies, chair of the House Special Committee to Investigate Un-American Activities (later the HUAC) in 1938, "are not always garbed in the uniform of foreign troops, nor do they always speak with a foreign accent. They may be native-born American citizens. Such figurative parachutists have already landed in the federal government. They await the 'zero hour' when Stalin gives the command to attack" (qtd Goldberg, p25).

The idea that "figurative parachutists" had already taken up residence on native soil was a convenient one for the Republican party, which was eager to reclaim control from the Democrats. Picking up the conspiratorial thread, the Republicans accused the Democratic party of taking the country in the direction of communism, step by incremental step, using as evidence the social reforms brought in by the New Deal. During the 1946 House elections during President Truman's first term, the House Republican leader warned that the voters' choice was a stark one: "The people will vote tomorrow between chaos, confusion, bankruptcy, state socialism and Communism, and the preservation of American life" (qtd Goldberg, p27). Such scare tactics clearly had the desired effect: for the first time since 1928 the Republicans had a majority in the House and Senate (although this would swing back in the Democrat's favour in 1948, during Truman's re-election year).

Conspiracy as a political tactic was clearly successful, and the Republican party continued to emphasize a connection between Soviet communism and US liberalism. In 1947 alone, 22 investigations took place to discover the extent of communist infiltration of the US, from government institutions to the film industry. A small-time actor called Ronald Reagan referred to the "Communist plan to…take over the motion picture business". The language of fear, infiltration, secrecy and duplicity was everywhere in political discourse, with Republican vice-president nominee (later chief justice) Earl Warren warning in 1948 that: "While we spend billions to halt the Communist conspiracy abroad, we find this same conspiracy reaching its stealthy fingers to grab the framework of our own free institutions and tear them down" (qtd Goldberg, p28).

Accusations of conspiracy were now a convenient and commonplace political weapon and created an atmosphere of suspicion that only continued to breed mistrust. It was in such an environment that Wisconsin Senator Joseph McCarthy was able to make his political mark.

The dawning of the McCarthy era took place on February 9th, 1950, at a meeting of the Women's Republican Club in West Virginia. It was here that McCarthy made his infamous speech alerting the country to the widespread communist presence in the US government:

> While I cannot take the time to name all of the men in the State Department who have been named as members of the Communist party and members of a spy ring, I have here in my hand a list of 205 that were known to the Secretary of State as being members of the Communist party and who nevertheless are still working and shaping the policy of the State Department.

That "list of 205" would be evoked time and again by McCarthy, like a talisman. And in evoking an accusatory list, one can't help but hear the ghostly echo of Jedidiah Morse's list of Illuminati members reverberate down the centuries. Little did it matter that McCarthy had no such list; the senator had found his cause (in which he was aided by an enthusiastic Richard Nixon). From now on his aim was to sniff out and eradicate these covert communists in US government positions. He was no rhetorician, no master of the finely tuned argument; crude and pugnacious in style, he was prepared to grab his single policy by the scruff of the neck and shake it until its teeth rattled, as in this speech to the Senate, made in 1951:

> How can we account for our present situation unless we believe that men high in this government are concerting to deliver us to disaster?... This must be the product of a great conspiracy, a conspiracy on a scale so immense as to dwarf any previous such venture in the history of man. A conspiracy so black that, when it is fully exposed, its principals shall be forever deserving of the maledictions of all honest men.

Like all conspiracy theorists, McCarthy was able to distil a complex situation into a single argument, evoking with a few broad brush strokes the tense world of plots and subversion that threatened the US, and providing a solution in equally simplistic terms. He gave good newspaper copy, speaking in slogans that translated easily to the front page. Up until now, his political career had been distinguished only by an ability to alienate himself from his colleagues in the Senate. Now he had the ear of the Senate, the press and the president. A Senate committee was convened to investigate the allegations. And although McCarthy's crusade to identify actual communists within the US government was spectacularly unsuccessful (he didn't identify a single one), his vehement accusations, untroubled by supporting evidence, ruined many careers. As his crusade gathered momentum, his opponents were browbeaten into submission, fearing that their dissent would be taken as a sign of disloyalty; those who disagreed, if not openly accused of communist sympathies were at the very least "dupes of the Kremlin" (qtd Goldberg, p31).

Over the next four years McCarthy took centre stage in the US political arena. His strategic manoeuvring to become chairman of the Permanent Subcommitee on Investigations gave him the authority to investigate all levels of government, leading to further accusations of communist activity at even higher ranks of government and the military. Among the accused were Assistant Secretary of State, William Benton, in 1951, and, later in 1953, Secretary of the Army, Robert Stevens. Much of the information that formed the basis of McCarthy's campaign came from the Federal Bureau of Investigation, whose head, J. Edgar Hoover, was convinced of the extent of the rot that had taken hold of the US. In his words: "Something utterly new has taken root in America during the last generation, a Communist mentality representing a systematic, purposive and conscious attempt to destroy Western civilization and roll history back to the ages of barbaric cruelty and despotism" (ibid). And the American people agreed: in the early 1950s surveys revealed that 70 percent of Americans believed the aim of the Soviet Union was to rule the world.

McCarthy was both a Catholic and Midwesterner and could represent the common American in much the same way as Father Coughlin had. Like Coughlin, he too emphasized the gulf between the moral values of the American heartland and the Eastern elite. When he described US communist sympathizers as "born high with silver spoons in their mouths" the implicit connection with the East Coast elite was instantly clear, and set the liberal East in ever greater contrast to the conservative Midwest. When Hollywood got in on the act with its spate of anti-communist films in the 1950s, such as *Big Jim McLain*, star-ring none other than John Wayne, this idea of a collusion between the Eastern elite and Soviet communism continued, with red-blooded American values on one side and the com-munist subversives with their effete "country club ways" on the other. Suspicions of the East Coast, with its Ivy League intellec-tuals, centres of finance and big business, and general air of privilege would become inextricably entwined with the con-spiracy-laden atmosphere of the post-war era and would feed directly into Robert Welch's theory about the identity and *modus operandi* of the Insiders.

By 1954, however, McCarthy's credibility had been destroyed and the red scare was on the wane. His spectacular fall from grace took place during what became known as the Army-McCarthy hearings, in which one of his aides was accused of threatening the US Army with communist investigations if the aide did not get preferential treatment for a colleague. McCarthy's performance during the hearings was broadcast nationwide, and allowed the American public to see his hyster-ical, accusatory style for what it was worth. By the end of the year McCarthy had been officially censured by the Senate, and although he remained in the Senate until his death in 1948, his political significance was negligible. At the same time, World War II hero Dwight Eisenhower, elected president in 1952 and committed anti-communist, introduced measures which reas-sured the public that, even if the US were under threat from communism, its agents would not be found in the government. By the end of 1954 only 4 percent of Americans believed that the greatest threat facing the country was the infiltration of gov-ernment by communists.

McCarthy's influence would endure, however, in the attitude toward political opposition. Communism was no longer simply a different ideology, it was the polar opposite of American freedoms, establishing a worldview composed of black and white extremes: US democracy vs Soviet totalitarianism, Christianity vs atheism, and openness vs secrecy, all of which could ultimately be distilled down to good vs evil. This worldview would inform Robert Welch's and contributed to the foundation of the John Birch Society. The difference was that Robert Welch made it his own by introducing the Illuminati into the mix.

If the McCarthy era of witch hunts and denunciations was effectively over by 1958, anti-communist feelings in the US still ran high. The events of the next few years – 1961 saw the construction of the Berlin Wall, the successful launch of the Soviet Sputnik satellite and the failed Bay of Pigs invasion, followed by the Cuban Missile crisis the following year – gave added urgency to the society's message, and Robert Welch's proposals for defeating communism spread across the country. His anti-communist campaign was mainly one of education. Members were assigned reading lists, comprising 100 titles (known as "One Hundred Steps to the Truth"), and were expected to keep up with the monthly bulletins and weekly newsletters. They were also exhorted to campaign by writing to congressmen and other officials, to open bookshops and to attend anti-communist lectures.

Like Joseph McCarthy and Father Coughlin before him, Robert Welch appealed to the church-going, patriotic small businessman, whose life was far from the world of the elite players on the East Coast. This is not to say they were ignorant; many JBS members were extremely well off and well educated, and although many did not accept Welch's theory of Eisenhower as a communist agent, Welch's premise clearly struck a chord.

Welch's equating of communism with elitism provided his members with a visible foe: they might not have met any communists personally, but the liberal East Coast, with its air of privilege, centres of academic excellence, financial and business institutions and general aura of entitlement, was plain for all to see. As Welch described in *The New Americanism* (qtd Lipset and Raab, p257), the idea that communism was an ideology for and of the people was a smoke-screen and a sham:

> From the beginning Communism has been presented as a movement of the proletariat, as a rising of the supposedly shackled and downtrodden poor against the powerful, who were exploiting them. And this itself is one of the biggest lies in all history. For Communism has always been imposed from the top down by the very rich, the highly educated, and the politically powerful on the suffering masses.

And Welch is very clear where these rich, educated and politically powerful figures are to be found:

> When you look at the Communist strength in America today, you don't find it in the poor struggling beatniks who by and large comprise the small and insignificant officially presented Communist party. That Communist party exists primarily for propaganda needs in this very pretence. But the strength of the Communist conspiracy lies in the very top social, economic, educational, and political circles in our country... I can find you a lot more Harvard accents in Communist circles in America today than you can find me in overalls.

And this wasn't all: in opposing the elite powers, Welch calls upon his members to stand vigilant against a too-powerful government. From the very first meeting of the John Birch Society, Welch was clear on this: "The greatest enemy of man is, and always has been, government; and the larger, the more extensive that government, the greater the enemy" (*Blue Book*, p108). Later he stated: "For all governments, with very rare exceptions indeed, are thoroughly dishonest." Among the many dangers of "big government" for the Birchers, was the fact it was likely to be trading with anti-capitalist countries – and as capitalism was the very foundation of US democracy this essentially threatened the US people. A 1966 Bircher document emphasized the importance of self-reliance and local self-government: "The history of liberty is very much the history of local self-government; despotism can come only when local self-government is destroyed."

Robert Welch was not alone among right-wing groups in suspecting the motives of "big government" but he was among the first to draw attention to what he felt were patterns in history, coming to the conclusion that world events did not arise out of a complex series of circumstances, but were carefully orchestrated. As his overarching conspiracy theory developed, it became increasingly clear to him that there was nothing "natural" about the spread of communism: from the very first rumblings of the Bolshevik revolution, the spread of a communist ideology, in Welch's view, had been planned step by incremental step, and was inching its way ever nearer to the heart of US government.

Eisenhower was clearly a dupe of the communists who had "destroyed" Senator McCarthy. "[T]he Communists just had to get rid of McCarthy and went to such extreme lengths to do so" because he had tried to expose the truth. If further evidence of foul play were needed, a JBS bulletin of 1959 pointed to McCarthy's death at the age of 48, claiming: "We... know there will be no proper investigation [of McCarthy's death] under the present [Eisenhower] Communist-infested administration."

By the early 1960s Welch's theories expanded to incorporate the Council on Foreign Relations (CFR) as further evidence of the power of "big government". The CFR had been founded at the end of World War I to study foreign policy with the aim of preventing another "war to end all wars". Supporters of the CFR saw in the organization's internationalism a move toward global peace, while its critics, of which the JBS became an increasingly vocal one, saw the organization's aims as nothing less than creating a one-world government. Where it did confirm Welch's suspicions is in its elite make up: members were and are quite spectacularly well placed in government and the worlds of finance, law and the media. All presidents since 1945 have been members, and several, including Nixon and Carter, went on to appoint many CFR colleagues to their administrations. In the same vein, the United Nations (UN), founded in 1945 to promote international peace and security, too, fell under suspicion, and its agenda for peace masked a more sinister motive, as Welch explained in "Truth in Time":

> Another manifestation of the same principle at work was the establishment of the United Nations. This organization was conceived by Communists, founded by Communists, has always been controlled by Communists, and has been used increasingly – and ever more brazenly – to carry out Communist purposes. But it was sold by propaganda and pretence to the American people, and to most of the rest of the world, as a means of maintaining peace and preventing Communist aggression.

By the mid-1960s Welch's conspiracy theory had become so large and all encompassing it was in danger of getting out of control: big business and government officials, intellectuals and East Coast liberals, and all major leaders of both the Republican and Democratic parties were implicated. Welch needed a unifying thread to tie the whole theory together before it became too large to be creditable. And it was around 1964 (one year after the assassination of President John F. Kennedy) that the works of Barruel and John Robison, particularly, re-enter the scene. For

Welch, Robison's theories about the causes of the French Revolution made perfect sense; he added to this the theories of Nesta Webster and felt, clearly, that communism was but one aspect of a much larger plot – and that plot was the work of the Illuminati.

At this time the JBS had been at its most influential in US politics, when it had backed Republican candidate Barry Goldwater as presidential candidate against Lyndon B. Johnson in 1964. The campaign suffered a catastrophic defeat, and it was following this bitter disappointment that Welch's theories were ratcheted up another notch, as if, now that the JBS was confined irrevocably to the political wilderness, Welch decided to hit back at his enemies with ultra-conservative vengeance. Simple communism could no longer carry the weight of his suspicions; it had to be just one element in a much more extensive web. (When the nucleus of the remaining Goldwater supporters formed the basis of what was to become known as the New Right – the ultra-conservative face of Republicanism – Welch's conspiratorial view would resurface in the guise of Christian fundamentalism.)

Welch's 1966 essay "The Truth in Time" describes those at "the inner core of conspiratorial power", whose aim "always has been, and still is, to impose the brutal tyranny of their rule over the whole human race". He attempts to expose the unimaginable reach of the central conspiracy, but from the outset realizes the near futility of the endeavour:

To make the history of the great conspiracy both clear and convincing, we need a hundred volumes of a thousand pages each. And we hope that those scholarly volumes will all be written in due course, as a guide and a warning to future generations. But at present we have a more immediate and more urgent task. We want to give you simply an outline of the progress of this organized evil force, from its beginning up to the present time.

Clearly informed by the key Illuminati conspiracists, Robison, Webster *et al*, Welch explains the shadowy nature of the conspiracy and those behind it:

We must hunt the first steps largely in the shadows rather than in the substance of history. For the conspiracy is deep-rooted. Two hundred years ago, or during the last half of the Eighteenth Century, there were in Europe many secret societies with grandiose dreams of overthrowing all existing human institutions, and of rising out of the resulting chaos as the all-powerful rulers of a "new order" of civilization. Of these groups the Illuminati, founded in Bavaria by Adam Weishaupt on May 1, 1776, was undoubtedly the most important.

Then he enumerates the Illuminati's crimes: causing the French Revolution, establishing the origins of communism, overthrowing governments and destroying religion:

By 1789 the Illuminati were already strong enough to have had a great deal to do with planning and precipitating the holocaust known as the French Revolution. In that upheaval we find many elements of Communist strategy and purpose with which we are familiar today. One was the ruthless undermining of rulers and governments in order to destroy them. Another was the destruction of all religion by substituting the worship of "reason" in its place.

Perhaps aware that his fellow Birchers would find the suggestion of a direct descendant of Adam Weishaupt striding the corridors of power on Capitol Hill hard to accept, Robert Welch coined the term the "Insiders" to describe these faceless but all powerful figures:

> Whether or not this increasingly all-powerful hidden command was due to an unbroken continuation of Weishaupt's Illuminati, or was a distillation from the leadership of this and other groups, we do not know. Some of them may never have been Communists, while others were. To avoid as much dispute as possible, therefore, let's call this ruling clique simply the Insiders.

From this point on, the Illuminati conspiracy was an official part of the Bircher philosophy, and its effect was two-fold. It distanced many Bircher members, who, although alert to the perceived dangers of communism in the US, were less prepared to accept wholesale Robert Welch's theories of a global, centuries-old conspiracy. On the other hand, it fed into a growing conspiracy industry, and introduced or expanded ideas about Illuminati/Insider involvement in aspects of government and world affairs. The Illuminati myth would, in the latter part of the 20th century, become so large and all-encompassing it would become all things to all people, and the Bircher theories played into that.

In 1967, for example, the John Birch Society, in its role as bookseller and publisher, reprinted John Robison's *Proofs of a Conspiracy*. In bringing the book to the attention of a new generation, the anonymous Bircher-written introduction draws specious parallels with the present, and even attempts to give the shadowy Insiders a more concrete identity. Reprising an earlier target, the introduction refers to the role of the intellectual in the greater conspiracy:

This was a conspiracy conceived, organized, and activated by professionals and intellectuals, many of them brilliant but cunning and clever, who decided to put their minds in the service of total evil.... It is obvious that this conspiracy, appealing to the conceit of half-baked intellectuals, would attract educators, writers, philosophers, publishers, and cler-gymen. Their counterparts who run America today...have the same self-conceit, the same arrogance which seems to characterize the overly bright and overly sadistic in any age and any civilization.... One tends to think of professors, philosophers, and writers as sitting in their ivory towers, per-fectly harmless to the world. Robison and history prove oth-erwise... [W]e have had nothing but presidents surrounded by professors and scholars.... All of which brings to mind Weishaupt's plan to surround the ruling authorities with members of his Order.

Today's Illuminati, "this conspiracy of intellectuals" repre-senting "the cleverest and most diabolical minds" the introduc-tion continues, are to be found in the following institutions: "the great subsidized universities, tax-free foundations, mass-media communications systems, government bureaus such as the State Department, and a myriad of private organizations, such as the Council on Foreign Relations."

By this stage, although the idea of the Illuminati may have provided the model for the Insiders, the latter concept had become so vast it was probably easier to list those who weren't part of the plot. The unlikely named Revilo Oliver, associate editor of the JBS journal *American Opinion* until the mid-1960s, linked the Illuminati/Insiders to just about everybody, and was the first Bircher to raise the connection with the (genuinely elite and secretive) Bilderberg group. Oliver states in *American Opinion* in March 1964:

Since it was clear that there was a conspiracy inside the outer (Marxist) shell, it was only natural that attempts should be made to identify it. Various sincere and thoughtful writers have positively identified the inner conspiracy as composed of one of the following: ... Illuminati, Satanists, "Bilderbergers", Zionists, Pharisees, Khazars, Fabian Socialists, International Bankers, Rockefellers, Rothschilds, or a gang of otherwise unidentified "messianic materialists".

He was also one of the most vocally anti-Semitic members of the JBS, and was finally expelled from the society for publicly declaring at a rally in July 1966: "If only by some miracle all the Bolsheviks or all the Illuminati or all the Jews were vaporized at dawn tomorrow, we should have nothing more to worry about." (He was also one of the first conspiracy theorists to address the Kennedy assassination, claiming that Kennedy's death was caused by an international communist conspiracy.)

Sensitive as the JBS was to accusations of anti-Semitism, the society's endorsement of a book by Gary Allen, *None Dare Call it Conspiracy*, in 1971, suggest that the JBS may have been concerned more about degrees of anti-Semitism. In addition to the by now usual JBS conspiracy theories, the book discusses the role of the [Jewish] Rothschilds and international bankers in the wider plot. Allen's book claimed that "Anti-Semites have played into the hands of the conspiracy by trying to portray the entire conspiracy as Jewish" and "it is...unreasonable and immoral to blame all Jews for the crimes of the Rothschilds". However, the fact remains that his diagrams charting a "supra-government" which includes, among other organizations, international banking institutions and major corporations, is an updated variation on the Jewish world conspiracy myth.

In other respects, Allen's book picked up the baton supplied by the JBS and ran with it, reprising the society's theories point for point. Using the familiar conspiracy theorist technique of repetition and accumulating details and questionable "facts", Allen claims to have proof of the origins of the *Communist Manifesto*:

> All Karl Marx really did was to update and codify the very same revolutionary plans and principles set down seventy years earlier by Adam Weishaupt, the founder of the Order of the Illuminati in Bavaria. And, it is widely acknowledged by serious scholars of this subject that the League of Just Men [alleged to have hired Marx to write the *Communist Manifesto*] was simply an extension of the Illuminati which was forced to go underground after it was exposed by a raid in 1786 conducted by the Bavarian authorities.
>
> (Allen, pp25–6)

Elsewhere Weishaupt is denounced as "the monster who founded the Order of the Illuminati" whose "role…in such horrors as the Reign of Terrror is unquestioned" (Allen, p80). Allen found today's Illuminati in the Council on Foreign Relations – "active in working toward its final goal of a government all over the world – a government which the Insiders and their allies will control" (Allen, p87); among America's elite ("While the Insiders are serving champagne and caviar to their guests in their summer mansions in Newport [Rhode Island, US], … their agents are out enslaving and murdering people. And you are next on their list". (Allen, p97); and among the secretive and super elite Bilderberg group. And if the JBS admires Allen, the feeling is mutual. If only the rest of the world could realize the error of its ways, Allen wondered:

> The organization which is the leader in this field [ie, of exposing the conspiracy of the Insiders], has had the most expe-

rience, and is doing the best job of exposing the conspiracy is the John Birch Society. Doesn't it appear strange that this organization, which worked toward decentralization of political power and the exposure of the Insiders should be so vilified by the mass media, while the Council on Foreign Relations, which promotes centralization of power in the hands of a few within a world government is practically never mentioned?

It was not only JBS supporters who were guilty of unpalatable conspiracy theories. The JBS itself has strayed dangerously into racist territory. In several JBS bulletins the Insiders/Illuminati are claimed to be behind the civil rights movement, in which "the Black Panthers...are being used by agents of the Insiders far above them, to beat their breasts and make loud noises, like the gorillas whom they so much resemble" (qtd Lipset and Raab, p257). Several other extreme rightwing groups either formed in the wake of the JBS, or picked up on the Insider theory to put forward their own racist agenda, in which a vast Illuminati/Jewish/communist world conspiracy could be used as justification for disseminating hate. The Fiery Cross, the journal of the Ku Klux Klan, reprinted and expanded on JBS theories on the role of the Illuminati, repeating claims that there was a vast international conspiracy to control the US government that dates back to the Illuminati, who themselves date back to the pre-Christian era, who instructed Marx in the tenets of communism, which is bankrolled by the Jewish banking system, and so on and so forth...

As the society became associated with more politically extreme and historically absurd theories many of its ordinary members fell away, numbers dropped dramatically, and former allies publicly criticized the group. Prominent conservative organizations such as the American Conservative Union issued statements denying any affiliation with the JBS, and prominent conservatives such as Ronald Reagan were openly critical. When, in 1985, Robert Welch suffered a stroke and died the following year, the society appeared to be in permanent decline. By 1986 the organization was $9 million in debt and by the end of the decade the society was down to an estimated 18,000 members.

Events at the start of the 1990s added new impetus to the society. George H. W. Bush's reference to a New World Order in 1991 was a clarion call to conspiracists, and the Bircher's warning of an impending one-world government loomed large. Its members advanced the idea that the war against Iraq was falsely manipulated by the US president as part of a larger scheme to increase the powers of the UN and reduce that of the US. By 1995 its membership, reportedly, had swelled to 55,000; where the membership stands today is difficult to come by, as the society claims not to keep records.

Although the Bircher philosophy may not sit comfortably with many Americans, the society's legacy nonetheless extended into a larger arena. By the 1970s conspiratorial thinking was no longer the preserve of the extremist few. The assassination of John F. Kennedy in November 1963 and the findings of the Warren Commission, investigating the case and published in September 1964, launched the beginning of what has been described as "the mother of all conspiracy theories". The year 1963 is seen as the time that the US lost its innocence, and when it became acceptable – if not rational, or even obligatory in some circles – to question official versions of events. Events over the next few years seemed to bear this out, reaching a climax with the Watergate affair in 1972 – in which Republican agents broke in to the offices of the Democratic National Committee – and the subsequent impeachment of Richard Nixon. This instigated a widespread atmosphere of suspicion and distrust that allowed conspiracy theories to flourish in a mainstream environment.

Criticism of the authorities and suspicion of official explanations could be seen as a sign of healthy scepticism, rather than dismissed as paranoia. With regard to the Illuminati myth specifically, Welch and his allies had extended its definition to embrace just about every major development and organization of the late 20th century. By the millennium's end, the Illuminati/Insiders plot myth would encompass the Bilderbergers, the CFR and Trilateral Commission, international banking institutions, the Internal Revenue Service, the Federal Reserve System, every US president since the end of World War II, the assassination of President Kennedy, and the symbols on the dollar bill, to name but a few. And once the Christian Right got in on the act, the results were apocalyptic.

Chapter Six: Agents of the Apocalypse – the Illuminati and the Christian Right

At the end of the Gulf War, on March 6th, 1991, George Bush made a speech to Congress that would have a profound impact on some of his fellow Americans:

> Until now, the world we've known has been a world divided – a world of barbed wire and concrete block, conflict and Cold War. Now, we can see a new world coming into view. A world in which there is the very real prospect of a new world order. In the words of Winston Churchill, a "world order" in which "the principles of justice and fair play...protect the weak against the strong..." A world where the United Nations, freed from Cold War stalemate, is poised to fulfil the historic vision of its founders. A world in which freedom and respect for human rights find a home among all nations.

Never mind the rhetoric of fair play, freedom and respect for human rights, the 41st President of the United States had explicitly referred to a "New World Order".

For some Americans he might just as well have announced he was the Antrichrist: the phrase, for the conspiracy minded, was the verbal equivalent of the Mark of the Beast, a blatant indication of the US government's role in this New World Order and of its intentions to sell out its citizens to create a one-world government. Yet, many of the government's most vociferous critics came from the very circles that might have been expected to support their Republican president: the conservative right. Their fears of a one-world government would combine conspiracy theories ancient and modern, in which religious apocalypticism would merge with suspicions of international bodies, such as the Council on Foreign Relations and the Trilateral Commission, to create the beginnings of a vast, global conspiracy belief. The lynchpin of the whole plot, holding the various elements together, is identified by Pat Robertson, in his 1991 book *The New World Order*, as none other than the Illuminati. Robertson's book can be seen as a descendant of Robert Welch's "The Truth in Time", and develops the Illuminati myth to reflect Robertson's Christian fundamentalist agenda.

From the 1980s, fundamentalist Christian groups had an increasingly public, political presence, aided by the growth of televangelists, such as Jimmy Swaggart (at his height drawing the largest audience of all the media preachers, seen in 80 countries around the world), Billy Graham, Pat Robertson and Jim Bakker. Whereas evangelists of old had concentrated solely on spiritual matters, this new breed of preacher used their television programmes as a platform to air their political concerns, such as the erosion of "family values" by a liberal agenda, and other social issues. With their ability to reach out to huge swathes of conservative Americans and their enormous success at fund-raising, these preachers became a political force to be reckoned with and one that the Republican party could not afford to ignore. However, by the early 1990s some members of the Christian right were displaying evidence of a chasm between their ideology and that of their president, George Bush, and his administration. They had worrying evidence that the president, wittingly or not, was under the sway of dark forces bent, as dark forces tend to be, on world domination. Pat Robertson described in *The New World Order*, his concern that even such upstanding statesmen as former president Jimmy Carter or George Bush,

might, in their ambassadorial roles and involvement in organizations for world peace such as the United Nations, be carrying
out a much darker agenda, unknown even to themselves. He
offered the theory that, possibly in all innocence, such world
leaders were parroting the slogans of a "tightly knit cabal", who
were manipulating those around them to bring about a new
order under the domination of Lucifer.

In the last third of the 20th century, the fear of this "tightly
knit cabal" would surface again and again in many conservative
right-wing circles. It would be interpreted in different ways –
sometimes as the nation's own government, sometimes as an
international body such as the UN, and sometimes as the hench-
men of the devil himself – and employed for different purposes.
Across a wide swathe of the conservative right, from the
Christian fundamentalists to the most extreme militia movements, the rhetoric of good vs evil, of openness vs secrecy, and
of God vs Satan would help to shape the prevailing worldview.
And whether referred to directly or merely alluded to, the name
of the Illuminati is rarely far from the story.

Although "fundamentalism" first began to be used to
describe a strand of US Protestantism that emerged in the early
20th century, it shares some ideological similarities with the
earliest American colonists. Christian fundamentalists of the
20th century saw in the mainstream Protestant denominations,
such as the Episcopal church, worrying evidence of a growing
liberalism, of an acceptance of the secular humanism espoused
by modernism and, much earlier, the Enlightenment.
Conservative Protestant leaders therefore prescribed a list of
fundamental beliefs intrinsic to true Protestantism, seeking to
restore traditional values as explained in the Bible. Central to
this belief is an apocalyptic worldview that sees the world as
undergoing a struggle between good and evil, and that society
is in danger of being undermined by an evil conspiracy. To

combat this, evangelical fundamentalists urge a return to the true faith, and call upon their followers to maintain a constant vigil to identify the conspiracy. This might take any of a number of forms, but all threaten the bedrock of society, and all are manifestations of something much more sinister: the reign of the Antichrist. In the latter half of the 20th century, US fundamentalists have pointed to, variously, the forces of liberalism, feminism or rock music as a threat to Christian values. However, this tradition stretches back to the very foundation of the country. Pilgrim preacher Cotton Mather, having fled the religious repression of Europe, saw in the pope the embodiment of the conspiracy; during the American War of Independence many devout Protestants saw the work of the Antichrist in the reign of King George III.

Christian belief is imbedded in American history. When the pilgrim fathers founded their "city upon the hill" it was a concrete expression of their manifest destiny, proof that God was behind their mission, and that the founding of America was an expression of His will. The Bible was key to this, and within its pages the early Puritan colonists were able to find strength, interpreting the Scriptures literally for proof of their mission. The New Testament's Book of Revelation, which describes the Apocalypse, and the cosmic battle between God and Satan before the return of the Messiah, was of particular significance, and its powerful imagery informed the colonists' view of themselves in the world. Revelation tells how man's sinful behaviour incurs the wrath of God, who sends a warning in the shape of the four horsemen of the Apocalypse to spread war, disease and other disasters throughout the world. Satan takes advantage of this time of strife, called the Tribulation, by sending his agent, the Antichrist, to fool Christians into believing he is the Second Coming of the Messiah. The real aim is the destruction of Christianity. Those Christians who are not fooled by the

Antichrist are told they must renounce their Christian faith and are threatened with death, until God intervenes and is victorious in the final battle of Armageddon with Satan. Early colonists in the New World were able to understand their trials and hardships as an example of the Tribulation described in Revelation, a period of suffering to be endured before the thousand-year period of peace on Earth, which occurred with the true Christ's Second Coming. But such a reading reinforced a sense of living in the End-Times, the period when Satan's heir, the Antichrist (or beast), and his agent, the false prophet, rule on Earth before the final battle:

> Men worshipped the beast and asked, "Who is like the beast? Who can make war against him?" The beast was given a mouth to utter proud words and blasphemies and to exercise his authority for forty-two months.
> (Revelation 13:4-5)

Therefore, if this was the case, then it was important to remain on guard for the appearance of the Antichrist, the false prophet who would "exercise his authority". During the 18th-century Illuminati scare, the Reverend Timothy Dwight identified the *philosophes* and the Illuminati with the Antichrist, seeing in Revelation's description of the "unclean spirits coming from the mouth of the papal beast" an allegory for the deism and Enlightenment philosophies espoused by the French thinkers. In his sermon of July 4th, 1798, entitled, tellingly, "The Duty of Americans in the Present Crisis", he described his present era as one in which "false doctrines" and "impious teachers" were in danger of ushering in a period of godlessness, and urged his fellow Americans to be vigilant in order to protect themselves from the persuasiveness of these new ideas:

One great characteristic and calamity of this period is, therefore, that unclean teachers, or teachers of unclean doctrines,
will spread through the world, to unite mankind against God.
They are said to ... originate in those countries, where they
have principally co-operated against the kingdom of God; to
be *unclean*; *to resemble frogs*; i.e. to be lothesome [sic], and per-
tinacious; to be the *spirits of demons*, i.e. to be impious, malicious, proud, deceitful, and cruel; *to work miracles*, or wonders;
and *to gather great multitudes of men to battle*, i.e. to embark
them in an open, professed enterprise, against God Almighty.

Throughout America's history, this quest to identify the
Antichrist resurfaces in various guises – from the 18th-century
Illuminati scare to the anti-Semitism and anti-communism of
the first half of the 20th century, through to suspicions of the
UN, EEC, barcodes and black helicopters – but will always reinforce the sense of the US under siege from unseen forces, from
the Other. From a late 20th-century Christian fundamentalist
standpoint, it explicitly fed into and was in turn reinforced by
the Illuminati myth.

Christian fundamentalism relies on a literal reading of the
Bible to interpret the world. The infamous "Monkey Trial" of 1925,
for example, was the result of former Populist politician turned
fundamentalist William Jennings Bryan's challenging the teaching of Darwinism in Tennessee public schools, because it posed
a direct challenge to the origins of man as described in Genesis.
(Alarmingly, 80 years later the debate was revisited when the
Kansas Board of Education lobbied to allow the creationist
theory to be taught in science classes.) Fundamentalists look to
the Bible to understand the world's future as well as its past.
Most believe in "dispensationalism" – the idea that the world's
history is divided into a series of ages or "dispensations", each
marked by a particular attitude of God toward mankind.

According to dispensationalists, we are currently living in the last of these ages. At the end of this will occur the Rapture, when Christ will return to Earth to lift the saved to heaven. Premillennial dispensationalists believe that the Rapture will begin with a seven-year period of Tribulation, during which time the world will see a series of natural disasters, wars, plague and famine, after which the saved will ascend to heaven. The prophecies of Revelation and the Book of Daniel, particularly, are believed to contain the clues to when this will happen. The prophetic imagery within the text is interpreted in the light of world events, and is used both as a key to understanding them, and as a means of establishing the timing of the Rapture. Throughout US history, fundamentalists have poured over the Scriptures to establish the date of the Second Coming. In 1843–4, evangelist William Miller led a mass movement known as the Millerites, who anticipated the return of the Messiah. A close reading of the Bible had led Miller to calculate a timeline to predict the date of the Second Coming, which he established (with some reluctance, it appears) as some time between March 21st, 1843 and March 21st, 1844. When the appointed time came and went, a second date was suggested. When again this passed without incident, it was subsequently referred to as the Great Disappointment, yet it has not dissuaded premillennialists from attempting to predict the date of the end of the world by poring over the Bible. Postmillennialists also believe history to be divided into a series of dispensations, but that Christ's return will be brought about when Christians have established His kingdom on earth.

The 1970s saw a resurgence in fundamentalist belief in the US. The growth of televangelism allowed fundamentalist preachers to become celebrities with followings stretching from coast to coast. In the uncertainty of the post-Watergate years Scripture provided answers. The best-selling book of the decade was

Hal Lindsey's *Late Great Planet Earth*, a work of premillennial dispensationalism published in 1970. By the end of the decade it had sold 19 million copies. At last count it was over 35 million copies, and had been translated into 50 languages. Lindsey was a missionary and preacher in the late 1960s. His intention was to write a book that would explain the Rapture to a younger, more cynical and questioning readership. Reading current events in terms of biblical prophecy, Lindsey saw in the founding of Israel in 1948 the beginning of our current dispensation. Proof, too, that we are reaching the End-Times is the emergence of the EEC, which Lindsey sees as the return of the Roman Empire as described in Daniel. The Soviet Union, according to Lindsey, was clearly Gog, the invader from the north as described in Ezekiel (the collapse of which later necessitated a quick reinterpretation of events).

Although not all Christian fundamentalists, and not all of Lindsey's readers, were necessarily of a conspiratorial mindset, Lindsey's interpretation of events nonetheless contributes to a wider conspiratorial agenda. When Greece became the EEC's tenth member in 1979, Lindsey understood this to represent the last of the ten horns of the beast described in Revelation ("and behold a great red dragon, having seven heads and ten horns and seven crowns upon his head"). From this he extrapolated that the EEC "will be headed by the Antichrist. And I believe that leader is alive somewhere in Europe; perhaps he is already a member of the EEC parliament" (qtd Fuller, *Naming the Antichrist*, p166). In 1981, in Lindsey's *Countdown to Armageddon*, the aims of the Trilateral Commission came under attack, whether intentional or not:

> I believe the Trilateralist movement is unwittingly setting the stage for the political-economic one-world system the Bible predicts for the last days.... What the Trilateralists are

trying to establish will soon be controlled by the coming world leader – the Anti-Christ himself.

Elsewhere, Lindsey claims: "[The Anti-Christ] will have a magnetic personality, be personally attractive, and a powerful speaker. He will be able to mesmerize an audience with his oratory" (*Late Great Planet Earth*, p97). Such an adaptable description has meant that numerous public figures, including Prince Charles, Bill Clinton and Saddam Hussein, have been named as the Antichrist by one group or another; Hal Lindsey is particularly suspicious of King Juan Carlos of Spain. It might be simpler to assume that at any given time anyone in the public eye has been or will be considered a candidate.

For fundamentalists such as Lindsey, Revelation holds the key to understanding every aspect of our world, and is infinitely adaptable to whatever situation arises. Yet its imagery of plagues, fire and brimstone, of seductive and charismatic false prophets helps to reinforce a worldview in which the good are perpetually under threat from evil, and the world is forever teetering on the brink of annihilation. With such a mindset comes an endless propensity for suspicion and intrigue, one that sees sinister motives behind even the most potentially philanthropic endeavour. For example, Mikhail Gorbachev's policies of Glasnost and Perestroika, rather than being seen in the context of ending the Cold War, were instead considered to be evidence of moving dangerously toward a one-world government. For fundamentalists, a one-world government threatened to undermine the superiority of the Christian faith, and thus was the work of the Antichrist. With such logic, it made perfect sense to see another candidate for the Antichrist in Pope John Paul II, with his message of tolerance and multicultural understanding.

In this way, Revelation not only holds the key to understanding the world, it can be used as a confirmation of one's worldview. Don't agree with European social policies? Suspect your government has a hidden agenda? Suspicious of what they're getting up to over in Brussels? Obviously the work of the Antichrist – who is in league with the usual suspects. One fundamentalist newsletter makes a link between a vast computer network in Brussels and the all-encompassing phrase "sinister organizations" to prove the existence of the Antichrist:

> The European Common Market computer at Brussels, Belgium...[is] prefixed by the numbers 666. It is called the Beast by those who built it and worked on it.... The Beast has many tentacles in the Mafia, the CIA, the Knights of Malta and other sinister organizations which have been working for many years together to bring this enslavement about.... In January of 1997 we were told that the current pope in Rome is an actor, a look alike for the real pope who was murdered in the world wide conspiracy.
>
> (Awakenings Newsletter, qtd Fuller, p181)

With fundamentalism's propensity to see vast, overarching connections between seemingly disparate events, it was not long before the Illuminati were reintroduced into the mix. And although they may have been alluded to on the fringes, evangelist and former presidential candidate Pat Robertson was to bring the Illuminati name to the foreground.

A graduate of Yale Law School, Robertson had been raised a Southern Baptist, but his early, lucrative, business career in New York had been marked by material success and a playboy lifestyle rather than any evidence of Christian faith. This was to change abruptly. In the 1950s, dissatisfied with his success, he turned to God, gave away most of his possessions and enrolled at the New York Theological Seminary. It was at this evangelical establishment that he was introduced to the idea of dispensationalism, and the charismatic evangelical concept of "spiritual gifts" such as faith healing and speaking in tongues. Shortly after graduating, he described how, after fasting and praying for seven days, he had a sign from God to buy a near-defunct television station in Virginia: "God Spoke, 'Go and possess that television station. It is yours'" (qtd Goldberg, p85). By October 1960 he was on the air, broadcasting his Christian message to a small audience. The early years were fraught with financial difficulties, but with the financial support of his audience the station became a success. Viewer assistance helped to found the *700 Club* programme, the result of a drive in which 700 viewers pledged to donate 10 dollars a month to support the station. The *700 Club* was a 90-minute current affairs programme with an avowedly Christian interpretation of the news and an active viewer participation element, in which members of the public would ring in with requests for prayers to be read on the air. Robertson's "spiritual gifts" also played a part, with acts of faith healing performed live on air for viewers phoning in. By the end of the 1960s, an estimated 10 million people were tuning in to one of the five television or six radio stations on Robertson's Christian Broadcast Network. During the next decade, the popularity and influence of the *700 Club* grew. It was sold to other networks, and by the end of the 1970s was seen on 150 US channels and 35 channels around the world.

The 1980s saw a series of high-profile scandals in the world of televangelism. Robertson's network remained as successful as ever, but the *700 Club* adapted with the times and was now a more conventional current affairs programme, albeit with a conservative Christian slant. Robertson's newsletters, however, were less restrained, and thundered with prophetic doom and moral outrage, seeing in the current climate with its "plague of abortion, homosexuality, occultism and pornography; ... widespread family disintegration; genocide in Cambodia; Russian troops and

planes in Cuba; the Afghanistan invasion", proof of a world near-
ing the End-Times, in the form of aa "potential Middle East War"
or even World War III (Newsletter, February–March 1980, qtd
Goldberg, pp87–8). And if the world were facing a countdown to
the Apocalypse, the Antichrist could not be far behind: "there is
a man alive today approximately 27 years old, who is now being
groomed for the Satanic messiah" (ibid). Later in 1984, he warned
of the danger of succumbing to the power of the Antichrist, linking, in one breathtaking rhetorical sleight-of-hand, the threat of
a murderous dictatorship with that of secular humanism. The
Antichrist he explained, in Answers to 200 of Life's Questions,
would appear, initially, like Jesus, until the time was right to
reveal his true colours as a combination of the worst of the
world's dictators – Adolf Hitler, Joseph Stalin, Genghis Khan and
Mao Tse-tung. His warning continued in describing the
Antichrist as present in anyone who tries to lead people to turn
away from Christ, and anywhere today where human individuals are given undue veneration. In that respect, the secular
humanism taught in schools and found in the media or intellectual arenas was the first of humanity's incremental steps
toward worshipping the Antichrist.

By the late 1980s, Robertson was preparing to take his message all the way to the White House, believing it to be God's will.
He explained how the voice he "had known so well" had told
him, "You will not want to do it, but I want you to be President
of the United States" (qtd Goldberg, p88). In 1987 he ran as a
Republican candidate, with a conservative Christian agenda.
Taking a leaf from the John Birch Society's book, he traced the
root of the country's decline back to the foundation of the
Federal Reserve System, taking in Roosevelt's New Deal and
the US role in Vietnam along the way. The current culprits
were the government bureaucrats, academics, feminists and
homosexuals who were promoting liberal agendas that

undermined the country's Christian values.

Although he spent more on his campaign than any other presidential candidate in history, Robertson lost spectacularly. Despite a promising start, and the copious funds of his many willing supporters (mostly viewers of his television programme), his campaign was derailed when scandals about his personal life became public. He was alleged to have used family connections to avoid active duty in Vietnam. Possibly even worse, for a candidate who inhabited the moral high ground, his wife was rumoured to have been expecting their first child before they were married. Undeterred by this bruising defeat, he launched the Christian Coalition two years later, a conservative political advocacy group which today has over one million members.

Robertson's agenda grew more extreme with the turn of the new decade. His biblical prophecies became more unpleasant – one prediction was that a hurricane would strike Orlando, Florida, as punishment for its support of gay rights – and his theories more conspiratorial, claiming for example that he had information about secret missile bases in Cuba, or that he alone knew the location of the American hostages in Lebanon. Always a critic of large corporations and their quest for profit at the expense of morality, he increasingly criticized the world of international finance, of the Council on Foreign Relations and the Trilateral Commission. Once he began to suspect a larger, hidden agenda at work, it wasn't long before references to the Illuminati made an appearance.

In 1991, Robertson published *The New World Order*, containing (according to his publishers) "striking documentary evidence" about who is really running the world, and shaping its future. Although it takes its cue from Welch's "The Truth in Time", Robertson's interpretation of the Illuminati myth reflects his Christian fundamentalism. As with Welch (and Nesta Webster, all the way back to the Abbé Barruel and John Robison),

Robertson is convinced that historical events are the result of sinister contrivance rather than accident and describes in *The New World Order* how public policies are planned, with malice aforethought and are the result of malign connivance that spring "from the depth of something that is evil".

Robertson is convinced that this conspiracy stretches back millennia, and although he resurrects many of the theories and culprits of his conspiratorially minded predecessors, he views them through the prism of the Scriptures, describing in *The New World Order* how the plot to establish a one-world government in the 1990s has its origins in the Tigris-Euphrates Valley, and is clearly described in Bible prophecy.

Using George Bush's reference to a New World Order as his starting point, Robertson looks for evidence of its implications, and charts its history. In an ever-increasing conspiracy theory, he claims to identify the thread that connects the White House, the State Department and the Council on Foreign Relations to secret societies and "extreme new agers". Their aim is to create a "world government, a world police force, world courts, world banking and currency, and a world elite in charge of it all". The usual elite suspects rear their heads, starting, this time, he says, with Cecil Rhodes, who is connected to the Federal Reserve Board; the administration of Woodrow Wilson; the Council on Foreign Relations, the United Nations and Trilateral Commission; the Carnegie, Ford and Rockefeller Foundations; Henry Kissinger, Jimmy Carter, and George H. W. Bush. So just about everybody, then.

Developing his premise from Robert Welch, Robertson describes the Illuminati as founding communism, drawing attention to the fact that the order was founded on May 1st, a "key annual holiday for communists". Proof, too, of the Illuminati's hand in the creation of communism was Robertson's perception of Weishaupt's aims: to overthrow the government, overturn the Church, and abolish the idea of private property, and in so doing create a one-world government under the control of a few carefully chosen "illumined" individuals.

Yet Robertson's fundamentalist suspicion of the Illuminati stems from two opposing concepts. On the one hand, the Illuminati represent secular humanism, an ideology that, since its conception, has threatened the Church. Modern Christian fundamentalism sees such an ideology as literally the work of the Antichrist as it offers an alternative to the word of God. At the same time, Robertson's suspicions of New Age philosophies and non-Western religion (as again, they distract from the Christian church) become intertwined with perceptions of the Illuminati, who thus are seen to represent the occult.

Robertson's placing the Illuminati myth within a biblical framework is significant for several reasons. It reinforces the idea of the Illuminati as satanic and agents of the devil. It is no longer the ideas of the Illuminati that are heretical, it is the group itself, which has become positively supernatural in its capacity for evil. It also extends Illuminati history back to the beginning of time; the Illuminati is now as old as original sin, is timeless, the embodiment of sin. Whether intentional or not, Robertson's take on the Illuminati story will contribute to its association with the occult, mysticism and the esoteric.

At its first appearance, Robertson's book had little impact beyond his immediate circle of supporters. This was to change when, three years later, it attracted attention from the Jewish Anti-Defamation League, who saw in its references to the machinations of "European Bankers" and quotations from extreme right-wing writers such as Nesta Webster an anti-Semitic agenda developed from the more extreme theories of the John Birch Society. A 1994 *Washington Post* article by Michael Lind added to the argument, and described the claims in *The New World Order* as making "Bircher conspiracy theories look tame" (qtd Durham, p117). In another article he traced the origins of Robertson's book to "the underground literature of far-right populism", which was "far more bizarre and sinister" than anything proposed by the John Birch Society. The strength of Robertson's Christian Coalition movement meant, however, that more mainstream conservative politicians had to tread carefully: a complete denunciation of Robertson might alienate a large portion of his supporters.

Yet Robertson's take on the Illuminati myth and the New World Order had points in common with other extreme right groups, so far on the margins of society that they already felt alienated from mainstream politics. Robertson may have been instrumental in bringing the conspiratorial worldview into the mainstream, but on the farthest reaches of the political spectrum they had been common currency for some decades. The far-right militia movements in rural America shared many of the theories voiced by Robertson and other fundamentalists. Among these was the idea that the US government was under the thumb of the United Nations; that this would lead to a one-world government ruled by international banking interests; and that because of this the rights of US citizens, as enshrined in the Constitution, were slowly being eroded. Robertson and his followers aimed to take on the US government by forming their own political party. The militias' route was to go on the all-out offensive by stockpiling weapons and declaring war on their own government.

The militia or Patriot movement is an umbrella term for a collection of disaffected extreme right-wing groups in the US, with roots in the earlier Christian Identity movement. Christian Identity itself encompasses a number of extreme right, racist groups – one of the most high profile being the Ku Klux Klan – who use a distorted reading of the Bible to justify their white supremacist ideology. Militia membership swelled in the early

1990s in response to the incidents at Ruby Ridge, Idaho and Waco, Texas, both of which involved a standoff between federal agents and heavily defended compounds which ended in tragedy. Within the larger framework of the militia movement are groups with varying agendas, which may range from issues of gun control, to religious fundamentalism, and the farthest reaches of neo-Nazism, but they share many points in common. Among these are a belief that the American way of life is under threat – that a centuries-old plot to bring about a one-world government and the reign of the Antichrist is being carried out by a secret, master group, which might be the communists, the US government, the United Nations or the Illuminati – and that the way to combat this threat is to create self-sufficient, self-defending groups of "citizen's militias" to withstand the coming onslaught.

Historian Michael Barkun describes the militia groups' responses to the perceived threat as falling into distinct camps: some take an, arguably, legal route to opposing the government, seeking to bring it into line with what they believe to be fundamental, immutable laws as described in the Bible. A second, grey area, is occupied by the survivalist groups. They might, but do not necessarily, have a specifically Christian agenda, and have such an overriding suspicion of the government, and society at large, that these groups retreat into their own, autonomous compounds, cut off from the rest of the world. As these groups are founded on a mistrust of the wider world and live in isolation, for the most part heavily armed, the potential for violent clashes with the authorities is huge. The final group is avowedly illegal. Wielding their beliefs like weapons, they attempt to justify their overtly racist, white supremacist agenda, by claiming some Biblical precedent.

Many of the militias subscribe to the theories of a one-world government conspiracy as described by the extreme right-wing writer Des Griffin. Drawing on the work of earlier Illuminati theorists, such as Lady Queenborough's *Occult Theocrasy*, Griffin describes the French Revolution as the work of "the Money Barons – the Illuminati" who also funded the Russian Revolution. The New Deal, according to Griffin, was but the latest phase in a centuries-old plot to destroy the US government, which originated with an ancestor of the author of the New Deal himself. The real aims of the New Deal were "to inflict on the nation every last phase of Clinton Roosevelt's Illuminist blueprint for destroying our constitution and our government" (qtd Martin Durham, *The Christian Right*, p132). The most recent suspects in the plot – the Trilateral Commission or the Council on Foreign Relations – are simply a continuation of the master plan, the Illuminati in another guise, as described in this End-Times scenario website (www.benabraham.com):

> Called the Jacobin Clubs in France in the 18th century, this aristocratic revolutionary movement today in America is called THE COUNCIL ON FOREIGN RELATIONS, INC. and its off-shoot is the TRILATERAL COMMISSION. The Council on Foreign Relations, Inc. is the political side of the Illuminati today. They have produced Congressmen, Senators and even Presidents, that they have used to pass laws that have little by little led America into becoming a Socialist country.

Crucial to the militias' ideology is the idea that the US Constitution describes a set of unalienable rights, of fundamental truths that transcend human interpretation. Many of the militias claim that the Constitution came not from the founding fathers, but directly from God. As one militia leader described it: "The source is the Bible, otherwise known as the common law" (Barkun, *Religion and the Racist Right*, p207). This idea of a Biblical common law forms the bedrock of the militias' identity, and is significant for several reasons. Firstly, it illustrates a belief in a set of core truths, of immutable values that do not allow any room for negotiation or interpretation. Secondly, it trumpets the militias' sense of righteousness. As the upholders of this so-called common law, they are carrying out the word of God. This immediately places any opposition in an un-Godly position. If you oppose or question the militias in any way, you are under-mining Christianity and at the furthest extremes it proves you are literally in the camp of the Antichrist. This view explains the paradox of groups who call themselves patriots believing their own government to be a corrupt body bent on enslaving its cit-izens: the militias believe themselves to be answering to a more fundamental set of values. If the government appears to be encroaching on these values, it only proves the nefarious nature of its enterprise.

Evidence of this is seen in the militias' understanding of the role of the US Constitution. Believing it to be describing God's "common law", any later amendments after the first ten described in the Bill of Rights are considered unconstitutional. Which means that later amendments pertaining to, for exam-ple, the paying of income tax, are genuinely believed to be unconstitutional, and therefore illegal. It would be one thing if this simply meant militia members were penalized for tax eva-sion, but this topsy-turvy logic can extend to incorporate a much more odious and dangerous set of beliefs, for example, that the Fifteenth Amendment of 1870, granting voting rights to Americans of all races, is unconstitutional. The idea of "common law" is therefore brandished to justify overt racism and anti-Semitism.

Perhaps most significant of all to the militias is the Second Amendment. Contained within the Second Amendment is not only the origins of the term used to describe the various groups, but also one of the most politically galvanizing issues in the US today: gun control. The Second Amendment states: "A well regulated militia, being necessary to the security of a free state, the right of the people to keep and bear arms, shall not be infringed." And the right to keep and bear arms is of fundamental significance to the groups' identities.

When in 1993 the Brady Bill was passed (the act required a waiting period before the purchase of a firearm), the militias responded with alarm. Such an act was seen as an infringement on their constitutional rights, and the beginning of the slippery slope toward total subjugation by their own government. Kenneth S Stern's compelling investigation into the militia movement, A Force Upon the Plain, quotes a militia commentator who describes the phenomenon of the conspiracy mindset as being like a funnel, which draws people in with issues that have a broad appeal, such as gun control laws or environmental restrictions, and gradually narrows to embrace a general ethos of anti-government:

> Then, further in, you get into the belief systems. The conspiracy. The Illuminati. The Freemasons. Then it's about the anti-Semitic conspiracy. Finally, at the narrowest end of the funnel, you've drawn in the hard core, where you get someone like Tim McVeigh... [T]he bigger the front end of the funnel is, the bigger the number that get to the core.

When the Militia of Montana organized a rally to protest against the Brady Bill in March 1994, around 800 people attended. Many of those in attendance may have come to genuinely protest the passing of a law they disagreed with, as is their right. However, they would have been confronted with pamphlets with titles such as "Executive Orders for the New World Order". These aimed to prove the US government's real agenda, which is to create a one-world government and enslave its own citizens:

There are individuals in this world, within this country, and in our own government, who would like to rule the world... These power hungry individuals have corrupted our government and are working on sabotaging our freedom by destroying the constitution of the United States in order to establish the New World Order (aka "Global Community").

To bring about the New World Order, and ultimately the single World Government, there are several things that must come about.... Because the Constitution is a document that safeguards the sovereignty of our nation it must be destroyed. Because of a genuine threat of the American militia, the American people must be disarmed...and thus become "sheeple".

    (qtd Stern, p73)

In rural communities where issues of gun control or environmental restrictions have a more immediate impact on the local community than in major cities, or the corridors of Capitol Hill, the perception of a distant federal government that interferes unnecessarily is a relatively easy one to understand, in theory. Some militia groups have taken this feeling of disenfranchisement to extremes, claiming that all government above the local level is, in fact, illegal, and that citizens are answerable only to their local sheriff. The group known as Posse Comitatus – literally "the power of the county" – derives its name from the old West practice of the local sheriff's ability to summon a "posse" of local men to maintain law and order. The Posse Comitatus Act of 1878 was passed with the aim of removing the US army from domestic law enforcement, returning it to the local level. The group claims that the Articles of Confederation, the document that defined the national government from 1781–9 prior to the establishment of the Constitution, continues to be the sole true expression of American law. According to the Posse Comitatus, and its leader, William Potter Gale, the Articles of Confederation are based on fundamental truths as enshrined in the Bible, and even the earliest version of the US Constitution cannot override the law as laid down in the Articles:

> They've never been altered, amended nor repealed. They cannot be... The sources of the Articles of Confederation for a Perpetual Union is the Holy Bible... It contains God's laws for his people, for their nations and their governments.
> (qtd Barkun, p207)

For the Posse Comitatus and many other militia groups, a malignant force, whether the US government, a New World Order, or a hybrid Illuminati/banking elite, has sought to pervert these fundamental truths to suit its own ends. Following this logic, any amendment to the Constitution is illegal, as it seeks to redefine or override the core truths of the common law. The Internal Revenue Service, the government body for tax collection, is, according to Gale, guilty of "a string of unconstitutional abuses which attempt to require a citizen's consent to the repudiation and violation of his God-given and Constitutional rights". In other words, not only are US citizens not obliged to pay income tax, it is illegal to try to force them to do so. In any event, many militias subscribe to the popular conspiracy theory that the whole of the US banking system is, as a Christian Identity pamphlet describes it, "the modern version of the 18th-century Illuminati" whose aim is to "get control of the monetary power of the major countries of Europe and ... create a one-world government" (qtd Barkun, p205).

To that end, the Posse vowed to "remove from office" any government employee who tried to enforce payment of taxes or to arrest those who failed to pay. This ominous threat is even more so when coupled with the belief that the right to bear arms is also a fundamental right, and leads to stockpiling of weapons.

The Posse's fundamentalism as regards the US government went further still. Referring again to the Articles of Confederation, William Potter Gale and his followers established an organization which called itself the Committee of the State, after the committee mentioned in the Articles, which was intended to take on the government of the country when Congress was not in session. Gale interpreted this to be a body capable of overruling Congress, and on July 4th, 1984 issued a "Compact" signed by like-minded extreme right-wing activists, which claimed to reinstate the Committee of the State (i.e., themselves). Part of the Compact included a statement known as the Caveat, which was, essentially, a death threat to federal employees: "Any interference or attempt to interfere with the functions and activities of this Committee of the State shall result in the death penalty being imposed upon conviction by said Committee sitting as the Congress of the United States" (qtd Barkun, p208). In place of income tax returns, many Posse Comitatus members sent the copies of the Caveat instead; in 1986 Gale and five other members were arrested and convicted for mailing death threats to tax employees.

Gordon Kahl, a North Dakota farmer and member of the Posse Comitatus (and former John Birch Society member) ceased paying taxes in 1967, and saw in the enforcement of payment of income tax the work of a satanic-communist conspiracy:

> If you've been paying tithes to the synagogue of Satan, under the second plank of the Communist Manifesto to finance your own destruction, stop right now, and tell Satan's tithing collectors, as I did many years ago, "Never again will I give aid and comfort to the enemies of Christ."
>
> (qtd Barkun, p210)

Kahl later killed two federal marshals who had a warrant for his arrest for violating the terms of his probation for tax evasion. In a statement he left after fleeing the crime he lamented the fact that "our nation has fallen into the hands of alien people" and that "these enemies of Christ have taken their Jewish Communist Manifesto and incorporated it into the Statutory Laws of our country and thrown our Constitution and our Christian Common Law (which is nothing more than the Laws of God as set forth in the Scriptures) into the garbage can" (qtd Barkun, p206). He was on the run for four months, and died in a subsequent shootout. For many among the extreme right he is hailed as a folk hero, and proof of the US government's conspiracy to deny its citizens their rights.

The Posse Comitatus are not alone in taking the law into their own hands, and believing not only in their fundamental right to do so, but that they have no other choice. Once the central premise – that the US government is an illegal agency – is in place, a world of looking-glass logic follows. Any perceived interference on the part of the government is seen as evidence of its being "out to get you", which in turn promotes marginalized behaviour which does, indeed, prompt investigations by law enforcement agencies. And on it goes, with isolated communities creating a world of self-fulfillng prophecy, in which the central image – that of being under attack by all-powerful shadowy forces – is constantly seen to be reinforced by the world around them. This, coupled with a literal reading of Revelation, leads to ever-more complex ways of finding proof of a larger threat.

For instance, convoluted numerological theories find the Mark of the Beast in just about any permutation of numbers, from the Social Security number allocated to all adult US citizens, to the use of bar codes, cash cards or other electronic numerical systems. Revelation describes how "all [will] receive a mark on their right hand or on their foreheads, and that no one may buy or sell except one who has the mark or the name of the beast, or the number of his name...and his number is Six hundred, threescore and six." The alleged preponderance of three sixes in barcodes is seen as proof of the impending reign of the Antichrist, and proof that Americans were already buying and selling with the number of the beast. Further evidence of three sixes point to evidence of the Antichrist in government agencies: President Bill Clinton's proposed health care plan in the mid-1990s involved an identification number comprising 18 digits, that is, three sixes. Agents of the Bureau of Alcohol, Firearms and Tobacco, a target of many conspiracy theories among the militia movement, for, among other things, its enforcement of gun control and involvement in the Ruby Ridge and Waco incidents, allegedly wear badges with 666 on them. Once on the quest for evidence of three sixes, they crop up everywhere: televangelist Jerry Falwell has found that the numerical equivalent of the letters in Henry Kissinger's name add up to 666, while other televangelists have managed to find 666 encoded in the letters that make up "New York City" – a centre for international banking and the ruling Eastern elite.

At one end of the spectrum, this tendency to see the world through complex numerical codes and biblical portents is, arguably, an expression of harmless eccentricity. What danger is there in someone devoting a website, say, to analysing the number of bricks in the unfinished pyramid on the back of the dollar bill (not, incidentally, any permutation of three sixes, no matter what might be claimed otherwise)? On the furthest reaches of the extreme right, however, this tendency fuels a dangerous paranoia, and an already entrenched sense of righteousness.

The Christian Identity group calling itself the Covenant, Sword and Arm of the Lord (CSA), based in southern Missouri, has concocted an elaborate racist conspiracy theory that, combined with the fact that they are among the most heavily armed of the militias, has the potential for terrifying consequences. For them, the time of Tribulation prior to the Rapture needs to be confronted head on, and they are very clear on who they believe to be the agents of Satan in the present day – the Jews. The CSA's *Survival Manual* of 1982 is full of tips on how to survive the coming Tribulation:

> For now, in the period before the collapse of the world as we know it... Christians are headed for the Tribulation. The days ahead are a chance to truly show our love and faith in God. Do not let the judgements that are about to fall turn you against God. Understand that this is the cleansing process needed before the kingdom of our Lord Jesus Christ can be established... [T]he planet earth is about to become the battleground between the forces of God, led by Jesus Christ...and the serpent father of deceit, Satan and his seed, the satanic blood-line Jews.
>
> (qtd Barkun, p216)

Once the Jewish-Satanic link had been revived, it was a short step to widening the conspiratorial net to incorporate the Illuminati, a term which is increasingly used as a handy catchall to represent the threatening "Other". As alleged historical "proof" of its conspiracy theory, the CSA regurgitates myths about the *Protocols of the Elders of Zion*. Although not specifically a Christian Identity writer himself, Des Griffin's conspiratorial view in *Fourth Reich of the Rich* contributes to this strand of anti-Semitism by describing (emphatically):

> "the MASTER PLAN": THE MEN WHO CONCEIVED THE DIABOLICAL CONSPIRACY AS LAID OUT IN THE PROTOCOLS, WERE NOT ATHEISTS, THEY WERE MEMBERS OF THE

ILLUMINATI, FOLLOWERS OF THE ORIGINAL "LIGHT BEARER", SATAN THE DEVIL. THEY WERE WORSHIPPERS OF SATAN. THIS IS THE PLAN OF SATAN.
(qtd Barkun, p193)

An anonymously written CSA publication, *Witchcraft and the Illuminati*, clearly takes its cue from Griffin's theory, and makes a connection between the Illuminati and the Jews by claiming a conspiracy between Adam Weishaupt and the Rothschilds to bring about the New World Order. In this they have so far been successful in making their mark on history by establishing communism, orchestrating the assassinations of both Lincoln and Kennedy, and causing two world wars.

Many of the extreme right militias use the term ZOG – Zionist Occupational Government – to describe this Illuminati-Jewish-communist cabal at the heart of the US government. This term derived from a 1978 novel, *The Turner Diaries*, written by William L Pierce under the pseudonym Andrew MacDonald. *The Turner Diaries* is a crucial text for many extreme militia groups (although, ironically, Pierce himself is reportedly extremely contemptuous of the movement), and describes a guerrilla uprising by white Christian patriots against ZOG, a government hell-bent on subjugating its citizens by stripping them of their rights. Crucial to the uprising is the fictional "Cohen Act", a piece of legislation that denies citizens their right to bear arms and which would be seen as a prophetic foreshadowing of the Brady Act in the early 1990s. The protagonist, Earl Turner, describes in the book how he joins a group known as the Organization to combat ZOG. In an irony that seems to have passed by the militias, the description of Turner's initiation into the Organization relies heavily on the rites and rituals associated with occult secret societies and beliefs about the Illuminati themselves. Turner is eventually made part of the secret, innermost circle (unknown to the foot soldiers on the outer edges of the Organization), and in a ceremony involving oaths, candles and robes believes the members of the Organization to be "truly the instruments of God in carrying out his Grand design" (qtd Barkun, p226). In the ensuing war, Turner goes down in a blaze of glory, on a suicide mission, flying a plane armed with a nuclear missile into the Pentagon. A postscript describes the Organization's victory in the US and spread to Europe.

It is easy to see why *The Turner Diaries* would appeal to the militias, as it clearly parallels the fears of an illegal, occupying government and the success of a small band of committed citizens (crucially, with the might of the Lord on their side) in combating it. But reality began to echo fiction with the formation in the early 1980s of an extremist group called the Order (or, the Silent Brotherhood to its members) who vowed to overthrow ZOG. In so doing the group was responsible for carrying out a string of armed robberies and counterfeiting operations to fund its so-called cause. One robbery alone of an armoured Brinks truck in July 1984 yielded $3.8 million, much of which went to funding extreme right causes and most of which was never recovered. The Order was also responsible for the murder, by submachine gun, in June 1984 of popular and controversial radio talk show host Alan Berg, who had criticized and mocked its members on air. The group's plans to assassinate members of the Rothschild family, Henry Kissinger and David Rockefeller also came to light. The extent to which the Order modelled itself on the fictional Organization was revealed in court, when its oath was read out, in which members swore "a sacred duty to do whatever is necessary to deliver [our] people from the Jew and bring total victory to the Aryan race". It continued:

I, as an Aryan warrior, swear myself to the complete secrecy of the Order and total loyalty to my comrades.... Let me bear witness to you, my brothers, that should an enemy agent hurt you I will chase him to the ends of the earth and remove his head from his body. And... if I break this oath, let me be forever cursed upon the lips of our people as a coward and an oath breaker... We hereby invoke the blood covenant and declare we are in a state of war.

(qtd Barkun, p229)

In November 1987 two members of the Order responsible for Berg's death were sentenced to 150 years in prison; a third died in a house fire during a two-day standoff with the FBI. David Lane, currently in prison for his part in Berg's murder, continues to believe in the US government's part in the conspiracy: "The political entity known as the United States of America has attempted to destroy any white territorial imperative.... Genocide of the White Race has been the aim and result of the American political entity" (qtd Barkun, p111).

The notoriety of *The Turner Diaries* gained a wider audience when it was discovered to have been a favourite book of Timothy McVeigh, convicted of the April 1995 bombing of the Alfred P. Murrah federal building in Oklahoma City, in which 186 people were killed and 500 wounded. McVeigh shared many of the militia's beliefs, chief among them being the US government's intentional infringement of the rights of its citizens by way of gun control, but took them to their extreme. Bolstered by texts such as *The Turner Diaries* (which, among its many scenarios, contains a detailed account of an explosion outside FBI headquarters in Washington DC), McVeigh acted on his belief that the US government was ruled by a shadowy conspiracy, and carried out the bombing in order, allegedly, to prevent another Waco-style incident. The bombing took place two years to the day of the end of the Waco standoff between the FBI and David Koresh and members of his Branch Davidian sect. McVeigh was convinced the FBI had orchestrated the incident and had covered up the extent of its role. In this he was not alone: Waco had been instrumental in galvanizing the militias into action. For those who believed in the US government's guilt in that incident, it was a short step to believing a government conspiracy was behind the Oklahoma bombing.

Shortly after the bombing, the extreme-right rumour mill went into overdrive. Aided by the Internet, the theories were able to proliferate and became distorted beyond recognition. Leaflets circulated proclaiming "Clinton Ordered Oklahoma Bombing" or that, *Manchurian Candidate*-style, McVeigh had been "programmed" to carry out the bombing and was nothing but a pawn in the government's conspiracy. Others claimed that evidence of the FBI's role in Waco had been in the building and that the government had planned the bombing to destroy the evidence. Charlie Duke, at the time a Colorado state senator and active Patriot member who enjoyed the support of the militias and Christian Coalition, was among those who claimed the government's involvement in the bombing. Long an advocate of states' rights over the federal government, he had, a year earlier, publicly identified the nature of the rot at the heart of US government:

We are dealing with something that's evil here. We're dealing with something that took over a nation led by Christ, created by Christ, and put in place by Christians. If you listen real close, if you really turn up your sensitivity, you can hear the evil that flows through the [legislative] body... You can hear cackling in the ceiling, you can hear the smiles of the beast as it's trying to force its puppets to do its bidding.

(qtd Stern, p217)

The far right's appropriation of the Illuminati myth allowed for extremist anti-government activity to be played out under the guise of Christian righteousness. By equating the machinations of a secret elite with End-Times prophecy, the idea of the Illuminati became indistinguishable from the devil himself. At the same time, the idea of a global conspiracy in which "everything is connected" was to become commonplace, absorbed into popular culture wholesale to the extent that a conspiratorial worldview became almost mainstream. The Illuminati myth became absorbed into the mainstream along with it, although under this new guise, its earlier, unpleasant antecedents – its anti-Semitic and xenophobic roots – were left by the wayside, leaving instead an all-encompassing umbrella theory of conspiracies. And just when it appeared it could go no further, the counter culture got in on the act, and the plot went inter galactic.

Chapter Seven: Pyramids and UFOs – the Illuminati Go Cosmic

On June 4th, 1969, the latest issue of the underground paper the *East Village Other* contained an elaborate chart documenting the interconnectedness of, among other organizations, the US Communist Party, the Federal Reserve and the Bank of America, plus the usual conspiracy targets, such as the "House of Rothschild" and the "Elders of Zion", and secret societies such as the Rosicrucians, the "Ancient Craft Masons" and the Shriners. On this information alone, it could have been an article from the John Birch Society. However, what made this document different was the presence of the lynchpins of a counterculture: among the interconnected boxes labelled "the Republican Party" and "Bank of Hong Kong" were references to Yippies, Black Panthers and Students for a Democratic Society.

At the core was a pentagram surrounded by five circles, with each circle representing a "sphere" of the conspiracy: "Confusion", "Discord", "Chaos", "Aftermath" and "Bureaucracy". Each sphere was overseen by a pair of rulers, intriguing in their incongruity: the Aga Khan, "Primus Illuminatus", occupied the Sphere of Aftermath with Saint Yossarian, the bewildered protagonist of Joseph Heller's anti-war satire *Catch-22*; elsewhere, Richard Nixon, "Grand Illuminatus", ruled over the Sphere of Chaos with a character called "Mordecai the Foul".

Other key figures included Mark Lane, a leading Kennedy-assassination conspiracy theorist of the time, "Saint McMurphy", a reference to the anarchic anti-hero from Ken Kesey's novel

One Flew Over the Cuckoo's Nest, and Mao-Tse-Tung. The chart was entitled "Current Structures of the Bavarian Illuminati Conspiracy Theory and the Law of Fives" and it opened up the Illuminati myth to another realm, embracing left-wing fears as comprehensively as those on the right, while at the same time resuscitating the mystical-occult myths of old.

The chart was an elaborate spoof of conspiracy theories, the work of Robert Anton Wilson who was editor of *Playboy* magazine at the time. Anton Wilson had become interested in the Illuminati myth through the many readers (clearly some of whom *were* buying the magazine for the articles) who wrote in enquiring about the alleged activities of the Illuminati. Since the assassination of President Kennedy in 1963 and the subsequent assassinations of Robert Kennedy and Martin Luther King, Jr, conspiracy had become a household word in the US, and conspiracy theories a mainstream and accepted way of interpreting the world. The Warren Commission investigating the president's assassination had done nothing to quell the rumour-mill which sprang into action following his death; if anything it contributed to the mythology, as every discrepancy and apparent contradiction was picked over and held up to scrutiny. Jim Garrison, flamboyant district attorney for New Orleans and leading Kennedy-assassination conspiracy theorist, had been instrumental in bringing numerous sensational theories to the attention of the underground, left-wing press, one of which had introduced the Illuminati into the equation. Anton Wilson, exasperated that the left seemed as gullible as the right when it came to conspiracy theories, began planting some of his own, including the "Structure of the Illuminati" chart. "We accused everybody of being in the Illuminati – Nixon, Johnson, William Buckley, Jr, ourselves, Martian invaders, all the conspiracy buffs, everybody," Anton Wilson explained, with undisguisable glee. The parody became too big to be contained in a single flow chart, and led to Anton Wilson writing, with fellow *Playboy* editor Robert Shea, the *Illuminatus!* trilogy, in 1975, which was an elaborate, satirical in-joke about fears of conspiracies played out through myths about secret societies. This began a new direction for the Illuminati myth. Up until this point, it had been the sole preserve of the political right for whom the idea of the Illuminati could be used in the service of ideological scaremongering. Now, the Illuminati would become part of the left-leaning counterculture's mythology, representing both suspicion of the establishment and the burgeoning interest in esoterica and mysticism that was part of 1970s hippy culture (and continues today in various New Age guises).

The trilogy comprises the novels *The Eye in the Pyramid*, *The Golden Apple* and *Leviathan* and incorporates possibly every permutation of the Illuminati myth, while introducing some of its own. "Actually, *Illuminatus!* began with the idea of satirizing conspiracy mania," Shea said in a magazine interview of 1976. "Conspiracy mania is a cop-out...a way of ending our responsibility for history." And to that end, the novels exuberantly pick up and run with prevailing fears, holding both the political right and left up to ridicule along the way.

The densely plotted trilogy begins with the discovery, through a series of memos, that the Illuminati are plotting to take over the world, the culmination of which will be the epic slaughter of an audience gathered outside Ingolstadt for a rock concert. Along the way the book takes in favourite American conspiracy theories, such as the assassinations of presidents Lincoln and Kennedy; supernatural elements such as Nazi soldiers kept in suspended animation in an underground lake outside Ingolstadt; and the mystical-anarchic Discordian Society, a religion created by Greg Hill and Kerry Thornley (under the names Malaclypse the Younger and Omar Khayam Ravenhurst) in the late 1950s, of which the book's authors were members and which attracted more followers following the success of the trilogy.

Discordia has been described by its followers as "a religion disguised as a joke disguised as a religion". Its central premise is that disorder and chaos are the natural states of the universe and it embraces this notion with relish, worshipping the ancient Greek goddess of discord, Eris. Its key text, the *Principia Discordia*, shares many characteristics with the *Illuminatus!* trilogy, by parodying literary techniques and genres including abrupt switches of points of view and elisions of time, all serving to disorient the reader and to reinforce the joyful anarchy of the Discordian philosophy. The *Principia* sets itself up in opposition to authority, yet at the same time sends up the idea of any kind of establishment conspiracy. Like the *Illumintatus!* trilogy its targets are left and right alike. Tongue-in-cheek references to the Illuminati include a spoof advertisement in which the "Ancient Illuminated Seers of Bavaria invite you to join the World's Oldest and Most Successful Conspiracy". It further advises, "May we warn you against imitations! Our is the original and genuine", and asks, "Is there an esoteric allegory concealed in the apparently innocent legend of Snow White and the Seven Dwarves?" A letter purporting to be from a member of the Illuminati pokes fun at both ends of the political spectrum when it reveals:

Our teachings are not, need I remind you, available for publication. No harm though, in admitting that some of them can be found disguised in Joyce's *Finnegans Wake*, Burroughs' *Nova Express*, the King James translation of the Holy Bible (though not the Latin or Hebrew) and [the John Birch Society's] *The Blue Book*. Not to speak of Ben Franklin's private papers (!), but we are still suppressing those.

(*Principia Discordia*, p72)

The *Principia Discordia* and the *Illuminatus!* trilogy extend the parameters of the Illuminati myth by emphasizing its alleged esotoric/mystical antecedents. Both elaborate on the strand of Illuminati beliefs that say the order is much older than its 18th century origins (the *Principia* claims it dates to 18,000 BC and originated in Atlantis). Both books are at once a celebration and a parody of esoterica, concocting an elaborate system of meanings and symbols as a key to the mysteries of the universe, only to undermine this propensity for finding deeper, hidden significance in absolutely everything. The *Principia* presents its key as "The Law of Fives" which "is one of the oldest Christian Mysteries..." The Law of Fives states that: "ALL THINGS HAPPEN IN FIVES, OR ARE DIVISIBLE OR ARE MULTIPLES OF FIVE, OR ARE SOMEHOW DIRECTLY OR INDIRECTLY APPROPRIATE TO FIVE." Furthermore "The Law of Fives is never wrong." Unfortunately, as Wilson was to write: "You have achieved Discordian enlightenment when you realize that, while the Law of Fives [is] not literally true, *neither is anything else*. Out of the hundred million buzzing, bright, busy signals received every minute, the human brain ignores most and organizes the rest in conformity with whatever belief system it currently holds" (qtd Johnson, *Architects of Fear*, p183).

The *Illuminatus!* trilogy is an anthology of these million buzzing, bright, busy signals, all seemingly battling to form some sort of coherent narrative but liable to short-circuit at any moment. In *The Eye of the Pyramid*, the first of the novels, the paper trail of memos created by the authors allows them to introduce every prevailing and often conflicting theory about the Illuminati, to comment on its absurdity while still incorporating it into the plot as a possibility. "I think I've found the clue as to how Zoroaster, flying saucers and all that lunatic-fringe stuff fits into the Illuminati puzzle", one memo is prefaced. Another begins: "Here's some more info on how Blavatsky, theosophy and the motto under the great pyramid on the US Seal fit into the Illuminati picture (or *don't* fit into the picture. It's getting more confusing the more I dig into it!)" Once the readers are up to speed on the wealth of Illuminati legends and conspiracy theories (so comprehensively covered that cultural historian Mark Fenster has called the book "a virtual encyclopedia of conspiracy theories") the authors embroider what they know to be the prevailing myths into one vast, conspiratorial wink. Here, for example, is their theory about the fate of Adam Weishaupt after the Illuminati was made illegal in Bavaria in 1786:

> No historian knows what happened to Adam Weishaupt after he was exiled from Bavaria ... and entries in [George] "Washington's" diary after that date frequently refer to the hemp crop at Mount Vernon [Washington's house]. The possibility that Adam Weishaupt killed George Washington and took his place, serving as our first President for two terms, is now confirmed.

This is just one of many instances in which the book plays with established conspiracy theories and embellishes them with knowing irony. For example, it is a historic fact that many of the founding fathers were Masons, including Washington himself, and Masonic rites and imagery had a public presence in the early days of the country. When the Revolutionary Army retook Philadelphia from the British in 1778, Washington celebrated by leading a contingent of Freemasons through the city while wearing his Masonic regalia. However, the contemporary image of Freemasonry doesn't sit comfortably with the unimpeachable reputation of a hero like Washington. The authors of the *Illuminatus!* trilogy knew this, and neatly dispense with the apparent discrepancy, at the same time reinforcing the idea that there is undeniably something peculiar about the Masonic elements in the foundation of the US. Later, in one of the book's many in-jokes, a throwaway reference is made to the Templars' alleged role in the French Revolution, in a scene in which a quietly scheming Weishaupt writes to an imperilled Thomas Paine in France: "he finished the letter, explaining to Paine why he couldn't help him; and...murmured to himself, 'Jacques de Molay, thou art again avenged!'" (This fleeting reference to de Molay – the last Grand Master of the Knights Templar, executed by the French King Philippe IV in 1413 – is a playful allusion to the old myth that the French Revolution was instigated by the Illuminati in retribution for de Molay's death.)

In the same scene, Weishaupt seals his letter with "the Great Seal of the United States whose meaning only he knew", while, at the same time, in one of the book's many elisions of time, reference is made to a present-day character puzzling over the portrait of Washington on the one dollar bill: "It isn't Washington at all, it's Weishaupt. Compare it with any of the early, authentic pictures of Washington and you'll see what I mean." The hidden meaning in the design of the Great Seal of the United States and the dollar bill have inspired conspiracy theories that are positively Byzantine in their complexity. Anton Wilson and Shea encapsulate the most popular, and throw in their own embellishments for good measure. (According to the *Illuminatus!* version of events, the design of the Great Seal was given to Thomas Jefferson by a mysterious man in a black cloak, quite possibly a time-traveller from outer space.)

Wilson and Shea's interpretation of the Great Seal myth embellishes existing theories, putting a baroque spin on an already convoluted legend. As with the reference to the de Molay legend, it relies on the reader's prior knowledge of the actual conspiracy theory to fully enjoy their exaggerated flourishes, although theirs characteristically take the existing theories that one absurd step further. As the 20th century neared its end, however, their parodies of conspiracy theories would appear relatively sane compared to the grand overarching theories that were to develop in the wake of the trilogy.

Actual historical references to the creation of the Great Seal of the United States show that several people were involved in its design. The initial effort originated with Benjamin Franklin, Thomas Jefferson, John Adams and French artist Pierre du Simitère, who were appointed by the Continental Congress in 1776 to come up with a design. In August of that year they unveiled their effort: a disc containing a shield, above which is a triangle radiating light and containing a single eye. Under the shield is the motto E *Pluribus Unum* ("Out of Many, One"). Further developments were needed before the finished design was accepted; six years, and three committees later, in 1782, Secretary of Congress Charles Thomson incorporated the imagery into the seal as we know it today. On the front is an eagle clutching 13 arrows in its left foot (for the 13 original colonies) and an olive branch in its right, while on the back is an unfinished pyramid, with 13 steps leading to its apex. At the base of the pyramid are the roman numerals MDCCLXXVI (1776, the year America declared its independence) and above the pyramid hovers the all-seeing "Eye of Providence". The back features the words *Annuit Coeptis* ("He Has Favoured our Undertaking") and *Novus Ordo Seclorum* ("A New Order of the Ages").

In 1935 the imagery of the Great Seal was incorporated into the design of the one dollar bill, at the proposal of Franklin D. Roosevelt's vice president, Henry P. Wallace. A portrait of George Washington is on the front, and on the back appear the two discs of the Great Seal. Those involved in the creation of the design offer benign explanations for its symbolism. Thomson described the images: "The pyramid signifies Strength and Duration: the

Eye over it & the Motto allude to the many interpositions of providence in favour of the American cause." Wallace was fascinated with the Great Seal for the way it symbolized the idea of unity emerging from diversity and therefore provided an apt metaphor for the US; for him the pyramid represented human endeavour and the quest for knowledge.

But for the conspiratorially minded, benign explanations are never good enough. The symbolism of the Seal and the story of its creation indicated the presence of secret, and therefore malevolent, forces, whose aims are encoded in the imagery. Probably the most problematic image is that hovering eye over the pyramid. Both eye and pyramid clearly hark to a pre-Christian tradition and, no matter how many apologists point to the all-seeing eye as a traditional representation of an omniscient (Christian) God, the conspiracy theorist chooses to see it otherwise. The eye, for them, is the eye of the Egyptian sky-god Horus, who took the form of a falcon, and whose right eye was the sun and left the moon. With this reading, the eye represents the worship of the Sun, and of light in general. Extrapolating further, the worship of light is synonymous with the worship of the Bringer of Light, that is Lucifer, and thus the symbol is a blatant satanic/Masonic/Illuminati symbol. William Guy Carter, conspiracist-extraordinaire explains the significance of the Seal in the introduction to *Pawns of the Game*:

> The significance of the design is as follows: the pyramid represents the conspiracy for destruction of the Catholic (Universal Christian) Church and the establishment of a "One World" [sic], or UN dictatorship, the "secret" of the Order; the eye radiating in all directions, is the "all-spying eye" that symbolizes the terroristic, Gestapo-like, espionage agency that Weishaupt set up under the name of "Insinuating Brethren", to guard the "secret" of the Order and to terrorize

the population into acceptance of its rule.

Not a symbol of strength and unity, nor of endeavours blessed by a benevolent God, but instead an overt sign of the malevolent aims of the Illuminati. (No one seems to question why an allegedly secret group would choose to make such a public display of their presence and intentions. But watertight arguments are not the conspiracists' strong point.)

While the image of the eye in the pyramid does appear in Freemasonry, it also appears in Ancient Egypt and the all-seeing eye itself is also referred to in the Bible on more than one occasion (for example, Psalm 32:8: "I will instruct thee and teach thee in the way which thou shalt go: I will guide thee with mine eye"). What it is not, despite countless unsubstantiated claims to the contrary, is an Illuminati symbol. There is no documented evidence that Weishaupt's Illuminati used any such imagery, although the theory has been repeated so often that in some circles it is accepted as truth. There are no "documents in the British library" substantiating this claim, despite the insistence of innumerable conspiracy websites. But it is, undoubtedly, an intriguing image to find in your wallet, issued by the US government.

Once you go down that route, however, the whole design bristles with arcane symbolism. For numerologists, the prevalence of the number 13 is laden with significance – quite apart from the fact that the original colonies were 13 in number. The conspiracists point to the 13 arrows in the eagle's talons, the 13 berries and 13 leaves on the olive branch, the 13 bars on the shield, and the 13 stars above the eagle's head, which – coincidence, or something more sinister? – also seem to form a six-pointed star. There really is something for everyone: apparently the eagle has 32 and 33 feathers, symbols of the highest degrees of Freemasonry. Then there are the Latin mottoes, the most problematic of which, for conspiracy theorists, is *Novus Ordo Seclorum* ("A New Order of the Ages"), commonly, and repeatedly (and erroneously), translated as "A New World Order". And finally, that date – 1776 – which, as every US citizen, young or old, knows, is the year America declared its independence. What would make more sense than that it should be commemorated on the back of the dollar bill? Apart from the fact that, as every conspiracy theorist will tell you, it is also the date of the founding of the Illuminati.

Pat Robertson's interpretation encapsulates many popular theories about the Seal, as he describes in *The New World Order*. The eye, for example, is "an ancient Egyptian deity, Osiris, who is revered in the secret high ceremonies and sacred rites of the Masonic Order". For Robertson, this implied that 1776 heralded the dawning of a new age – a new world order – for the Masons, under their omniscient guardian, Osiris. Yet, he asked, what exactly was meant by this new order? What was the "old order" it was breaking with? Was there a meaning hidden within the phrase, known to only a select few within the inner coterie of founding fathers? In this Robertson, perhaps inadvertently, perhaps intentionally, is picking up on the idea of "hidden superiors", on the idea that, even those seemingly within the inner circle, or at the top of the pyramid, may themselves be at the mercy of an even more hidden elite. And for him, this elite was planning to replace the old Christian world order of Europe and the US with a "mystery religion".

Robertson's theories seem mild compared with some of the highly creative and exhaustively detailed readings of the Seal. Entire books have been written, painstakingly connecting the central points of the eagle's eye with the base of the pyramid, or counting each last feather and brick (and dividing by the number of founding fathers) to prove categorically that the entire device is a Masonic/Jewish/occult/Illuminati/satanic calling card, and that the US government is run by aliens.

The authors of the *Illuminatus!* trilogy play with this tradition of obsessive interpretation, and clearly enjoy themselves by inventing their own occult reading. In one deft sleight-of-hand they claim the US flag itself symbolizes the link between the Illuminati, the order of the Assassins (referred to as the Hashishim) and the Hell's Angels. Oh, and cannabis:

> The two main colours of the American flag are, excluding a small patch of blue in one corner, red and white: these are also the official colours of the Hashishim. The flag and the Illuminati pyramid both have thirteen horizontal divisions: thirteen is, of course, the traditional code for marijuana...and is still used in that sense by the Hell's Angels among others.
>
> (*Illuminatus!*, p42)

In bringing into the plot references such as the Hashishim (the ancient Order of the Assassins who terrorized the Muslim world from the 11th century and used copious amounts of drugs to induce a trance-like state), the authors acknowledge the Illuminati theories that allege the group belong to a much older, occult tradition, one that seems to recede further back in time with each retelling. As the idea of one all-encompassing conspiracy theory begins to dominate the conspiracist mindset in the late 20th century, the idea that Adam Weishaupt himself was a dupe of a much more ancient secret society gains ground. Ishmael Reed's 1971 satirical novel *Mumbo Jumbo* asserts that possibility with its epigram: "The history of the world is the history of the warfare between secret societies."

As the *Illuminatus!* trilogy fed into and playfully embellished prevailing conspiracy theories of the time, it brought the idea of conspiracy, and the Illuminati story, to a new audience: a hip, knowing demographic that was both in on the joke, but by its nature suspicious of establishment ideology. The ceaseless punning and in-jokes made the reader complicit in the idea of the absurdity of the conspiracy, yet at the same time left room for suspicion of "official" accounts of history. And in piling on so many different theories, doubts and legends, and by creating one vast super-conspiracy, all theories become equally possible and therefore impossible. As one character says, doubtfully:

> It sounds plausible, ... but it also sounds plausible that the Illuminati is a Jewish conspiracy, a Catholic conspiracy, a Masonic conspiracy, a communist conspiracy, a bankers' conspiracy, and I suppose we'll eventually find evidence to suggest it's an interplanetary scheme masterminded from Mars or Venus.
>
> (*Illuminatus!*, p200)

As the book reaches its climax during a rock concert on May 1st, 1976, it parodies apocalyptic rhetoric, and in a final plot twist, reveals the true identity of the Illuminati.

The book clearly struck a collective chord. Its knowing irony, absurdist humour and literary game-playing led to its being, 13 years after publication, the best-selling science fiction paperback in the US. In 1977, the National Theatre in the UK produced an eight-hour stage version, with Robert Anton Wilson appearing in a cameo role. Although Shea and Wilson did not collaborate again, Wilson continued exploring conspiracy theories and the Illuminati myth in a prolific writing career that includes titles such as *Cosmic Trigger 1: Final Secrets of the Illuminati* (1977), *Masks of the Illuminati* (1981) and *The Widow's Son* (1985). The book has also inspired a game, the Illuminati, in which the aim is, of course, to take over the world. There is both a card and a role-playing version, in which players can choose to assume one of a number of identities, all parodies of the usual suspects in the conspiracy line-up from both right and left: "Big Media", UFOs, "the gnomes of Zurich" and the IRS, as well as some unexpected culprits, including "Congressional Wives", convenience stores and boy scouts. As cultural historian Peter Knight writes on this parodic strain of conspiracy thinking:

> There seem to be ... almost as many spoof versions on the Web of [conspiracy theories] as there are serious ones. What's more, many of the straight-up accounts bear an uncomfortably close resemblance to the *Illuminatus!* trilogy.... The serious and the entertainment versions of conspiracy theories are thus caught up in a spiralling mutual feedback loop, which, even if it doesn't produce more fully paid-up members, certainly makes the culture of conspiracy theory more prominent.
> (*Conspiracy Nation*, p6)

Yet as much as the book was part of a hip, countercultural awareness of ideas about conspiracy, its parody of conspiratorial thinking would soon appear in reality. In creating a vast, uber-conspiracy, in which everything is literally connected, the book provides a foreshadowing of some of the more extreme conspiracy theories of the late 20th century. As Wilson explained, the book contained "so many alternative paranoias ... everybody could pick a favourite, if they were inclined that way. I also hope that some less gullible souls, overwhelmed by this embarrassment of riches, might see through the whole paranoia game." On the contrary, for some, this embarrassment of riches could be seen as a challenge. As conspiracy commentator Robert D Hicks wrote: "If the evidence doesn't seem to fit a particular conspiracy theory, just create a bigger conspiracy theory." By the late 20th century some conspiracy theories had become so vast they

were literally out of this world and the Illuminati became associated with shape-shifting aliens.

Conspiracy theorist Milton William Cooper elaborated on this
theme in a number of books and articles which attempt to prove
that the Illuminati have, in fact, come from another planet with
the express aim of taking over the Earth. His book, *Behold a Pale
Horse* (1991), comes from a background of right-wing fundamentalism, but puts an otherworldly spin on proceedings. In an
all-embracing conspiratorial stew, of which the authors of the
Illuminatus! trilogy would be proud, Cooper explains the infinite
interconnections and nefarious aims of the Illuminati, their role
in the secret world government and their involvement with little
grey creatures from space.

Cooper came from a military background, which dated from
1961 when he enlisted in the US Air Force upon graduating from
high school. He served more than 10 years in both the air force
and navy, and by all accounts had an exemplary record, earning
several medals. In 1966, he volunteered to work on submarines,
and it is from this date that he claimed to have seen his first
flying saucer. While on watch one night he claims to have seen
a contraption the size of an aircraft carrier rise up from below
the waves and disappear off into the sky. Others, he claimed,
saw it, but all had had orders from navy superiors to keep quiet
about it. Two years later Cooper saw active service in Vietnam,
where his sightings of UFOs proliferated, and which he described
in *Behold a Pale Horse*:

> The whole time I was in Vietnam ... I had noticed that there
> was a lot of UFO activity. We had individual 24-hour crypto
> code sheets that we used to encode messages, but because
> of the danger that one of them could be captured at any time,
> we used special code words for sensitive information. UFOs,
> I was told, were definitely sensitive information. I learned

exactly how sensitive when all the people of an entire village disappeared after UFOs were seen hovering above their
huts. I learned that both sides had fired upon the UFOs, and
they had blasted back with a mysterious blue light. Rumours
floated around that UFOs had kidnapped and mutilated two
army soldiers, then dropped them in the bush. No one knew
how much of this was true, but the fact that the rumours
persisted made me tend to think there was at least some
truth in them. I found out later that most of those rumours
were true.

(pp25-6)

It was these experiences, and his alleged access to highly
classified documents later in his career that led Cooper to write
Behold a Pale Horse over a period of nearly 20 years. This book
exemplifies the direction of late 20th-century conspiracy theories in that it appears to embrace every fear, threat, myth and
rumour since John Robison's book hit US shores in the late 18th
century. It traces the role of secret societies in the history of a
covert government plot since the time of Ancient Egypt, bringing it up into the Space Age:

I hope to show that most modern secret societies ... are really
one society with one purpose. You may call them whatever
you wish – ... the Roshaniya, the Qabbalah, the Knights
Templar, the Knights of Malta, ... the Jesuits, the Masons, ...
the Illuminati, the Nazi Party, the Communist Party, the
Executive Members of the Council on Foreign Relations, ...
the Rosicrucians, ... the Trilateral Commission, the Bilderberg
Group ... – they are all the same and all work toward the
same ultimate goal, a New World Order.

(p80)

Along the way he explains the truth about the Kennedy assassination (the president was killed because he was going to alert the public about an alien presence in the US) and the government's involvement in underground experiments on its own citizens. In the book, Cooper claims to have found evidence of an alliance between aliens and a secret government, which he traces back to 1947, claiming that between then and 1952, 16 alien aircraft crashed in the US, from which 65 alien bodies – including one living – were recovered. This was all kept secret from the public of course, although President Eisenhower, with the help of members of the Rockefeller family, was working to keep the invasion in check. Cooper was not a lone voice: he broadcast a radio show five times a week and was something of a celebrity among the militia movement. And since 1947, the year of the Roswell incident, he was not the only American who genuinely believed in UFOs.

Roswell, New Mexico was the scene of a mysterious incident that will be forever synonymous with the little rural town. The bare bones of the case relate to the discovery on June 14th, 1947, of unexplained debris on a ranch on the outskirts of the town. The rancher who discovered the debris took some samples to the nearby Roswell Army Airfield, where some days later the press officer issued a statement that made reference to a "flying disc" or "flying object". Shortly afterwards the mystery seemed to be solved: officials at the airfield identified the debris as the remains of a radar reflector and weather balloon (part of a project approved by the Joint Chiefs of Staff in 1946, and probably unknown to any but the highest military officials) to measure the effects of possible atomic fallout over the US. The next day a local paper carried the headline "Flying Disc Explained". As the idea of government cover-ups had not yet become common currency, this official explanation seemed to suffice, and the case appeared to be closed. Had that been the end of it, the Roswell incident would still be notable for introducing the idea of the flying saucer into popular culture, and lodging the idea of the UFO into the public consciousness. Within a few months of the incident, polls showed that 90 percent of Americans had heard of UFOs. In the decades following the Roswell incident, however, public perception and belief in UFOs would change dramatically. In 1966, 96 percent of Americans had heard of UFOs and 46 percent believed in their existence. By the 1980s, UFOs had become part of the conspiratorial mindset, entwined with ideas of government cover-ups, secret governments and the New World Order. A poll in 2000 revealed that 49 percent of the population believe the US government to be withholding information on UFOs.

In this climate, the strange case of Roswell was revisited, with the first of many books purporting to explore the truth of the incident appearing in 1980. The first of these Roswell testimonials, *The Roswell Incident*, was the work of Charles Berlitz and UFOlogist William Moore, who interviewed key witnesses at the time. Thirty years after the event, the story had changed dramatically: one military official who claimed to have recovered the debris alleged that the material was unlike any he had seen before, unable to be burnt, dented or damaged in any way and, in his words, like "nothing that came from earth". Other witnesses claimed that the debris had been torn from a spacecraft that had crashed elsewhere and the remains of which had never been recovered. This testimony gained wide acceptance among the UFO community, and opened a floodgate of Roswell titles. The stories have conflicting details but they all agree that the material found at Roswell was no weather balloon, and that the government had gone to great lengths to cover up what exactly was recovered that day – because among the wreckage were four humanoid aliens, which had been spirited away to government laboratories for analysis.

This version of the Roswell incident feeds into the wider cultural phenomenon of distrust of government and authority in general. By the end of the 20th century it had become quite normal to believe in government cover-ups, even if you didn't believe in UFOs themselves. This in turn means the idea of the "official" version of the incident is easier to doubt, and thus the "true" version ever more important to uncover. Roswell became part of what has been described by cultural historians as "fusion paranoia" in which both far right and far left become united in their suspicion that the government has been subverted from within. Once this has been accepted as a frame of reference, it allows conspiracy theories from right and left to feed into one another in seemingly endless permutations and variations.

The UFO community has its own tradition of conspiracy beliefs, mainly focussing on the government's suppression of the truth about alien activity, but it has tended to distance itself from the extreme views of someone like Milton William Cooper. Cooper's theories take the extreme right's belief in the government's complicity in the creation of a New World Order and grafts on to it the UFOlogists belief in extraterrestrials. In so doing, he has united the extremist views of the militias – always too bigoted to be absorbed into the mainstream – with what had hitherto been perceived as a relatively harmless, if eccentric, belief in extraterrestrials, and one which had been readily accepted into the wider pop culture. Cultural historians have seen his theories as a bridge between two cultures, providing a two-way exchange in which popular UFO theories feed into the extreme right, and vice versa. In the 1970s, for example, new developments in UFO beliefs fed directly into theories about the New World Order, which in turn reflected back on the UFO community. A direct example of this could be seen in the development of the "alien abduction" story in the 1970s, in which "abductees" claimed to have been kidnapped by aliens, usually forced to undergo some kind of invasive scientific procedure, and then sent on their way. Many "abductees" reported having had some kind of device implanted into their bodies, which had direct parallels with the extreme right, Apocalyptic belief in the idea of the Mark of the Beast, and by extension, the government's use of barcodes and scanning devices as a means to control the US population. The government was clearly not only in league with the Antichrist, but with aliens, too.

The idea of a secret government working within the government had been an accepted part of extreme right ideas about the New World Order since the 1970s; by the mid-1980s this was given an intergalactic spin with the publication of *Extra-Terrestrials Among Us* (1986), by George C. Andrews, which claimed that a secret group of elite humans was working with aliens to control the rest of humankind. The outward manifestation of this super elite was the CIA, whose covert activities were clearly part of a more sinister agenda. The idea of a government within a government became part of common currency; and the fabled "Men in Black", those nameless government officials allegedly sent to investigate and (cover up) extraterrestrial activity, would become an accepted (and eventually spoofed) part of popular culture.

It had been a hoax itself that brought this idea to the attention of a wider public. In 1977 Anglia Television in the UK broadcast a spoof documentary, *Alternative 3*, which was based on the idea that the US and Soviet Union were co-operating on plans to establish a colony in space, creating a haven for a select few to escape to when the earth's environment became irreparably damaged. Although the credits made it clear the documentary was a piece of fiction – and the programme's airing on April 1st should have given the game away – many took the programme at face value. A book version was published a year later, reaching a readership who had either forgotten the original programme, or, as in the US, had never seen it. The book provoked a host of questions and established or consolidated many UFO conspiracy theories. Key among these was the identity of the select group chosen to be saved. Who were they, and what was their role in the plot? Their alleged involvement was understood in different ways: some claimed that this elite was in league with aliens, either as their conspirators or as their dupes (either way, the common rabble was done for); or, that this elite had concocted the whole scenario of an alien invasion to detract attention from their real aim, which was to create a one-world government. No matter what the consensus, the outcome for the human race looked bleak. In terms of the Illuminati myth, it cemented their position in this new fusion-paranoia theory; the spoof map drawn by Wilson in which they were at the centre of an elaborate, mythical, power structure was now being put forward as truth, and the Illuminati were now seen as the force behind a secret, millennia-long plot to control mankind.

For Cooper, the spoof documentary provided proof that the elite Bilderberg group was part of the plot. And the fact that the "documentary" was revealed as a hoax by its producers? A double-bluff:

> I read while in Naval Intelligence that at least once a year … representatives of the Soviet Union meet with the Policy Committee of the Bilderberg Group. … Items on the agenda include the combined efforts in the secret space programme governing Alternative 3. … A BBC-TV documentary entitled "Science Report" revealed these same facts but subsequently issued a retraction … that the show had been fiction. … Never in its history had it aired fiction. … Is Alternative 3 true, or is it part of a plan to ring in the New World Order?
>
> (*Behold a Pale Horse*, p95)

Further "evidence" of the government's complicity in hiding the truth about alien activity seemed to be confirmed with the appearance in 1987 of the so-called MJ-12 papers. William Moore, the UFOlogist who had first brought the Roswell incident back into the public eye, claimed, along with two others, to have received a roll of film containing images of a classified document marked "Top Secret/Majic-Eyes Only". It was subtitled "Briefing Document: Operation Majestic-12; Prepared for President-Elect Dwight D. Eisenhower", and dated November 18th, 1952. The papers supposedly contained details of a government programme begun by President Harry Truman to investigate extraterrestrial activity in the US – particularly at Roswell. The programme was run by 12 men drawn from the highest ranks of the military, intelligence and scientific communities, and the briefing paper contained details of the programme's findings, including the apparatus alleged to have been recovered from numerous UFO crashes, and the discovery of their alien occupants. The programme demanded the highest level of security to prevent public hysteria and contained, for example, details of the hastily concocted weather balloon story to conceal the truth about Roswell from the public. The MJ-12 document divided the UFO community almost immediately. Various discrepancies in the text style pointed to the document being a forgery, including the fact that the style of typewriter it appeared to have been written on was not developed until the early 1960s, and an ill-disguised forgery of Truman's signature. The timing of the discovery itself was suspiciously fortuitous: Moore was working on a documentary about Roswell at the time, and the contents of MJ-12 conveniently confirmed all his theories. As a hoax, though, it had considerable mileage: the document was realistic enough that it was assessed by the Department of Defense, and once it began to be taken seriously it would contribute to expanding the parameters of the Illuminati myth. And although the document may have caused a rift among UFO believers, for alien-New World Order conspiracists like Milton William Cooper, MJ-12 simply provided more ammunition. For Cooper, the individuals who made up MJ-12 were not solely from the military-intelligence community, they were also part of the Council on Foreign Relations:

> I read Top Secret documents while with Naval Intelligence that stated that President Eisenhower had appointed six of the Executive Committee members of the CFR [Council on Foreign Relations] to sit on the panel called Majesty Twelve, also known as Majority Twelve for security reasons. Majesty Twelve is the secret group that is supposed to control extra-terrestrial information and projects.
>
> (*Behold a Pale Horse*, p85)

Cooper's wholesale adoption of the MJ-12 hoax allowed him to elaborate on the belief shared with the extreme right militias, that the government is ruled from within by a secret government whose aims are ultimately to enslave the population. Absorbing belief in UFOs into this worldview opens the conspiracy up to cosmic dimensions: this is no longer a question of one-world government, but potentially a one-galaxy government. Cooper developed this theory in a document entitled "Top Secret/Majic", which underwent several revisions. In this, the wildly distorted views of the militias are seen through the prism of UFO beliefs, resulting in a conspiracy theory of baroque complexity. Referring to his military background, Cooper claims to have seen alien spacecraft marked with "trilateral insignia", clearly implying a cosy relationship between members of the Trilateral Commission and their extraterrestrial brethren. The government's secrecy about alien activity has nothing to do with preventing a public panic, but is proof of its complicity in a plot to enslave its own citizens, part of a treaty entered into between the US government and alien nations. Under the terms of the treaty the US government will provide aliens with humans whose organs will be harvested to further the alien race:

> They would furnish us with advanced technology and would help us in our technological development. They would not make any treaty with any other earth nation. They could abduct humans on a limited and periodic basis for the purpose of medical examination and monitoring of our development with the stipulation that the humans would not be harmed, would be returned to their point of abduction, that the humans would have no memory of the event, and that the alien nation would furnish MJ-12 a list of all human contacts and abductees on a regularly scheduled basis.
>
> ("Majestic 12 and the Secret Government")

Unfortunately, the terms of the treaty go horribly wrong. The aliens renege on the deal and abduct far more than their allocated number of humans; the Soviet Union has been involved in secret, separate negotiations with the aliens, allowing them sole access to new technology; and in an attempt to combat this threat, President Eisenhower turns to the Rockefellers. ("Asking Rockefeller for help with the alien problem was to be the biggest mistake Eisenhower ever made for the future of the United States and most probably all of humanity," Cooper claimed.) Cooper describes an elaborate scenario of American citizens abducted and held in government-run concentration camps, of the CIA profiting from the international drugs trade as a means to fund its extraterrestrial research, and the whole culminating in an End-Times scenario in which the time-travelling aliens have exploited humanity's religious faith for their own ends:

> The aliens explained that they had created us through hybridization and had manipulated the human race through religion, satanism, witchcraft, magic, and the occult. ... The aliens showed a hologram which they claimed was the actual Crucifixion of Christ, which the Government filmed. We did not know whether to believe them or not. Were they using our GENUINE religions to manipulate us? Or, were they indeed the source of our religions with which they had been manipulating us all along?
>
> (*ibid*)

This ludicrous plot could have come straight from the pages of the *Illuminatus!* trilogy, but instead, by the late 1990s, it brought Cooper closer than ever to the extreme right. He began to refer to the *Protocols of the Elders of Zion* to prop up the creaking edifice of his conspiracy theories, appending the text to *Behold a Pale Horse*, with instructions to replace reference to the "Jews" within the text to "Illuminati" and, indeed, his descriptions of the aliens as a sinister race bore disturbing traces of the rhetoric of the *Protocols*. In an interview with UFO sceptic Jacques Vallee in 1992 he described four types of aliens, one of which, a "grey", is characterized by its large nose, as opposed to another type which is "Nordic", tall, blond and "Aryan". He then makes a clear parallel between the Nordic types of aliens and the angels of Scripture, versus the greys, which "could well be the demonic ones. After all, the Bible talks about a pact with the Devil in the last days...leading to Armageddon."

By this time Cooper had strayed to the outer reaches of paranoia. In a 1998 memo, he claimed that he and his family were "targeted for imprisonment or extermination by the federal government ... for documenting and sourcing the truth about the tyranny and despotism of the Illuminati's coming socialist totalitarian new world order." He joined the ranks of those on the extreme right who saw the US government as the chief culprits in the Oklahoma bombing, and described then US Attorney General Janet Reno as the "Butcher of Waco" and Bill Clinton as the "Illuminati Socialist President of the United States".

Cooper's beliefs brought him up against the authorities on several occasions. He adhered to the militias' belief in "common law", rejecting as unconstitutional, for example, the payment of income tax, licensing of vehicles, or law-enforcement above the local level. He had often claimed that he would resist any attempts at arrest, and was true to his word when a confrontation with law-enforcement agents in 2001 ended in a shoot-out in which Cooper was shot and killed after shooting one of the deputies in the head. Before the incident he claimed to have information about the role of the secret government in the attacks on the World Trade Center, and his death is still considered suspicious by members of the militias who see it as evidence that the Illuminati had to silence him.

They say that if you go far enough to the right you'll meet the left on your way round. The staggeringly eccentric theories of David Icke complete the circle, coming at the Illuminati from a New Age perspective, but reaching very similar conclusions to that of Cooper and his followers. The key difference with Icke – and what differentiates his from all other conspiracy theories – is that in his worldview the Illuminati are not in league with the aliens, they are the aliens, and shape-shifting lizards at that.

David Icke had several successful careers before embarking on his incarnation as a purveyor of intergalactic, New Age conspiracy theories. He played professional football until rheumatoid arthritis curtailed his career, then worked as a sports writer and commentator for the BBC. From the early 1980s concern over environmental issues led to his becoming spokesperson for the Green Party. In 1990, during a consultation with a psychic healer to relieve symptoms of his arthritis, he describes undergoing a profoundly spiritual experience, which set him on his current path. According to Icke, during the consultation he received a strong psychic message telling him his role was to heal the Earth, and in doing so he would become world famous. Later, on a spiritual quest in Peru, he experienced another vision in which he described an overwhelming surge of energy, "pouring from my hands with fantastic power", so strong that "my feet continued to vibrate for some 24 hours". Shortly afterwards he began the latest phase of his career, writing and lecturing on his unique worldview.

Historian Michael Barkun has traced the development of Icke's theories through the course of his first four books. From the publication of the first in 1994, Icke begins from a familiar conspiratorial premise that quickly spins off into jaw-droppingly surreal territory. The first of these books, *The Robot's Rebellion* of 1994, covers familiar conspiratorial ground, in which a group that Icke chooses to call the Brotherhood is responsible for manipulating world events with the aim of bringing about a New World Order. The Brotherhood is in fact a collective term for a vast network of secret societies, organized according to the familiar pyramid structure, at the top of which sits the Illuminati. In this book Icke's views are very much within the tradition of Nesta Webster; he even refers to the *Protocols*, but, like Webster, urges his readers to substitute "Illuminati" for "Jews". The Illuminati, through the extensive network of the Brotherhood, according to Icke, control the world through the usual methods, particularly the world financial system, with the aim of creating a one-world government.

This was followed by ...*And the Truth Shall Set You Free* (1995), which developed the pyramid premise: those at the lower levels of the pyramid are unaware of the machinations being carried out above them, and are merely pawns in the greater conspiracy.

Even the select group at the top of the pyramid, called the "global elite", are under the control of another, extraterrestrial group, the Prison Warders, and above them is another level still: the "Luciferic Consciousness", an alien force that controls the world below it by employing a field of "negative energy" encircling the planet. This negative energy is the means by which the highest echelons will bring about a New World Order, by blocking the world's ability to achieve spiritual redemption. But it was with the publication of *The Biggest Secret* in 1999 that Icke distinguished his from all other conspiracy theories: "I wish I didn't have to introduce the following information, because it complicates the story and opens me up to mass ridicule," he wrote. But he had discovered the identity of the super elite ruling the earth: reptilian creatures from the hitherto undiscovered planet, Draco, who lived in underground caves on earth, and plotted to control humanity by interbreeding with humans. It is these hybrid creatures, with their human appearance and reptile blood, that control the world. *The Children of the Matrix* (2001) reveals the part they play in the Trilateral Commission, the Council on Foreign Relations, the Bilderbergers, international banking, etc., bringing the usual conspiracy targets into the realm of science fiction, by way of an ancient reptilian "bloodline" that dates back to ancient Babylon. All the world's ruling families and leaders share this bloodline ("The incessant interbreeding between these family lines is not due to snobbery, but their desire to hold a specific genetic structure"), one which "would appear to go back to an extraterrestrial intervention which created hybrid bloodlines". And it is this group – "call it the Illuminati for want of a better word" – who control the world.

A former Green Party member said of Icke that he "never met a conspiracy theory he didn't like" and you would be hard pressed to find a theory, myth or legend that is not included in his vast conspiratorial worldview, from the ancient pre-Christian mysteries of the pyramids to an intergalactic new world, all seen through the nebulous lens of a vaguely New Age philosophy. Icke's theories represent the point at which an End-Times scenario collides with the world of pulp science fiction, all overlaid with an interest in esoteric, "alternative" philosophies. His warning at the approach of the new millennium – a false millennium created by the Illuminati to harness the world's energy – is an example of this in miniature. In his essay "The Illuminati Rituals on the False Millennium and Coming Age of Light", he described how the coming millennium was only a result of the adoption of the Gregorian calendar, introduced in 1582, he believed, by the Illuminati working within the Vatican. According to Icke, this calendar was not introduced to measure time, but to coincide with a number of crucial solar cycles and astrological configurations – all important to the Illuminati's main agenda. He then pointed to the surfeit of millennial celebrations as evidence of the Illuminati's master plan, particularly at purportedly significant places such as the pyramids in Egypt, all attended by a "stream of Illuminati names" such as George Bush.

On the one hand it is difficult to fit David Icke into the conspiracy web; as anyone will know who saw his appearance on Terry Wogan's chat show in the UK in 1991, in which the audience and presenter openly laughed at him, there is the uncomfortable feeling that the man, more than most conspiracy theorists, may suffer from some form of clinical paranoia. However, that doesn't explain or excuse the vast numbers of his followers. His successful lecture tours take him through the UK, US, Canada, Australia and South Africa, and his appearances are often sold out. Many of his appearances are at the kind of militia expos where his brand of New Age spirituality and energy healing would appear to sit uneasily with the world of survivalism and unfettered gun ownership, and yet somehow his theories seem to form a bridge between the two. His 2002 book on the attacks on the World Trade Center shares common ground with the anti-government right in finding the US government – through the machinations of the Illuminati – responsible. And on top of the apparently harmless belief in the power of energy fields or the healing qualities of the colour turquoise, there is the underlying ugliness of the *Protocols*, which he has described as "a quite stunning prophecy of what has happened in the twentieth century" (*And The Truth*, pp54–5) and "very much the creation of the Rothschilds and the reptile-Aryans" (*The Biggest Secret*, p212. Both Barkun, p146).

With David Icke, the Illuminati myth seems to have been played out. His pick-n-mix approach to conspiracy beliefs results in a theory that collapses under its own weight. His theory is Robert Anton Wilson's parody, with its "embarrassment of riches" played out for real. He has literally appropriated everything, and there seems to be nowhere else for the theory to go. And yet, just as the idea of the Illuminati is impossible to pin down definitively, it is equally impossible to kill off. In the age of the Internet, when blogs and message boards allow ideas to be exchanged worldwide in the time it takes for current events to unfold, where does it go from here, and why does such a myth endure?

Conclusion: the Illuminati Today

Today, an Internet search engine will call up over one million sites that make reference to the Illuminati, in all of their many guises, from their original, historic definition as an obscure, short-lived philosophical society to the intergalactic shape-shifters of the more extreme conspiracist imagination. A random sample suggests that the Illuminati might be satanists, communists, Freemasons or Atlantans; that they are wise men, holding the key to ancient mysteries, or are bent on destroying the world as we know it; that they are time travellers or mystics, members of the Trilateral Commission, the CFR, or the CIA, the president of the United States, the pope or the devil himself.

What is impossible to establish is any kind of consensus view. Once the idea of the Illuminati departs from its actual, historical origins, there seem to be limitless permutations and interpretations of the myth, and no way of being certain in advance what the political charge of the stories might be. The Illuminati myth now crops up in surprising places, for example, the late gangsta rapper Tupac Shakur reworked elements of the Illuminati story into his heady brew of half-ironic, half-serious conspiracy theory and numerology on his album *The Don Killuminati: The Seven Day Theory* (released posthumously in 1996). Just how did the idea of the Illuminati develop over the course of 250 years from its origins as the brainchild of a provincial law professor to its present sci-fi incarnation, feared not merely as one secret society among many, but as the lynchpin of all secret societies?

The Illuminati myth has proven to be one of the most enduring of all the conspiracy theories, seemingly endlessly adaptable
and able to embody contemporary fears in a way that no other
conspiracy has been able to do. From the outset the group was
associated with the worst that their time could imagine. Their
Enlightenment philosophy, with its questioning of the authority of the Church, promoted deism, which was at odds with the
religious orthodoxy of the day. This led to charges of heresy, an
accusation that has stuck ever since. And as the perception of
what is considered heretical has changed, so the definition of
the Illluminati has mutated to reflect the darkest of society's
fears. Once the group became synonymous with dangerous
ideas, the Illuminati's original aims were forgotten, and the order
became a cipher, taking on the mantle of whatever society
feared most.

In 18th-century Europe, when fears of the Illuminati took
root, the order's principles of enlightened democracy were
deeply threatening to much of society, particularly the upper
echelons, who had most to fear from radical change. And as the
results of the French Revolution proved, these fears were justi-
fied: the power of the Church in France, the idea of the divine
right of kings, and the authority of the old guard had been irrevocably swept away. These anxieties about the power of revolutionary thought made an easy transition to the nascent US,
where the growing pains of the new country manifested themselves in the deeply conservative attitudes of the New England
clergy. By this time the Illuminati had become synonymous with
radicalism, and from here it was a short step to interpreting that
to mean sedition and atheism. For the Puritan-founded US, it
was hard to know which was worse: political agitation, or godlessness.

By the time the idea of the Illuminati resurfaced over 100
years later, the order's original aims had been forgotten. The

name, now, was a byword for secrecy, heresy and danger, and could be easily appended to early 20th-century fears of the mysterious "Other" in the person of the Jew. Revisionist historians such as Nesta Webster revived the Illuminati ideas of old, bringing the myth to a new audience in a series of history titles, and establishing the origins of the story as it is known today. But many of today's sources who quote her as an authority may not know – or worse, may be all too aware, yet simply not care – that Webster's ideas came from a deeply unpleasant legacy of anti-Semitism, and that one of the most notorious documents of the 20th-century, the forged *Protocols of the Elders of Zion*, informed much of her ideas about the Illuminati.

In the immediate post-war years, it was not long before a new foe rose to take the place of fascism. Communism became the menacing spectre threatening the free world, and as it spread successfully across Eastern Europe the idea that it might be setting its sights on the US took on an increasing sense of urgency. In the atmosphere of hysterical suspicion that defined the McCarthy era of the late 1950s, one man was personally responsible for dragging the Illuminati story onto centre stage: Robert Welch, founder of the ultra-conservative John Birch Society. Now the Illuminati were simply known as the "Insiders" and they represented a super-secretive elite who really pulled the strings – in government, big business and world affairs. For Welch they were bent on bringing in a New World Order in the guise of communism.

By the late 1960s to early 1970s, the Illuminati myth had spun off in two different directions. On the one hand the belief in the Illuminati's role in the New World Order continued to develop in extreme right circles, and now appeared in beliefs in End-Times scenarios, with the Illuminati in the role of agents of the Apocalypse or as the Antichrist himself. On the other hand, the role of conspiracy theories in popular culture underwent a seismic shift that is still being felt today. Robert Anton Wilson, author of several novels that playfully embellish both the Illuminati myth and the nature of conspiracy beliefs, set the ball in motion with the *Illuminatus!* trilogy, written with Robert Shea.

Wilson and Shea very much reflected the changing nature of conspiracy beliefs of their day, in which the idea of plots and subterfuge, of governments withholding information from the public, became common currency, part of the cultural landscape. In the aftermath of the Kennedy assassination (which, over 40 years after the event has spawned its own conspiracy-theory industry so vast it has taken on a life of its own) and the Watergate scandal, the idea of fixed, immutable truth became outdated, replaced by uncertainty and suspicion.

It is part of human nature to seek the truth: somewhere, under the official version of events lies the real story; it just needs to be uncovered. A character in the *Illuminatus!* trilogy voiced this attitude when he admitted his attraction to an alternative, conspiratorial view of history:

> You've just tied two hundred years of history up in a theory that would make me feel I should be committed if I accepted it. But I'm drawn to it, I admit.... Partly because the orthodox version of history that I was taught never made sense to me, and I know how people can twist history to suit their beliefs.... If I learned one thing in the last few years, it's that the crazier an idea is the more likely it is to be true.

Part of that alternative view of history, which the *Illuminatus!* trilogy resurrected, and which persists today, is the interest in the esoteric and mystical, which arose with the counterculture of the 1960s and 1970s – the predecessor to the popularity of New Age beliefs today. In this tradition, the Illuminati's perceived (although erroneous) links with a distant, mystical past, with the Assassins of ancient Persia, or the mystical Alumbrados of 16th-century Spain, imbue them with the idea of ancient, hidden knowledge, with holding the secrets to literal enlightenment. Drug culture certainly played its part in this: who better to embody the spirit of an expanded consciousness, of the quest for forbidden knowledge, than an ancient mystical group, especially one that for centuries – if not millennia – had been banned by the authorities because of its dangerous ideas?

At the same time, a distrust of government became commonplace in the second half of the 20th century. A US poll in 1964 revealed that 75 percent of respondents trusted the federal government "to do what is right always or most of the time". By the mid-1970s the legacies of Watergate and the Vietnam War had made a severe dent in the public's faith, with one in three answering yes to the same question. By the mid-1990s the public's cynicism had reached an all-time high: only 25 percent of those questioned believed their government would do what is right. The idea of a government involved in a self-benefiting conspiracy had become commonplace, with, by the turn of the new millennium, one in four believing that a government elite was involved in some sort of conspiracy.

Today, it seems we all believe in conspiracy theory as a way of explaining the world – to a greater or lesser degree. The 1960s saw the beginning of the end of our unwavering faith in authority figures and officialdom. We have almost come to expect revelations of government mendacity, cover-ups and scandal, and believe that we are right to question the official versions of events. For most of the population this will manifest itself as a degree of healthy cynicism, rather than extreme paranoia, but it still means that the idea of conspiracy itself is an accepted, even banal, way to interpret the world. This is clearly demonstrated in the way conspiracy beliefs have been absorbed into popular culture.

The wry, self-aware appropriation of conspiracy theories, as set in motion in the 1970s by Robert Anton Wilson, is widespread today, common currency in popular films, books, computer games and websites. The idea that "everything is connected", or (as *The X-Files* slogan says), "The Truth is Out There", can now be expressed almost in shorthand, a view that both openly expresses a distrust of authority while simultaneously commenting on the absurdity of conspiracy theories. Steve Jackson's Illuminati games and related websites, zines and Internet forums are both elaborate spoofs of conspiracy beliefs as well as expressions of anti-authoritarianism; underlying the parody, with its knowing wink to those in on the joke, runs the concurrent belief that, mad as such theories are, you would be equally mad to accept the "official" version of events. This allows a kind of countercultural having-your-cake-and-eating it, allowing those in the know to reject officialese, but at the same time to disassociate themselves from the wackier extremes of conspiracy theories.

One of the reasons for this is that conspiracy theories that had traditionally been the preserve of the right have now seeped into the left, through pop cultural references as well as through world events. The anti-globalization demonstrations of recent years – Seattle in 1999, Genoa in 2001 – saw demonstrators of all political affiliations take part. Yet the demographic of the anti-government left would be at pains to distance themselves from that of the anti-government right – these suspicions of the working of the World Trade Organization or the government's cosy relationship with big business, or the activities of the Bilderbergers, are not cut from the same cloth. They may meet at a common point, but they come from different directions. The ironic self-awareness that permeates most pop cultural references to conspiracy theories allows the left to make that distinction.

So what does this mean for the Illuminati myth? On the one hand it allows the name to be used as a yardstick for measuring conspiracy beliefs – you may suspect the government of lying, but if you believe the Illuminati are involved you've clearly crossed a line – while at the same time becoming a pop reference for vast, all-encompassing conspiracies. Two recent films demonstrate how the Illuminati have become appropriated in this way. In the recent *Lara Croft: Tomb Raider* movie, a fleeting reference to the villains' identities as members of the Illuminati is clearly meant to be sufficient to explain the driving force behind the plot. Whether through bad editing or an unwavering confidence that the film's intended audience would understand the reference, there is no explanation as to who the Illuminati are or what their aims might be; they seem to exist as part of the pop cultural vocabulary as a byword for global evil. Disney's recent foray into the action genre with the family-friendly *National Treasure* is an even more interesting development in the secret society myth, in that it acknowledges and positively revels in the idea that secret societies played an important role in the founding of the US, but now as a force for good. The Templars' hidden treasure – the purpose of a madcap dash around famous US monuments – is compared to the principle of democracy itself: too precious to be entrusted to one individual.

But although this is just another indication of the endless mutability of the Illuminati myth, (the Illuminati rehabilitated into a family-friendly Disney version) it does not represent the final incarnation of the story. The taint of the myth's origins – its roots in anti-Semitism and xenophobia – can never fully be removed from the Illuminati story. Of the myriad theories and rumours circulating on the Internet, many are clearly – although sometimes unwittingly – derived from the myth's more unpleasant origins.

As the Internet allows rapid and infinite exchanges of ideas without any regulation or filter, it facilitates the creation of an alternative history, one which appears to carry equal weight as the "official" version. In this parallel world, Nesta Webster and John Robison are considered eminent historians providing "well documented evidence" for the presence, and threat, of the Illuminati throughout history. When a novelist such as Dan Brown interweaves fact and fiction into wildly popular novels, the truth becomes even more obscured. Fully aware that controversy sells, he prefaces *Angels and Demons* with the statement that "the Illuminati are historical fact" then creates an entirely fictitious story of the order's origins, complete with bloody ceremonies and demented acts of vengeance. This later turns up on the Internet as historical truth, adding yet another layer to an already convoluted legend.

Beliefs in the Illuminati have become so far removed from the order's historical origins that the story can now be put to any use. The Illuminati even appeared in theories about the attacks on the World Trade Center, having allegedly duped their puppet Osama Bin Laden, and are no doubt currently training agents in the Muslim world. The myth will continue to grow and mutate wherever there is fear and suspicion, wherever people feel powerless, in the dark, and in need of easy answers.

The irony is that the actual Illuminati sought to spread the opposite. In encouraging the pursuit of enlightenment they aimed to fight the forces of obscurantism, bigotry and ignorance, employing, as Weishaupt himself wrote in 1787, "the sun of reason" in order to "dispel the clouds of superstition and of prejudice". And yet the lasting legacy of the Illuminati seems to be principally as a divining rod for fear and ignorance. Wherever references to the order appear, chances are it will indicate evidence of the anti-enlightenment at work, where hysteria, superstition and prejudice prevail over tolerance and reason.

If the Illuminati are remembered at all today, it is often as some nebulous force for evil; a symbol of an otherwise name-less dread that threatens the status quo. Yet if we return to the source of the myth – the Abbé Barruel – it is startling to discover that among the many heinous charges of which the group was accused were the following objectives, that: "[that] man [should] be equal and free; that the principle of all sovereignty essentially resides in the people; and that law is nothing more than the expression of the general will." Today we take these principles for granted. So just how did such a laudable mission become so misunderstood, so misrepresented that over the course of 200 years it came to represent its exact opposite? It is as if, over generations, the story was communicated through a series of Chinese whispers, which, consciously or not, distorted the message to reflect the concerns of the prevailing ideology of the day. As each story built upon the excesses of its predecessor, the Illuminati myth became a hybrid creation, a Frankenstein's monster composed of remnants of superstition and fear, with the veracity of the legend never called into question. As Weishaupt himself wrote: "O Mortal Man, is there nothing you cannot be made to believe?"

Bibliography

Barkun, Michael, *A Culture of Conspiracy*, University of California Press, 2003

Barkun, Michael, *Religion and the Racist Right*, University of North Carolina Press, 1994

Barruel, Abbé Augustin de, *Mémoires pour servir a l'histoire du Jacobinisme*, P Fauche, 1798–9

Bennet, David H., *The Party of Fear*, University of North Carolina Press, 1988

Berlet, Chip and Mathew N. Lyons, *Right-Wing Populism in America: Too Close for Comfort*, The Guilford Press, 2000

Billington, James H., *Fire in Men's Minds*, Basic Books, Inc., 1980

Bullock, Steven C., *Revolutionary Brotherhood*, University of North Carolina Press, 1996

Broyles, J. Allen, *The John Birch Society: Anatomy of a Protest*, Beacon Press, 1964

Cohn, Norman, *Warrant for Genocide*, Scholars Press, 1981

Davis, David Brion (ed.), *The Fear of Conspiracy*, Cornell University Press, 1971

Diamond, Sara, *Roads to Dominion: Rightwing Movements and Political Power in the United States*, The Guilford Press, 1995

Diamond, Sara, *Not by Politics Alone: The Enduring Influence of the Christian Right*, The Guilford Press, 1998

Durham, Martin, *The Christian Right, the Far Right and the Boundaries of American Conservatism*, Manchester University Press, 2000

Epstein, Benjamin R. and Arnold Foster, *The Radical Right: A Report on the John Birch Society and its Allies*, Random House, 1967

Fried, Richard M., *Nightmare in Red: The McCarthy Era in Perspective*, Oxford University Press, 1990

Fenster, Mark, *Conspiracy Theories: Secrecy and Power in American Culture*, University of Minnesota Press, 1999

Le Forestier, René, *Les Illuminés de Bavière*, Doctoral Thesis, University of Paris, 1915

Fuller, Robert, *Naming the Antichrist: The History of an American Obsession*, Oxford University Press, 1995

George, John and Laird Wilcox, *American Extremists: Militias, Supremacists, Klansmen, Communists and Others*, Prometheus Books, 1996

Gilman, Richard, *Behind World Revolution*, Vol I, Insight Books, 1981

Goldberg, Robert A., *Enemies Within*, Yale University Press, 2001

Gervaso, Roberto, *Cagliostro*, translated by Cormac O Cuilleanáin, Victor Gollancz Ltd, 1974

Hoffman, Amos, "Opinion, Illusion, and the Illusion of Opinion: Barruel's Theory of Conspiracy" *Eighteenth-Century Studies*, Vol. 27, No.1 (Autumn, 1993), 27–60.

Holms, Colin, *Anti-Semitism in British Society, 1876–1939*, Holmes & Meir Publishers, Inc., 1979

Howard, Michael, *The Occult Conspiracy*, Rider & Co. Ltd, 1989

Jacob, Margaret C., *Living the Enlightenment: Freemasonry and Politics in Eighteenth-Century Europe*, Oxford University Press, 1991

Johnson, George, *Architects of Fear: Conspiracy Theories and Paranoia in American Politics*, Jeremy P. Tarcher, Inc., 1983

Knight, Peter (ed.), *Conspiracy Theories in American History: An Encyclopedia*, ABC-CLIO, 2003

Knight, Peter, *Conspiracy Culture: From the Kennedy Assassination to "The X-Files,"* Routledge, 2000

Knight, Peter (ed.), *Conspiracy Nation: The Politics of Paranoia in Postwar America*, New York University Press, 2002.

Levine, Robert Steven, *Conspiracy Fears and the American Romance, 1789–1860*, Doctoral Thesis, Stanford University, 1981

Linehan, Thomas, *British Fascism 1918–39. Parties, Ideology and Culture*, Manchester University Press, 2000

Lipset, Seymour Martin and Earl Raab, *The Politics of Unreason*, Heinemann Educational Books Ltd, 1970

Luckert, Steven, *Jesuits, Freemasons, Illuminati and Jacobins: Conspiracy Theories, Secret Societies, and Politics in Late Eighteenth-Century Germany*, Doctoral Thesis, State University of New York at Binghamton, 1993

Marsden, Victor E., *Protocols of the Meeting of the Learned Elders of Zion* (translated from the Russian of Nilus), The Britons Publishing Society, reprint 1941

Marrs, Jim, *Rule by Secrecy*, HarperCollins, 2000

May, Henry F., *The Enlightenment in America*, Oxford University Press, 1976

McCalman, Iain, *The Last Alchemist*, HarperCollins, 2003

McGirr, Lisa, *Suburban Warriors*, Princeton University Press, 2001

McKay, Charles, *Extraordinary Popular Delusions and the Madness of Crowds*, Crown Publications. Reprint, 1995

Montjoie, Galart de, *Conjuration de Louis-Philippe-Joseph D'Orléans, surnommé Egalité*, Paris, 1831

Mortensen, Peter, *British Romanticism and Continental Influences*, Palgrave MacMillan, 2003

Ovason, David, *The Secret Symbols of the Dollar Bill*, HarperCollins, 2004

Perry, Marvin and Frederick M. Schweitzer, *Antisemitism: Myth and Hate from Antiquity to the Present*, Palgrave Macmillan, 2002

Pipes, Daniel, *Conspiracy: How the Paranoid Style Flourishes and Where it Comes From*, The Free Press, 1997

Pope-Hennessy, Una, *Secret Societies and the French Revolution*, John Lane, the Bodley Head, no date

Principia Discordia: How I found the Goddess and What I did to Her When I Found

Her, Illuminet Press, 1991

Lady Queenborough (Edith Starr Miller), *Occult Theocrasy*, Vol 1. Published posthumously for private circulation only, 1934

Ribuffo, Leo P., *The Old Christian Right: The Protestant Far Right from the Great Depression to the Cold War*, Temple University Press, 1983

Robison, John, *Proofs of a Conspiracy*, 1798, reprint 1967

Roberts, J.M., *The Mythology of the Secret Societies*, Secker & Warburg, 1972

Roberts, J.M., *The French Revolution*, Oxford University Press, 1978

Robertson, Pat, *The New World Order*, GK Hall & Co., 1992

Shea, Robert and Robert Anton Wilson, *The Illuminatus! Trilogy*, Dell, 1975

Stauffer, Vernon, *New England and the Bavarian Illuminati*, Russell and Russell, 1918, reissued 1967

Stern, Kenneth S., *A Force Upon the Plain: The American Militia Movement and the Politics of Hate*, University of Oklahoma Press, 1996

Thurlow, Richard, *Fascism in Britain: From Oswald Mosley's Blackshirts to the National Front*, IB Tauris Publishers, 1998

Webster, Nesta, *The French Revolution*, Bloomfield Books, 1918, reprint 1983

Webster, Nesta, *Secret Societies and Subversive Movements*, Boswell Printing & Publishing Co., Ltd., 1924

Webster, Nesta, *Spacious Days*, Hutchinson & Co. Ltd. No date

Webster, Nesta, *World Revolution: The Plot Against Civilization*, Constable and Company Ltd, 2nd edition, 1922

Webster, Nesta, "Cagliostro and the Queen's Necklace", *The Sphere*, April 23rd, 1927

Webster, Nesta, "The Rulers of Darkness", *The Sphere*, April 9th, 1927

Welch, Robert, *The Blue Book of the John Birch Society*, Western Islands Publishing Co., reprint 1961

Wilcox, Clyde, *Onward Christian Soldiers? The Religious Right in American Politics*, Westview Press, 2000, 2nd edition

Wilgus, Neal, *The Illuminoids*, Pocket Books, 1979

Index

Also available from Conspiracy Books:

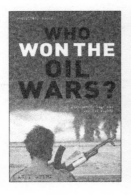

Warm thanks to Will at Essential Works for his advice and support; Birgit and Anna, for making work in Boston such a pleasure; and Val, for sending interesting articles my way. Thanks are due, too, to friends and family for their endless enthusiasm, especially Jo, Lisa, Lúise, Sam and James.

And, for his generosity with time and ideas, and his ceaseless encouragement, I am indebted to Peter, without whom this book would not have been written. This book is for him.